MIKE YAGE
Corvette Bible

SPECIFICATIONS • HUNDREDS OF PHOTOS • BUYING TIPS

By Mike Yager

©2007 Mike Yager

by

kp krause publications

An Imprint of F+W Publications

700 East State Street • Iola, WI 54990-0001
715-445-2214 • 888-457-2873
www.krausebooks.com

Our toll-free number to place an order or obtain
a free catalog is (800) 258-0929.

Library of Congress Catalog Number: 2006935658
ISBN-13: 978-0-89689-489-1
ISBN-10: 0-89689-489-4

Designed by Kara Grundman
Edited by Tom Collins

Printed in China

CONTENTS

Corvette
1953-2007

The 1953 Corvette was based on the 1952 EX-122 show car. It was one of the few Motorama dream cars to actually go into production with the styling virtually unchanged.

The Corvette was created as an economical sports car for young adults. It was also something that could be used as a performance-image builder while Chevrolet waited for its V-8. The car's fiberglass body was not only novel,

but practical. It lowered the cost of production in limited numbers and expedited the Corvette's debut. Steel-bodied models were originally planned for later model years.

Sales were so bad Chevrolet management was on the verge of killing the Corvette. However, when Ford came out with its two-passenger Thunderbird, the company was forced, for competitive reasons, to continue production.

Sales shot up dramatically in 1956. One of the main reasons was the Corvette now had looks to match its performance.

With the introduction of fuel-injection in 1957 advertising proclaimed, "For the first time in automotive history — one horsepower for every cubic inch."

The clean, classic styling of 1956 and 1957 was jazzed-up in 1958. Although the basic design was attractive, the chrome-laden 1958 is generally considered the gaudiest Corvette.

A four-passenger Corvette was considered for 1963. It might have been quite successful. Thunderbird sales soared when the T-Bird went that route in 1958.

The basic aerodynamic styling introduced in 1968 would remain until 1983. After the early 1970s, Corvettes became significantly tamer. It can easily be said that all Corvettes are collectible, yet some more so than others. The 1978 Indy Pace Car Replica is one and the '82 Collector Edition is another. Neither qualifies as rare as quite a few were produced. No doubt, strong demand will also keep the '86 convertible on the desirable list.

An exciting addition to the 1990 Corvette lineup was the ZR-1 coupe, which was engineered in conjunction with Lotus of England and the Mercury Marine Div. of Brunswick Corp., in Stillwater, Oklahoma. It bowed in September 1989, as a 1990 model, and production of 3,000 copies was scheduled for Bowling Green.

Rumors of the demise of the Corvette have been steady in recent years, but after 54 years of production and with it being a proven image-enhancing product for Chevrolet, the Corvette's future cannot be dismissed so easily.

FORWARD

"BIBLE"
BY DANA MECUM

I make my living watching Corvettes and other collectible cars change ownership. Mostly, I get to witness the magic that is created when people achieve a dream.

People regularly seek my advice on this matter. And here's what I always tell them: Buy what you like. Don't buy based on market trends— because someday you'll sell that car. And, have you ever tried to sell something you don't like?

This book can help you understand what you should pay attention to when you're researching the Corvette market.

The Corvette is the *number one* collector car in the world. For the past 30 years, Corvettes have shown consistent increases in value for investors, with the benefit being they are the most marketable to sell in the shortest timeframe anywhere in the USA. That fact is very important if an owner has the misfortune of an emergency-driven sale.

Mike Yager is the "Ultimate Corvette Package." There are all types of people in the Corvette community with many different motives: socializers, collectors, investors, restoration hobbyists, etc. Mike Yager is a unique animal— he fits all categories. He likes to talk about Corvettes. He likes to drive Corvettes. He likes to make money on Corvettes. He likes to maintain the history and tradition of Corvettes. And he wants you to share his passion for Corvettes.

Mike is my friend and always has been. I don't need a contract with Mike Yager – his word is gold. Enjoy his words here!

Dana Mecum is a star personality and an institution in the Corvette world. He is the owner of Mecum High Performance Auctions and Bloomington Gold Corvettes.

Using Mike Yager Comments:

In nearly 40 years in this hobby, I have met many different people with different objectives. And I've seen a lot of Corvettes! After a while, you start to see commonalities and similarities.

THE RATING GRAPHS:

In an effort to encapsulate collecting situations and activities, I've created a Rating Graph that I hope you find useful. I wanted to be able to accommodate a broad range of typical circumstances that just about anyone can identify.

At the top I've broken out three major categories. Trust me, your Corvette falls into one of these – you be the judge! A "Basket Case" may have the motor missing or have a lot of parts missing or disassembled. An "Average Driver" is a normal production Corvette without distinguishing attributes. A "Rare Unique" is a low production Corvette via desirable attributes such as motor, options, colors, etc. A "Complete Original" speaks for itself – it is 95% there or better.

Then I've offered conditional sub-categories for each status to help you define your situation even more. (Note: N-O-M stands for Non-Original Motor. O-M stands for Original Motor.)

Over on the left-hand side of the graph I have listed a variety of strategies that I would recommend you to consider.

Cross-reference the condition of your Corvette at the top with the strategies on the left side. Any areas that are highlighted underneath the condition of your Corvette are applicable.

"MIKE YAGER SAYS:"

The information I've listed under "Mike Yager Says" is a valuable collection of my observations based on my experience with Corvettes.

Generally, the "Cheers" point out new features and changes. The "Jeers" point out items that needed to be improved or that were lacking on the cars. Look at this information as a quick reference each Corvette model year. My Game Plan observations also will be quite valuable to you.

After reading "Mike Yager Says," I hope you will appreciate that some Corvettes are rarer or more valuable than others, but each one is fun to own and even more fun to drive!

— *Mike Yager*

1953 Corvette

"Don't Let The Stars Get In Your Eyes" was a hit tune in 1953, but Chevrolet Motor Division wanted to put stars in car buyers' eyes when it brought its 1953 Corvette dream car to life. Movie stars like John Wayne were given Corvettes to generate publicity for the new "All-American Sports Car." TV celebrity Dave Garroway—a well-known sports-car buff—praised the new model in a sales promotion film called "Halls of Wonder."

A prototype bowed at the 1953 GM Motorama in New York City, then the sleek Corvette roadster was rushed into production. The first Corvette was built on June 30, 1953 at a Flint, Michigan, assembly plant. All 1953s were constructed in an area at the rear of Chevrolet's customer delivery garage on Van Slyke Ave. in Flint. The company predicted that 10,000 Corvettes per year could be built and sold. They were wrong. Production actually reached only 300.

The Corvette was a brand new addition to the sports car world in 1953. *Tom Glatch*

A scene of the early Corvette assembly line. Note the early domed hub caps and no outside rearview mirror.

The 1953 Corvette was fiberglass bodywork at its best. *Tom Glatch*

1953 'VETTE FACTS	
VEHICLE IDENTIFICATION NUMBER	Corvettes for 1953 were numbered E53F001001 to E53F001300. The first symbol E = Corvette. The second and third symbols 53=1953. The fourth symbol F=Flint, Michigan assembly plant. The last six symbols were digits representing the sequential production number.
ENGINE	Type: Six Bore and stroke: 3.56 x 3.96 in. Displacement: 235.5 cid Brake hp: 150 at 4200 rpm. Induction: Three Carter Type YH 1-bbl. Options: None
VITAL STATS	Original Price: $3,498 Production: 300 Wheelbase: 102 in. Length: 167 in. Tires: 6.70 x 15
COOL STUFF	The '53 is the lowest production Corvette. *Life Magazine* reported, "If the tough plastic is punctured in an accident it can usually be patched like new with a blowtorch for a couple of dollars." Zora Arkus-Duntov joined Chevrolet Motor Division May 1, 1953 and would later become chief engineer of the Corvette.

A group of 1953 Corvettes took to the proving ground test track.

The carburetors stood out in the engine bay with their shiny silver caps. *Tom Glatch*

MIKE YAGER SAYS:	
CHEERS	Only 300 Corvettes can lay claim to the "birthright" of the marque. It was America's first postwar production sports car. The antenna was in the fiberglass trunk lid. These were the only Corvettes made at Flint, Michigan. A handmade, hand-formed fiberglass version.
JEERS	The Blue Flame six engine. The six-volt electrical system. Early carbs leaked and caused fires. Car interiors leaked due to no roll-up windows plus side curtains. No door locks. Large steering wheel, uncomfortable seating position and lack of head room. Expensive to restore correctly. Vacuum windshield wipers. Powerglide two-speed transmission. The convertible top frame and the correct non-Conelrad radio are hard parts to find today.
GAME PLAN	Collectors should look for as original and untouched example as they can find. Ownership history and provenance are important to get your return on investment. Buy as complete a car as you can find, as key parts are very expensive and extremely hard to find. The VIN tag is screwed onto the door jamb. Be sure your Corvette is not a 1954 model with a 1953 VIN tag.

The taillights hinted at a rocket flame, a modern design in 1953. *Tom Glatch*

The venerable Blue Flame six-cylinder was the engine of choice in the first Corvettes. *Tom Glatch*

Everyone knew the new-for-1953 sports car was from Chevrolet. *Tom Glatch*

The 1953 Corvette interior included a symmetrical dash with a large steering wheel. *Tom Glatch*

1953 Corvette nose included wire screen covers over the headlights. *Tom Glatch*

About 200 are known to survive today and early examples are still turning up. In fact the body of the second car built may have been discovered recently.

The first Corvette had a fiberglass body, a bright toothy grille and rounded front fenders with the headlights under wire screen covers. Like typical sports cars of the day, it had no windows or door handles. GM's innovative wraparound windshield was used and added to the Corvette "dream car" image. The taillights looked like a part stolen from Captain Video's spaceship.

Corvette Bible **11**

The Corvette interior featured bucket-style seats and an oddly-designed floor-mounted shifter for the transmission. The dashboard carried oil pressure, battery, water temperature and fuel gauges, plus a tachometer and a clock. This was very un-sports-car-like. The Powerglide two-speed automatic transmission from contemporary Chevrolet passenger cars was used.

Each 1953 Corvette was virtually a hand-built car and many minor changes were made during the production run. All of the first-year cars were Polo White with Sportsman Red interiors. All had black canvas convertible tops that could be manually folded and stored in a space behind the seats. A black oilcloth window storage bag was provided to protect the '53 Corvette's removable plastic side windows when stowed in the trunk.

Other 1953-only features included special valve covers, a one-piece carburetor linkage and a small trunk mat. Short exhaust extensions were used only on 1953 and early 1954 models. They were dropped because they were prone to drawing exhaust fumes into the car through the vent windows.

By early 1954, Chevrolet announced that production of the Corvette was being shifted to the assembly plant in St. Louis, Missouri. Programming, at that point, called for production of 1,000 Corvettes per month in St. Louis by June 1954.

1953 Corvette Status Guide	Basket Case		Average Driver		Rare, Unique or Completely Original		Restored
Condition of CORVETTE:	Production Status						
	Average	Rare/ Unique	N-O-M	O-M	Needs Work	Unrestored Low Mileage	Restored
Suggested Actions: Collect It							
Drive, Show and Enjoy							
Race, Autocross Competitively							
Store for a Future Project/Investment							
Candidate for Resto Rod							
Restore to Curb Appeal Condition							

1954 Corvette

"Ebb Tide" was a very moving song of 1954 that made it to "My Hit Parade" early in the year. Unfortunately, the Corvette didn't make the sports car hit parade and its sales ebbed. Chevrolet Motor Division had been poised to build 12,000 Corvettes at the new St. Louis factory, but dealers were not able to sell that many. Some books say half the cars built languished in showrooms, but the figure was more like 70 percent. Only 3,640 Corvettes were assembled.

To the naked eye, 1953-1954 Corvettes look identical, but collectors know the small differences. The window storage bag changed, as did the starter and the

fuel and brake line locations. A new type of valve cover was held on by four bolts through the outside and had decals with larger lettering.

The signal-seeking AM radio, a $145 option, now had Conelrad National Defense System icons on its face, a sign of the Cold War. Early in 1954, the original hood latch was changed to a single-handle design. Corvettes after serial number E54S003906 had integrated dual-pot air cleaners.

A major addition in the 1954 Corvette was color— like this Pennant Blue version owned by Mike Yager. *Mid America Motorworks*

MIKE YAGER SAYS:	
CHEERS	The first year with more color choices than Polo White. The improved 3 x 1 carburetors. The panel finish was improved. A new camshaft with more horsepower.
JEERS	Panel fit still suffered due to handmade nature of car. The Blue Flame six and the six-volt electrical system. The two-speed Powerglide transmission and the vacuum-powered windshield wipers. Side curtains and no windows to roll up meant leaks and wind noise. Large steering wheel, uncomfortable seating position and not much headroom for tall people. Very expensive to restore to NCRS standards. Convertible top frames are hard to find.
GAME PLAN	Look for as original and untouched example as possible. Ownership history and provenance are best for a return on your investment. This is where values lie in the 1953 through '55 Corvettes. The value of this Corvette often is overlooked in the marketplace.

Three Carter YH single-barrel carburetors were underneath the chrome air cleaner covers on the 1954 Corvette. *Mid America Motorworks*

Mike Yager's Pennant Blue version has the lowest mileage of any unrestored 1954 Corvette. *Mid America Motorworks*

1954 'VETTE FACTS	
VEHICLE IDENTIFICATION NUMBER	Corvettes for 1954 were numbered E54S001001 to E54S004640. The first symbol E = Corvette. The second and third symbols 54=1954. The fourth symbol S=St. Louis, Mo. assembly plant. The last six symbols were digits representing the sequential production number.
ENGINE	Type: Six Bore and stroke: 3.56 x 3.96 in. Displacement: 235.5 cid Brake hp: 150 at 4200 rpm. Induction: Three Carter Type YH 1-bbl. Options: None
VITAL STATS	Original Price: $2,774 Production: 3,640 Wheelbase: 102 in. Length: 167 in. Tires: 6.70 x 15
COOL STUFF	Mid America Motorwork's MY Garage museum features a Pennant Blue car that is the lowest-mileage unrestored '54 'Vette. There's a Polo White car with lower mileage, but it has been completely restored. Since they were virtually handmade, early 'Vettes did not carry standard Fisher Body Style Numbers like other GM cars. The Corvette model number, 2934, was also the body style code. At the end of the 1954 sales season, 1,100 1954 Corvettes were unsold. The Mid America Motorworks MY Garage museum features a Pennant Blue car that is the lowest-mileage unrestored '54 Corvette. There is a Polo White car with even fewer miles, but it has been fully restored. Since Corvettes were virtually handmade, they did not carry standard Fisher Body Style Numbers like other GM cars. The Corvette model number consisted of the four digits 2934, which also served as the body style number for the early production years. Over 1,100 of the Corvettes built to 1954 specifications were unsold when the model year ended.

Corvette sales still lagged behind estimates in 1954 but the cars were very good looking.

1954 Corvette Status Guide	Basket Case		Average Driver		Rare, Unique or Completely Original		Restored
Condition of CORVETTE:	Production Status						
	Average	Rare/Unique	N-O-M	O-M	Needs Work	Unrestored Low Mileage	Restored
Suggested Actions: Collect It							
Drive, Show and Enjoy							
Race, Autocross Competitively							
Store for a Future Project/Investment							
Candidate for Resto Rod							
Restore to Curb Appeal Condition							

A clip to hold the ventipanes (butterfly windows) closed was added in late 1954.

New colors were the most apparent change. Polo White was used on about 88 percent of 1954 models. Some 15 percent were Pennant Blue with a Shoreline Beige interior. About three percent were Red with a Red interior. Some Black cars with Red interiors were built. In addition, Metallic Green and Metallic Brown cars may have been built. A beige convertible top was offered.

The same engine was used at first, but later on a new camshaft raised the horsepower rating to 155. With the early-year engine, a 1954 Corvette could go from 0 to 60 mph in 11 seconds and from 0 to 100 mph in 41 seconds.

To help dealers sell Corvettes, Chevrolet dropped the price to $2,774. This didn't flood the showrooms with buyers and serious consideration was given to discontinuing the Corvette. Ford saved the day by launching the Thunderbird. "There was talk of the Corvette being discontinued," Zora Duntov once said. "But when the Thunderbird arrived, GM was suddenly reluctant to drop the Corvette. I believe the T-Bird got Ed Cole's competitive spirit going."

Cole – Chevrolet's chief engineer – was not the only Corvette booster. Another fan was Harley Earl, who had conceived the original Motorama roadster. Before long, Zora Duntov would join the team as well.

Three new "dream Corvettes" were exhibited at the 1954 GM Motorama in New York. The first was a coupe with a lift-off hardtop, the second was the Nomad wagon and the third was a fastback coupe called the Corvair. How interesting that two of these names were used later on production cars.

Changes in the 1954 Corvette were practical, such as a window storage bag.

1954 CORVETTE EX-87 TEST MULE

This is a special Corvette—the first V-8 test version. *Tom Glatch*

Installation of a potent small block was a "sneak preview" of 1955's new V8 power! *Tom Glatch*

Not only did the EX-87 test V-8 power and matching handling, it tested aerodynamics. *Tom Glatch*

The EX-87 took on a racing demeanor that was far more than fiberglass layers deep. *Tom Glatch*

The door area was stripped of essentials for lightness and more speed. *Tom Glatch*

1955 Corvette

With Ford bringing the Thunderbird out, Chevrolet decided it had to stick with the Corvette. The first 1955 models left the assembly line in St. Louis, Missouri on October 28, 1954. The exterior look was the same as before, but the construction and content kept getting better. The fiberglass used to make the body, was thinner, smoother and better than that used earlier.

An exciting new V-8 replaced the in-line six very early in the run. It provided 40 additional horsepower to Corvette buyers. A large gold "V" within the word Chevrolet on the front fenders called out the V-8. Corvettes with it also had a new 12-volt electrical system. Electric windshield wipers were standard.

Corvette's expanded color palette included Metallic Copper with a Beige interior and Harvest Gold (yellow) with Green-and-Yellow trim and a Dark Green top. Bright Gypsy Red replaced Sportsman Red on

In 1955, Chevrolet premiered its V-8 engine and Corvette now had one. *Tom Glatch*

MIKE YAGER SAYS:	
CHEERS	The new V-8 engine and three-speed transmission! The panel fit and finished was greatly improved. Additional new colors available were Harvest Gold, Corvette Copper and Gypsy Red. A 12-volt electrical system was added.
JEERS	With side curtains and no roll-up windows, the car leaked and suffered from wind noise. There were no door locks. The car had a large steering wheel, an uncomfortable seating position for tall people and not much headroom. The car is very expensive to restore correctly to NCRS standards. The convertible top frame and correct 265 cid engine block are very hard to find.
GAME PLAN	Of the big three years, 1953 through 1955, this is the one to grab and hold onto. Buy a 1955. The color choice and interior trim makes this a stunningly beautiful car.

It was the third year that Corvette used essentially the same styling.   *Tom Glatch*

1955 'VETTE FACTS

VEHICLE IDENTIFICATION NUMBER	Corvettes for 1955 were numbered VE55S001001 to VE55S001700 (the "V" was not used on sixes). The first symbol E = Corvette. The second and third symbols 55=1955. The fourth symbol S=St. Louis, Mo. assembly plant. The last six symbols were digits representing the sequential production number.
ENGINE (SEE 1954 FOR SIX-CYLINDER SPECS)	**Type: V-8** Bore and stroke: 3.75 x 3.00 in. Displacement: 265 cid Brake hp: 195 at 5000 rpm. Induction: Carter 4-bbl. Options: Six in about six cars
VITAL STATS	Original Price: $2,934 (with V-8) Production: 700 Wheelbase: 102 in. Length: 167 in. Tires: 6.70 x 15
COOL STUFF	Zora Arkus-Duntov used a prototype 'Vette V-8 to set a Measured Mile record at Daytona Beach in 1955. The T-Bird outsold the 'Vette 23-to-1 in 1955 and Zora decided to pull out all stops to up the performance of 'Vettes. They became true sports cars. The 265-cid/3-speed combo was powerful and made the 'Vette a real performance machine. '55 was the last year for "Gen I" styling motifs like tail fins and wire basket headlight covers.

body. A Light Beige Elascofab interior was new and had a "lighter and lovelier" appearance. Soft tops came in canvas and vinyl. New top colors included White and Dark Green.

After a half-dozen or so 1955 Corvettes were built with sixes, the V-8 came on stream and its impact was amazing. Now the Corvette could really move and that meant that it could win races, like sports cars are supposed to do. Chevrolet soon plugged the six-cylinder engine-mounting holes in the frame and went to producing only V-8s.

The first "small-block" Chevy V-8 had a cast-iron block, cast-iron cylinder heads and independent rocker arms. A special cam, an 8.0:1 compression ratio, solid valve lifters and a Carter four-barrel carburetor helped the "Corvette" edition produce more horsepower than the family-car version. The Corvette's ladder frame required modifications to accommodate the V-8 fuel pump. Since the V-8 retained less heat than the six, it could get by with a smaller radiator.

List price on the Corvette six was $2,799 and the V-8 added $135. The V-8 engine weighed 28 pounds less than the six, which added to the Corvette's performance numbers. With the V-8 it could zoom from 0-to-60 mph in 8.7 seconds and 0-to-100 mph took only 24.7 seconds.

Very late in the model year, a three-speed manual transmission became standard in Corvettes. A single dry-plate clutch was

The V-shape in the trim told everyone there was something special powering this car. *Tom Glatch*

1955 Corvette Status Guide	Basket Case		Average Driver		Rare, Unique or Completely Original		Restored
Condition of CORVETTE:	Production Status						
	Average	Rare/ Unique	N-O-M	O-M	Needs Work	Unrestored Low Mileage	Restored
Suggested Actions: Collect It							
Drive, Show and Enjoy							
Race, Autocross Competitively							
Store for a Future Project/Investment							
Candidate for Resto Rod							
Restore to Curb Appeal Condition							

A product called "Elascofab" gave the Corvette interior a new look in 1955. *Tom Glatch*

A new story was under the hood with 195 HP and a Carter four-barrel carburetor. *Tom Glatch*

used with this gearbox. The two-speed Powerglide automatic used previously was made optional. Only seven other options were offered: directional signals for $16.75, a heater for $91.40, a signal-seeking AM radio for $145.15, a windshield washer for $11.85, a parking brake alarm for $5.65, 6.70 x 15 white sidewall tires for $26.90 above the cost of standard "blackwalls" and a courtesy light package for $4.05.

1956 Corvette

The Corvette hit its stride as America's "Real McCoy" sports car in 1956. In its era, this year's design had panache. "A lot of people would have been perfectly content if Chevrolet had frozen Corvette styling with the 1956 model," is the way automotive historian Charlie Webb once put it. Chevrolet styling studio chief Clare MacKichan spearheaded the beautiful redesign and is known as "the man who made the 1956 and 1957 Corvette look as good as it ran."

To a large degree, the early Corvette styling motifs used in 1953 through 1955 were carried over, but in much-finessed form. A cross bar with slimmer chrome "teeth" filled the grille cavity. New Mercedes-inspired forward-thrusting front fenders housed the uncovered chrome-rimmed headlights. Important updates included the addition of roll-up glass windows, external door handles, chrome-outlined concave side body coves and sloping, taillight-integrated rear fenders.

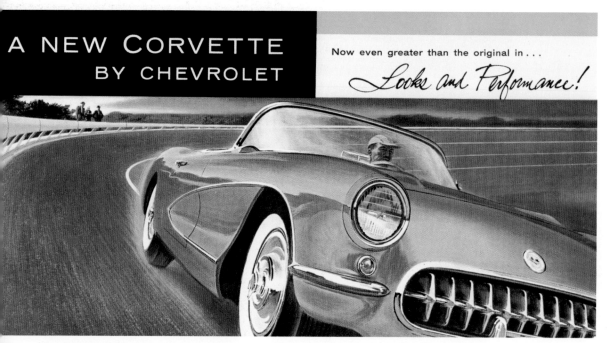

A NEW CORVETTE BY CHEVROLET

Now even greater than the original in . . .

Looks and Performance!

The 1956 Corvette had a new look and certainly was "greater than the original." *Phil Hall Collection*

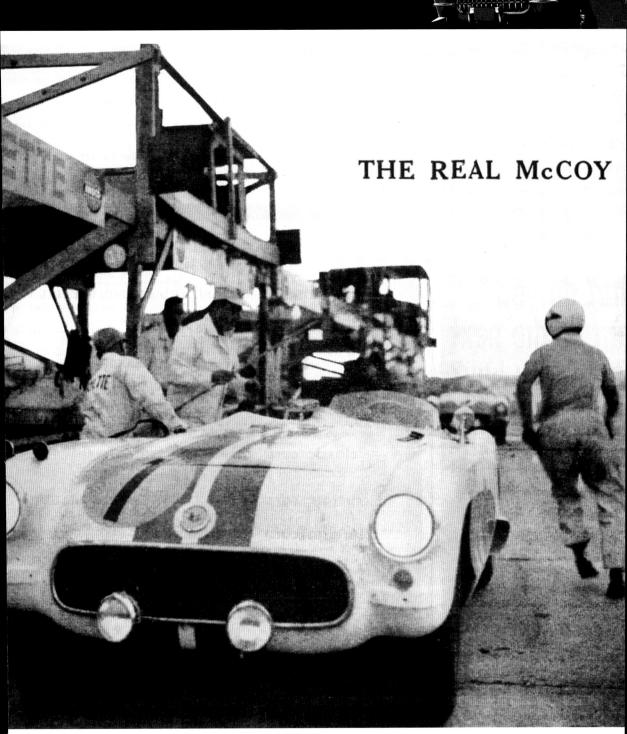

THE REAL McCOY

In July 1956, Chevrolet proudly touted the Corvette's racing success with an ad headlined "The Real McCoy."

MIKE YAGER SAYS:	
CHEERS	The first year for the hardtop. The first Corvette signature side coves. First time for multiple engine options and the 2 x 4 carbs were the most common choice. Weather-tight door locks and handles. Exterior door locks and handles as well as roll-up windows. Exterior two-tone, power window and power top options. Steering wheels, chassis parts and major interior restoration parts are easy to find.
JEERS	Both the two-speed Powerglide and three-speed manual transmissions. The bumpers were mounted on the fiberglass fenders. The convertible top frame, power top assembly, correct early hardtop, stainless trim, clock and gauges and the grille and chrome trim all are hard to find.
GAME PLAN	A 1956 Corvette can be a great buy and an enthusiast's car. Look for original, untouched examples. Many 1956 Corvettes have been cut up to build '57 cars. Look for 1956 values to rise.

Many recall the first time they saw a Corvette, like this Venetian Red 1956 version. *Phil Hall Collection*

The dashboard layout was themed the same as in 1953-1955 models. A new rearview mirror, located at the center of the top of the dash, was adjusted by using a thumbscrew. Carrying a $3,149 price tag, the 1956 Corvette roadster weighed 2,730 pounds. The model regained a little popularity and 3,467 were made – five times the amount sold in 1955. The wheelbase was unchanged, but overall length increased significantly. Large 6.70 x 15 tires were retained.

The fabric top was redesigned to provide better weather protection – a sore point with many other sports cars. Options included a power-operated top and a removable

Interiors were available in either beige or red in 1956. *Phil Hall Collection*

1956 'VETTE FACTS	
VEHICLE IDENTIFICATION NUMBER	Corvettes for 1956 were numbered E56S001001 to E56S004467. The first symbol E = Corvette. The second and third symbols 56=1956. The fourth symbol S=St. Louis, Mo., assembly plant. The last six symbols were digits representing the sequential production number.
ENGINE	**Type: V-8** Bore and stroke: 3.75 x 3.00 in. Displacement: 265 cid Brake hp: 210 at 5600 rpm. Induction: Carter WCFB 4-bbl. **Options:** 265-cid/225-hp w/ two 4-bbl. carbs 265-cid/240-hp w/ two 4-bbl. carbs
VITAL STATS	Original Price: $3,149 Production: 3,467 Wheelbase: 102 in. Length: 168 in. Tires: 6.70 x 15
COOL STUFF	The 1956 Corvette made its debut on New Year's Day at the Waldorf Astoria in New York during the 1956 GM Motorama. A series of 1956 ads featuring pencil sketches of Corvettes in sports car races came to symbolize the official start of Corvette racing history. A 225-hp 1956 Corvette could go from 0-to-60 mph in 7.3 seconds; from 0-to-100 mph in 20.7 seconds.

fiberglass hardtop. Six body colors could be combined with beige or red upholstery in specific combinations. Soft tops came in black, white or beige, also in specific combinations with certain body colors.

For the first time, the Corvette offered real engine options and some of the choices worked out by Zora Arkus-Duntov were designed to blow the doors off the competition. The 1955 V-8 – with hydraulic lifters and compression bumped to 9.25:1 -- was the base engine. Even this version made over 200 hp.

Two optional 265-cid V-8s were offered. The "Turbo-Fire" 225 featured solid valve lifters, two Carter four-barrel carbs and dual-exhausts. It was good for 225 hp at 5200 rpm. The Turbo-Fire 240 option added a high-lift camshaft to get up to 240 hp. A close-ratio three-speed manual all-synchromesh transmission with floor-mounted gear shifter was standard equipment. The two-speed Powerglide automatic transmission was a $175 option.

Ed Cole and Duntov decided it was time for the Corvette to go racing. In the spring of 1956, at Pebble Beach, dentist Dr. Dick Thompson finished second overall and first in class in the road race. He then went on to take the Sports Car Club of America (SCCA) 1956 championship with his Corvette.

1956 Corvette Status Guide	Basket Case		Average Driver		Rare, Unique or Completely Original		Restored
Condition of CORVETTE:	Production Status						
	Average	Rare/ Unique	N-O-M	O-M	Needs Work	Unrestored Low Mileage	Restored
Suggested Actions: Collect It							
Drive, Show and Enjoy							
Race, Autocross Competitively							
Store for a Future Project/Investment							
Candidate for Resto Rod							
Restore to Curb Appeal Condition							

1957 Corvette

Rock and Roll was catching on in America in 1957, with songs like "All Shook Up," "Party Doll," "Jailhouse Rock" and "Little Darlin'" zooming to the top of the Hit Parade. Corvette sales – as well as performance— were zooming, too. Zora Arkus-Duntov was off on a mission to transform the "'Corvette" into something more than a car that looked like Captain Video's boulevard cruiser.

In a short span of time, Chevrolet's two-seat dream machine had become a true sports car. Six cylinders under the hood was already a thing of the past. Six rockin' and rollin' V-8s were on the list for 1957. The small-block was bored out to 283 cubic inches and offered ratings from 220 to 283 hp. That last number was considered quite magical in 1957 – 1 H.P. per cubic inch! "Chevy puts the purr in performance," the ad copywriters of the era proclaimed.

The Corvette's appearance and style were improving as well. Seven colors were available: Onyx Black, Polo White, Aztec Copper, Arctic Blue, Cascade Green, Venetian Red and Inca Silver. White, Silver and Beige were optional color choices for

By 1957, the Corvette's reputation had been entrenched. It was a fine sports car. *Tom Glatch*

The 1957 Corvette was at the beginning of a very special era in Corvette history. *Tom Glatch*

MIKE YAGER SAYS:	
CHEERS	The new 283 V-8 was available with fuel injection, among six Corvette engine options. A four-speed transmission was available late in production meaning three transmissions were available. The unique two-year body style. The optional hardtop. Major interior restoration parts and chassis parts are easy to find.
JEERS	It is difficult to find a correct 1957 Corvette with a four-speed transmission. Only 10 percent of 1957 Corvettes originally had the four-speed transmission. Buyer beware in today's marketplace! Chrome and stainless steel moldings are hard to find.
GAME PLAN	Look for low production colors: Aztec Copper, Arctic Blue and Inca Silver. RPO684 (fuel injection) is a very desirable and rare option. RPO 579E, the 283-cid, 283-hp option, also included a fresh air intake and a steering column-mounted tachometer. Buyers should be aware that the desirability of this year's Corvette has created many bogus anon-original Corvettes. This car earned the distinction of "classic" and is a true piece of Americana.

The 1957 Corvette was one of the select Chevrolet models to receive a fuel injected V-8. *Tom Glatch*

the elliptical side cove. All "'Corvettes" also had a three-spoke competition-style steering wheel, an outside rearview mirror and a tachometer. The lock-nut-style rear view mirror required a wrench to adjust it, but didn't jiggle around at speed.

Chevrolet had been watching Ford's attempts to use the T-Bird as an "image car" to help sell standard Fords. So Chevrolet advertisements this year showed scenes such as a Cascade Green Corvette parked outside a garage shared with a red Bel Air Sports Coupe. Corvette sales increased 82 percent by the end of the year and the Corvette image helped sell other models, too.

Making headlines in the buff books was the top-of-the-heap 283-cid, 283-hp fuel-injected V-8. Its continuous-flow fuel-injection system was a team effort involving Zora Arkus-Duntov, John Dolza and General Motor's Rochester Division. Only 1,040 Corvettes were fuel-injected, but the "fuelie's" reputation on roads and racetracks was one reason for the sizeable gain in overall sales. The 283-hp Corvette could go from 0-to-60 mph in 5.7 seconds and from 0-to-100 mph in 16.8 seconds. It had a top speed of 132 mph.

The base 220-hp engine came with hydraulic lifters and a four-barrel carburetor. Adding dual Carter WCFB four-barrels created a 245-hp version that's very streetable and popular with collectors today. A second dual-carb "Super-Turbo-Fire" V-8 with a special Duntov–designed cam generated 270 hp at 6,000 rpm.

There were actually two "Ram-Jet" fuel-injected engines, both 283-based. The first, with a 9.5:1 compression ratio, generated 250 hp at 5,000 rpm and 305 foot-pounds of torque at 3,800 rpm. The second had a 10.5:1 compression ratio and did the 1-H.P. per cubic inch trick. Rated torque was 290 at 4,400. A race-oriented close-ratio four-speed manual all-synchromesh transmission with floor-mounted gear shifter was added to the options list in May.

Another important option was a competition suspension package RPO 684 which included heavy-duty springs, shocks and roll bars, 16.3:1 quick-ratio steering, a Positraction differential, special brake cooling equipment and Cerametallic brake linings. Dick Thompson and Gaston Audrey won the 12-hour Sebring race in Corvettes and Thompson took the SCCA B-production championship for the second year in a row.

1957 Corvette Status Guide	Basket Case		Average Driver		Rare, Unique or Completely Original		Restored
Condition of CORVETTE:	Production Status						
	Average	Rare/ Unique	N–O–M	O–M	Needs Work	Unrestored Low Mileage	Restored
Suggested Actions: Collect It							
Drive, Show and Enjoy							
Race, Autocross Competitively							
Store for a Future Project/Investment							
Candidate for Resto Rod							
Restore to Curb Appeal Condition							

1957 'VETTE FACTS	
VEHICLE IDENTIFICATION NUMBER	Corvettes for 1957 were numbered E57S100001 to E57S106339. The first symbol E = Corvette. The second and third symbols 57=1957. The fourth symbol S=St. Louis, Mo., assembly plant. The last six symbols were digits representing the sequential production numbers.
ENGINE	**Type: V-8** Bore and stroke: 3.875 x 3.00 in. Displacement: 283 cid Brake hp: 220 at 5600 rpm. Induction: Carter 4-bbl. **Options:** 283-cid/220-hp w/ 4-bbl. carb 283-cid/245-hp w/ two 4-bbl. carbs 283-cid/250-hp w/ Ram Jet fuel injection 283-cid/270-hp w/ two 4-bbl. Carbs 283-cid/283-hp w/ Ram Jet fuel injection
VITAL STATS	Original Price: $3,465 Production: 6,339 Wheelbase: 102 in. Length: 168 in. Tires: 6.70 x 15
COOL STUFF	The '57 'Vettes were coming when Larry Shinoda went to work for GM in September 1956. He would later gain fame for designing the Sting Ray. To tell a '57 'Vette from a '56, look for the new thumb-screw-adjustment inside rearview mirror. It requires a special wrench. Polo White was used for the last time on Corvettes in 1957. Correct '57 'Vettes are best-of-the-best cars in the collectors' market.

Corvettes were becoming well known as performance-oriented sports cars by 1957. *Tom Glatch*

The logo and flags told the story that this Corvette had something special under the hood. *Tom Glatch*

1957 CORVETTE SEBRING RACE CAR

The former air strip at Sebring, Florida and the sporty Corvette were made for one another. *Tom Glatch*

The engine was a big reason this Corvette won at the 12 hour Sebring race. *Tom Glatch*

The interior of this race car was meant for business on the track rather than comfort. *Tom Glatch*

1958 Corvette

Chevrolet called the Corvette "America's only authentic sports car," but some sports car purists argued the point. The two-seater took aim at the luxury market a bit this year. There was almost a "Cadillac" look to the four chrome-rimmed headlights. Long chrome bars extended from them and ran back down the fenders. Dummy air louvers decorated the hood. Three horizontal chrome strips were added to the side cove and the trunk now had a pair of chrome "suspenders." More massive wraparound bumpers were used front and rear.

Inside the Corvette, the gauges were now clustered in a panel directly in front of the driver. A center console and passenger side "grab handle" were added. Safety belts for the driver and passenger were made factory equipment. They had been a dealer accessory up to this time. In 1958, people associated seat belts with airplanes and racing cars, so the idea of the factory offering them in Corvettes enhanced the car's performance image at very low cost.

This year there were four horsepower options and eight distinct power teams.

The 1958 Corvette took on a new grille and quad headlights. *Tom Glatch*

MIKE YAGER SAYS:	
CHEERS	This was the first year for the quad headlights. Colors and minor exterior features make this car unique and very identifiable from the 1959 and 1960 versions. Very unique exterior and interior colors, including the only year for the Pebble Grain interior vinyl. The "washboard" style hood and trunk chrome spears are unique. The first year for the "Wonderbar" radio. Stock steel wheels and replacement three-speed transmissions are easy to find. So are major interior restoration parts and chassis parts.
JEERS	The 1958 Corvette is expensive to restore it and continued to use the same chassis and suspension as the 1953 version. Parts that are difficult to find include the convertible top frame, good trunk spears, the correct engine block and correct versions of the four-speed transmission. Chrome and stainless steel moldings and trim are hard to find.
GAME PLAN	Look for as original and untouched versions as possible. The ownership history and provenance are very important for the best return on investment. Beware of cars with rare colors and added options. This is one of my favorite years!

Corvette's taillight area was more refined than the grille, but still chrome-laden. *Tom Glatch*

All of them were once again based on the famous 283-cid Chevrolet small-block V-8 and even the standard 230-hp version (available with manual or automatic transmission) had a four-barrel carburetor and dual exhausts. A 245-hp option with dual four-barrel carbs was also available with both transmissions, A fuel-injected

version produced 250 hp and also came with both trannys. A solid-lifter V-8 with dual four-barrels made 270 hp. The top option was a fuel-injected solid-lifter V-8 with an 11.5:1 compression ratio and 290 hp. The last two engines came only with manual transmission.

To go along with the boost in luxury, the Corvette's option list kept growing. It included such non-sports-car-like amenities as a parking brake alarm for $5.40, windshield washers for $16.15, white sidewall tires for $31.55 extra, electric power windows for $59.20 and a power-operated

1958 'VETTE FACTS	
VEHICLE IDENTIFICATION NUMBER	Corvettes for 1958 were numbered J58S100001 to J58S109168. The first symbol J = Corvette. The second and third symbols 58=1958. The fourth symbol S=St. Louis, Mo., assembly plant. The last six symbols were digits representing the sequential production number.
ENGINE	**Type: V-8** Bore and stroke: 3.875 x 3.00 in. Displacement: 283 cid Brake hp: 230 at 4800 rpm. Induction: Carter or Rochester 4-bbl. **Options:** 283-cid/245-hp w/ two 4-bbl. carbs 283-cid/250-hp w/ Ram Jet fuel injection 283-cid/270-hp w/ two 4-bbl. carbs 283-cid/290-hp w/ Ram Jet fuel injection
VITAL STATS	Original Price: $3,631 Production: 9,168 Wheelbase: 102 in. Length: 177.2 in. Tires: 6.70 x 15
COOL STUFF	1958 was the last year for the "cumulative" tachometer that kept track of engine revolutions and it was not installed in all '58 models either. Acrylic lacquer paint was used on all '58 Corvettes, not just Inca Silver cars. A show car Corvette with a retractable hardtop was built for the 1958 GM Motorama.

The '58 Corvette had gauges placed in a centrally located cluster. *Tom Glatch*

Up to 290-hp was available for the more adventurous '58 Corvette drivers willing to order fuel injection.   *Tom Glatch*

1958 Corvette Status Guide	Basket Case		Average Driver		Rare, Unique or Completely Original		Restored
Condition of CORVETTE:	Production Status						
	Average	Rare/ Unique	N-O-M	O-M	Needs Work	Unrestored Low Mileage	Restored
Suggested Actions: Collect It							
Drive, Show and Enjoy							
Race, Autocross Competitively							
Store for a Future Project/Investment							
Candidate for Resto Rod							
Restore to Curb Appeal Condition							

folding top mechanism for $139.90. This was not your father's MG or Triumph!

Racing enthusiasts also found expanded competition components on the lengthy list of extras. In addition to hotter engines and a four-speed "stirrer" on the floor, they could tack on a Positraction axle with 3.70:1 or 4.11:1 gear ratios, a heavy-duty racing suspension and wider 15 x 5.5-inch wheels.

A 230-hp Corvette did 0-to-60 mph in 9.2 seconds and the quarter mile in 17.4 seconds at 83 mph. With the pedal to the floorboards you could push the needle up to 103 mph. With the 250-hp fuel-injection engine 0-to-60 mph took 7.6 seconds and the quarter mile disappeared in 15.7 seconds at 90 mph. Top speed was 120 mph. The 290-hp V-8 – used in about 11 percent of all cars built – took only 6.9 seconds to go from 0-to-60 mph. That was fast in 1958!

This photogenic 1958 Corvette was a scene stealer and very much at home around bodies of water—or any other scene where beauty played a part. *Trevor and Maria Yoho*

1959 Corvette

A popular 1959 song, "Everything's Coming Up Roses," could have been the latest Corvette's theme song. Chevrolet cleaned up the Corvette's hood louvers and chrome suspenders and sports car fans reacted positively. The car's basic technology was left pretty much untouched, but the steering gear was tweaked to enhance handling and performance driving.

Enthusiasts really started taking to the car's improvements this year. Actually, the Corvette had taken a quantum leap toward becoming a real sports car in 1958, but the over-styled decorative treatment had masked the realities of taut handling, strong drivability and blazing speed With the tinsel removed for 1959, Ray Brock gave the Corvette high ratings in his *Hot Rod* magazine road test. Even *Road & Track*, with its bias for imports, had to admit that that the Corvette was pretty… and speedy, too. *Motor Trend* pitted a Corvette against a Porsche and the German car won – at least in miles per gallon. The fiberglass wonder

A great color combination was the Inca Silver exterior with a red interior. *Tom Glatch*

Chevrolet got the most out of the 283-cid "small block" with up to 290-hp in 1959. *Tom Glatch*

Inside, the 1959 Corvette now featured a Madrid-grain vinyl interior. *Tom Glatch*

took all the other kudos. This was really the beginning of the Corvette being viewed as a reasonably-priced "world-class" sports car.

Chevrolet invested some studio time in interior design and came up with new bucket seats and door panels, a fiberglass package tray under the "sissy" bar and reflection-reducing concave gauge lenses. The inside door knobs were moved to the front of the door, so passengers would no longer get their clothing caught on them. Chevrolet also made the characters on the gauges more legible. Changing from pebble-grain vinyl to smooth Madrid vinyl made the seats look less like leather, but vinyl was "in" at this time. This was the first year you could get a true black (rather than charcoal) interior. A turquoise convertible top was also available.

A new 7,000-rpm tachometer, an outside rearview mirror, seat belts for the driver and passenger and an electric clock were standard features inside all Corvettes. Sun visors were optional, as were automatic transmission and power windows. Air conditioning, power brakes and power steering were not offered. The optional – and today very desirable – four-speed manual transmission had a new T-shaped reverse-lockout shifter with a white plastic shifter knob. The clutch was modified to permit a wider range of adjustments.

Under-hood options were the same as in 1958. All power options were based on the 283-cid "small-block" Chevy V-8. A 230-hp rating was standard and options included 245-, 250-, 270 and 290-hp engines. The respective torque ratings were 300, 300, 305,

MIKE YAGER SAYS:	
CHEERS	The new, clean exterior with the trunk spears and washboard hood gone. More exterior color choices. The unique interior with smooth vinyl. The four-speed transmission with its T-handle and reverse lockout shifter. 1959 was the first year for the "big tank" option. Major interior restoration and chassis parts are easy to find.
JEERS	Many 1959 Corvettes were modified and raced. The 1959 version is expensive to restore and is not showing the return of the 1958 version. The car still used the 1953 chassis and suspension. Parts that are difficult to find include the convertible top frame, original seat belts, the correct engine blocks and four-speed transmissions, inside door handles and the proper radios. Also, any chrome and stainless steel trim and moldings are hard to find.
GAME PLAN	Look for the most original and untouched examples as possible. The best examples of these cars often are "barn finds." Among the 1958 to 1960 Corvettes, this might be the best buy for a driver straight-axle Corvette. Again this year, be careful of cars with added options and rare colors. The 1959 Corvette has a lower price in the marketplace than either the 1958 or 1960. Look for ownership history and provenance. Choose a great-priced driver and enjoy!

High horsepower produced healthy torque ratings—as much as 305 lbs-ft in 1959. *Tom Glatch*

The fuel injection badge quickly told everyone who noticed what was under the hood. *Tom Glatch*

Rochester fuel-injection system is worth thousands today.

Chassis-wise, little changed, but mechanical improvements were made where needed. A new Saginaw re-circulating ball steering system had a 17:1 ratio, 3.7 turns lock-to-lock and a 38.5-foot turning circle. A new option was brakes with sintered metallic liners suitable for racing. Even harder springs were included in the optional heavy-duty suspension. Chevrolet advertised that the Corvette's Parallelogram Rear Suspension "nails all that torque right to the pavement." This setup used radius rods attached to the suspension to reduce axle tramp.

285 and 290 foot-pounds. A 3.70:1 rear axle ratio was standard with 4.11:1 and 4.56:1 options. The 290-hp fuel-injection engine with the 4.11:1 rear axle was the hot setup. It was a $484.20 option in 1959, but a restored

1959 'VETTE FACTS	
VEHICLE IDENTIFICATION NUMBER	Corvettes for 1959 were numbered J59S100001 to J59S109670. The first symbol J = Corvette. The second and third symbols 59 = 1959. The fourth symbol S = St. Louis, Missouri, assembly plant. The last six symbols were digits representing the sequential production number.
ENGINE	**Type: V-8** Bore and stroke: 3.87 x 3.00 in. Displacement: 283 cid Brake hp: 230 at 4,800 rpm. Induction: Carter WCFB four-barrel #2816. **Options:** 283-cid/245-hp w/ two 4-bbl. carb 283-cid/250-hp w/ Ram Jet fuel injection 283-cid/270-hp w/ two 4-bbl. carb 283-cid/290-hp w/ Ram Jet fuel injection
VITAL STATS	Original Price: $3,875 Production: 9,670 Wheelbase: 102 in. Length: 177.2 in. Tires: 6.70 x 15
COOL STUFF	*Road & Track* described the 1959 Corvette as "a pretty package with all the speed you need and then some." A 290-hp fuel-injected 1959 Corvette with the 4.11:1 rear axle could go from 0-to-60 mph in 6.8 seconds and from 0-to-100 mph in 15.5 seconds. It did the quarter mile in 14.9 seconds at 96 mph and had a top speed of 124 mph. Race driver Jim Jeffords won the Sports Car Club of America B-Production championship for 1959 with a Corvette.

On highways and race tracks, many saw only the rear angle of the 1959 Corvette. *Tom Glatch*

A new style of bucket seats was one of the additions to the 1959 Corvette. *Tom Glatch*

1959 Corvette Status Guide	Basket Case		Average Driver		Rare, Unique or Completely Original		Restored
Condition of CORVETTE:	Production Status						
	Average	Rare/ Unique	N–O–M	O–M	Needs Work	Unrestored Low Mileage	Restored
Suggested Actions: Collect It							
Drive, Show and Enjoy							
Race, Autocross Competitively							
Store for a Future Project/Investment							
Candidate for Resto Rod							
Restore to Curb Appeal Condition							

1960 Corvette

Chevrolet considered launching an all-new 1960 Corvette based on the experimental Q-model with a 94-inch wheelbase, fully-independent suspension and a rear-mounted transaxle. Market realities quenched that idea and Corvette started the 1960s as a bugs-in-your-teeth roadster styled in the old mold. It looked much the same as the 1959 model and had much the same technology.

The only model listed was a convertible. Owners could add a bolt-on hardtop. America's first rear sway bar suspension was introduced. The double sway bar setup improved the Corvette's handling immensely. So did a larger-diameter front anti-roll bar.

Aluminum "fuelie" cylinder heads were planned, but never used in production cars because they had design flaws and tended to warp if the engine got hot. They were 53 pounds lighter than the cast-iron heads. Clutch housings – and the radiators in cars with 270- and 290-hp engines – were also made of aluminum. The result was a lighter car. For example, the aluminum clutch

A new decade began with subtle changes on the popular 1960 Corvette. *Tom Glatch*

MIKE YAGER SAYS:	
CHEERS	There were performance-minded changes from the 1959 cars including the new sway bar suspension. The fuel injection system was refined. New exterior colors included Tasco Turquoise, Honduras Maroon, Sateen Silver and Horizon Blue. The stock steel wheels are easy to find and so are major interior restoration parts and chassis parts.
JEERS	The 1960 version is expensive to repair and does not show the return of the 1958 version. The chassis and suspension systems were virtually the same as the 1953. Many of these cars were modified, customized or raced. Parts that are difficult to find include the convertible top frame and power top assemblies. Also such parts as original seat belts, the correct heads, carburetors, engine blocks and either three- or four-speed transmissions, the inside door handles and the correct radios. The chrome and stainless steel moldings and trim also are difficult to find items.
GAME PLAN	Look for as original and untouched cars as you can find with full options and high horsepower. The fuel injection, heavy-duty brakes and 24-gallon fuel tanks are very desirable. Also look for cars with RPO 687, the heavy-duty brakes and suspensions. Check out cars with power tops and power windows. Check trader publications—these cars often are "barn finds" or back lot bargains. This might be the "sleeper" among the 1958 to 1962 Corvettes.

Horsepower choices available for the 1960 Corvette ranged from 230 to 290 hp.   *Tom Glatch*

housing cut the Corvette's weight by 18 pounds.

Standard equipment included a small-block V-8, a tachometer, sun visors, a dual-exhaust system, carpeting, seat belts, an outside rearview mirror and an electric clock.

A 1960 Corvette with the base 283-cid 230-hp V-8 could go from 0-to-60 in 8.4 seconds and do the quarter mile in 16.1 seconds at 89 mph. There were six optional V-8s with up to 290 horsepower and a choice of dual four-barrel carburetors or fuel-injection. One change for 1960 was that fuel-injected engines were only available in cars with the four-speed manual gearbox.

A blood-boiling aspect of '60 Corvette history was its race track performances. With support from Zora Arkus-Duntov, Briggs Cunningham took three Corvettes to Le Mans to run in the big-bore GT class. These were upgraded production cars with "fuelie" V-8s and Duntov tuned them more for durability than speed. When he had parts problems his old friend General Curtis Le May, of the U.S. Air Force, arranged to have

1960 'VETTE FACTS	
VEHICLE IDENTIFICATION NUMBER	Corvettes for 1960 were numbered 00867S100001 to 00867S110261. The first symbol 0=1960. The second and third symbols 08=Corvette. The fourth and fifth symbols 67 = convertible. The sixth symbol S= the St. Louis, Missouri, assembly plant. The last six symbols were digits representing the sequential production numbers.
ENGINE	**Type: V-8** Bore and stroke: 3.87 x 3.oo in. Displacement: 283 cid Brake hp: 230 at 4,800 rpm. Induction: Carter WCFB 4-barrel #3779178. **Options:** Base - 230-hp 283-cid/245-hp w/ two - 4-bbl. carb 283-cid/250-hp w/ Ram Jet fuel injection 283-cid/270-hp w/ two - 4-bbl. carb 283-cid/290-hp w/ Ram Jet fuel injection
VITAL STATS	Original Price: $3,872 Production: 10,261 Wheelbase: 102 in. Length: 177.2 in. Tires: 6.70 x 15
COOL STUFF	The majority of 1960 Corvettes, 50.1 percent, were sold with a detachable hardtop. Most 1960 Corvettes – 51.9 percent – had the four-speed manual transmission. The "Route 66" television series, featuring Martin Milner and George Maharis, debuted on October 7, 1960. The boys drove a new, light blue 1961 'Vette.

Drivers enjoyed a tachometer and an electric clock inside the 1960 Corvette.   *Tom Glatch*

the parts picked up from GM and flown to France.

One car hit 151 mph on the Mulsanne Straight, but later dropped out of the race. A second Corvette, driven by John Fitch and Bob Grossman, finished eighth. That was impressive, but it also happened because bad weather slowed down the competition. The overall message to European enthusiasts was the Corvette was on its way to earning some stripes in international competition.

In the United States, in SCCA events, daring dentist Dr. Richard Thompson piloted his "Sting Ray Special" to a Class C Sports/ Racing national championship. This car was the same experimental SS Corvette – known as the "mule" – that Zora Arkus-Duntov had prepared for Sebring racing in 1956. Design chief Bill Mitchell had purchased it from GM for a dollar and built it into a racing car with his own money. It could do 0-to-60 in four seconds and was fast enough for Thompson to take many checkered flags. Mitchell had to promise GM that he would not call the car a Corvette, but everyone knew it was and it established the image for the mold-breaking '63 Sting Ray's design.

Late in 1960, the "Route 66" television show debuted. It made a very positive effect on future Corvette sales, but the success of the series had little or no impact on the 1960 model, as the 1961 versions were out by the time the TV show was broadcast.

1960 Corvette Status Guide	Basket Case		Average Driver		Rare, Unique or Completely Original		Restored
Condition of CORVETTE:	Production Status						
	Average	Rare/ Unique	N-O-M	O-M	Needs Work	Unrestored Low Mileage	Restored
Suggested Actions: Collect It							
Drive, Show and Enjoy							
Race, Autocross Competitively							
Store for a Future Project/Investment							
Candidate for Resto Rod							
Restore to Curb Appeal Condition							

Shades of red always blend with Corvette styling. In this case, a 1960 edition. *Doug Mitchel*

This shade of green was popular in the early 1960s but it is overlooked today. *Doug Mitchel*

You couldn't see it from the outside but Corvette was a potent car in 1960. *Tom Glatch*

1961 Corvette

The new television "Route 66" TV show had a pretty basic plot involving two young men and a sports car. Actor Marty Milner played Tod Stiles, a silver-spoon-in-his-mouth type of guy whose father died and left his son a new Corvette. This inspired him and his pal Buzz Murdock (played by George Maharis) to a fit of wanderlust. For the next three years, they criss-crossed America in the car, learning about life and experiencing many adventures.

The show bowed on October 7, 1960 and took place in a different locale each week. There was a long list of guest stars. The acting wasn't great and the plots were somewhat predictable, but the changing cast and cities, combined with the freedom the Corvette roadster stood for, made "Route 66" a big hit. It was no fluke that Corvette sales jumped each year the show was on – from 10,939 in 1961, to 14,531 in 1962, to 21,513 in 1963.

Here's a Corvette that was meant for power and speed, the "Big Brake" Corvette. *Tom Glatch*

Heavy duty brakes and suspension were part of the goodies on this 1961 Corvette.   *Tom Glatch*

Inside, the "Big Brake" Corvette had a four-speed transmission.   *Tom Glatch*

MIKE YAGER SAYS:	
CHEERS	The fresh, new "shark" styling on the tail with the first use of the quad taillights. The new front grille. More trunk space and a cleaner exhaust exit. The new high-performance cylinder heads and all-aluminum transmission case. The new vinyl seat pattern. Parts that are easy to find include the stock steel wheels, correct replacement 283 engines and correct radiators. Chassis parts and major interior restoration parts also are easy to find.
JEERS	These cars are expensive to repair and don't show the return of the 1962 version. They still used virtually the same suspension and chassis as the 1953 Corvette. Many of these cars were customized, raced or modified. Watch for frame rust on the 1961 Corvettes. It is hard to find the correct engine block, heads, carburetors and both the three- and four-speed transmissions. The correct top frames, hardtops and seat frames are difficult to find. Original seat belts, inside door handles, exterior trim and radios also are difficult items to find. Generally, chrome and stainless moldings and trim are scarce in this era.
GAME PLAN	Look for as original and untouched versions as you can find. Look for fully-optioned cars with high horsepower, heavy duty brakes and suspensions, as well as unique trim and colors. Beware of rare colors and added options. The 1961 is a better value than the 1962 version but is not as desirable. Cars with fuel injection, the rare 24-gallon fuel tank and heavy-duty brakes are extremely desirable. Look for a low mileage car with unique options such as Powerglide transmission and the 245 hp V-8 with dual quads.

Here's a Corvette that was meant for power and speed, the "Big Brake" Corvette "fuelie." *Tom Glatch*

The popularity of "Route 66" made it an ongoing ad for Chevy's only two-passenger car. Maharis and Milner became famous and so did the car they drove. Every red-blooded male in America under the age of 30 soon dreamed of owning a Corvette and driving it coast to coast instead of working.

A refined, thin, vertical and horizontal bar grille quickly set the '61 Corvette apart from the 1960 model. To give the car a nastier, more functional look, the headlight bezels were done in body color instead of chrome. A new duck-tail rear end treatment with four cylindrical taillights was a predecessor to the Sting Ray-look coming in 1963. This was adopted from the XP-700 concept car that Bill Mitchell designed. It added more space to the Corvette's trunk.

Standard equipment included a tachometer, seat belts, sun visors, a dual-exhaust system, floor carpeting, an electric clock, an outside rearview mirror, a lockable rear-seat storage area and a new aluminum radiator. A temperature-controlled radiator fan was also made standard.

1961 'VETTE FACTS	
VEHICLE IDENTIFICATION NUMBER	Corvettes for 1961 were numbered 10867S100001 to 10867S110939. The first symbol 1 = 1961. The second and third symbols 08 = Corvette. The fourth and fifth symbols 67 = convertible. The sixth symbol S = the St. Louis, Missouri, assembly plant. The last six symbols were digits representing the sequential production numbers.
ENGINE	**Type: V-8** Bore and stroke: 3.87 x 3.00 in. Displacement: 283 cid Brake hp: 230 at 4800 rpm. Induction: Carter WCFB 4-barrel #3779178. **Options:** 283-cid/275-hp w/ Ram Jet fuel injection 283-cid/245-hp w/ two 4-bbl. carb 283-cid/270-hp w/ two 4-bbl. carb 315-hp w/ Ram Jet fuel injection
VITAL STATS	Original Price: $3,934 Production: 10,939 Wheelbase: 102 in. Length: 177.2 in. Tires: 6.70 x 15
COOL STUFF	This was the last year a contrasting color could be ordered from the factory for the side coves. This cost $16.15. Also, this was the final year the 283-cid Chevy small-block V-8 was used in the Corvette. And this was the last year wide whitewall tires were available on a Corvette. The extra charge was $31.55. A brand new baby blue '61 Corvette was used in the "Route 66" television series at first. Later, a brown Corvette was used. "Route 66" was one of the most massive mobile filming operations in television history. A crew of 50 people traveled throughout America in assorted vehicles and two tractor trailers to put the programs together.

There were five engines this year, one (230 hp) with a single four-barrel, two (245 and 270 hp) with dual-quad carb setups and two (275 and 315 hp) with fuel injection. Most Corvettes – more than 64 percent – had a three- or four-speed manual transmission. This year, the optional four-speed gearbox was improved with an aluminum transmission case. An optional Powerglide automatic transmission was a third choice.

The Corvette's exhaust pipes now exited under the car, rather than through ports in the rear bumper. The through-the-bumper styling looked great, but ruined many bumpers. This was the next-to-last year for a solid rear axle, which Corvette collectors now consider the dividing line between "classic" and the "midyear" (1963-67) models. The conventional suspension worked well. Road & Track said the Corvette had better "sticking ability on curves" than its competitors. It also said the Corvette was "unmatched for performance per dollar."

Interior styling followed the same theme as earlier, but there were numerous detail differences. The vinyl upholstery had a vertically-ribbed pattern with simulated machine stitching embossed into it. A heater was still optional equipment and cost $102.25 extra. A power convertible top mechanism cost $161.40 and a detachable fiberglass hardtop cost $236.75.

A Corvette first in class at the 12 Hours of Sebring seemed like a given by 1961, when Delmo Johnson and Dale Morgan garnered the honors. Ak Miller also repeated as first in class at Pikes Peak in a Corvette.

Meanwhile, Dr. Dick Thompson was racking up enough points for his second-in-a-row SCCA Class B-Production title.

Special production orders took a mild-mannered Corvette and made it a mauler. *Tom Glatch*

1961 Corvette Status Guide	Basket Case		Average Driver		Rare, Unique or Completely Original		Restored
Condition of CORVETTE:	Production Status						
	Average	Rare/ Unique	N-O-M	O-M	Needs Work	Unrestored Low Mileage	Restored
Suggested Actions: Collect It							
Drive, Show and Enjoy							
Race, Autocross Competitively							
Store for a Future Project/Investment							
Candidate for Resto Rod							
Restore to Curb Appeal Condition							

1962 Corvette

The 1962 Corvette is considered by many to mark a high point in the history of Chevrolet's sports car, and not without good reason. The '62 Vette represents the "Best of Both Worlds." It was the last Corvette based on the original "sports roadster" platform and the last "straight axle" car. When equipped with the new fuel-injected 327-cid 360-hp V-8, it was a preview of what was to come, performance-wise, in the muscle-car era. The 1962 was an almost ideal combination of classic beauty and future brawn. *Esquire* magazine opined that Chevrolet general manager Ed Cole and crew had "Brought into

The 1962 edition of the Corvette was the last of the original styling. It wore its look well. *Tom Glatch*

A new 327-cid V-8 was introduced in the 1962 Corvettes. *Tom Glatch*

The 1962 Corvette interior seemed to be the ideal cockpit for the active driver in 1962. *Tom Glatch*

full flower an American sports car that can hold its own with any marque in the world."

Design-wise, the '62 'Vette was essentially a carryover from the previous year's model. The most noticeable styling changes were the removal of the side cove chrome trim, the use of a blackout style grille and the appearance of ribbed chrome rocker panel moldings. For the first time since 1955, Corvettes were offered in solid colors only. Corvette wheels were available in black, beige, red, silver or maroon. The color of the car denoted the color of the wheel on the assembly line.

MIKE YAGER SAYS:	
CHEERS	The introduction of the new 327 V-8. It was the best engine combination with the 327 and fuel injection. It was the best year for fuel injection from 1957 through 1962. The car had a new front grille, a cleaner body and the optional cove colors were gone. There were new exterior emblems and trim. The interior restoration parts and chassis parts are easy to find. Stock steel wheels are easy to find. You might call the '62 Corvette "Beauty and the Beast."
JEERS	The 1962 Corvette is expensive to restore and has many unique, small parts, in addition to the chrome and stainless moldings and trim. While chassis and suspension was upgraded to true driving sports car status with additional options, it still was the same old 1953 design. Additional parts that were hard to find included the two-year only convertible top frame and hardtop, the correct engine block, carburetors and heads. The correct radios, both three- and four-speed transmissions, seat frames and headlight eyebrow trim also are hard to find.
GAME PLAN	This is the car that drew me to the Corvette hobby. Find yourself a Fawn Beige "fuel" version with full options or maybe a good driver with the incorrect engine. You can't go wrong with a 1962—a great driving car! Just ask Buzz and Todd! Look for as original and untouched an example as you can find—fully optioned, high horsepower with heavy duty brakes and suspension, fuel injection and a big fuel tank.

This Corvette had the 360-hp fuel-injection version of the 327-cid V-8 introduced in 1962. *Tom Glatch*

The 1962 Corvette interior seemed to be the ideal cockpit for the active driver in 1962. *Tom Glatch*

Standard equipment included: a small-block V-8, an electric clock, a dual-exhaust system, a tachometer, a heater and defroster, seat belts, an outside rearview mirror and windshield washers. Stiff rear leaf springs were reinstated as a Corvette performance option.

Under the hood is where the '62 Corvette really set itself apart. A new 327-cid small-block V-8 was introduced and used in all models. This was a bored-and-stroked version of the 283. A single fuel-injected version of the new engine was available. It was the most powerful Corvette engine

1962 'VETTE FACTS	
VEHICLE IDENTIFICATION NUMBER	Corvettes for 1962 were numbered 20867S100001 to 20867S114531. The first symbol 2 = 1962. The second and third symbols 08 = Corvette. The fourth and fifth symbols 67 = convertible. The sixth symbol S = St. Louis, Missouri, assembly plant. The last six symbols were digits representing the sequential production numbers.
ENGINE	**Type: V-8** Bore and stroke: 4.00 x 3.25 in. Displacement: 327 cid Brake hp: 250 at 4,400 rpm. Induction: Carter WCFB 4-barrel #3788246. **Options:** 327-cid/300-hp w/ 4-bbl. carb 327-cid/340-hp w/ 4-bbl. carb 327-cid/360 w/ Ram Jet fuel injection
VITAL STATS	Original Price: $4,038 Production: 14,531 Wheelbase: 102 in. Length: 177.2 in. Tires: 6.70 x 15
COOL STUFF	The 1962 was the last Corvette with exposed headlights. It was also the last Corvette to have a regular luggage compartment with a trunk lid until the 1998 convertible. 1962 was also the last year for a power-operated convertible top mechanism to be merchandised as optional equipment. Tires with thinner one-inch wide whitewalls were offered on Corvettes in 1962. The extra cost of $31.55 was the same as in 1961. The same circular rear emblem was used in 1961 and 1962, but in the later year the background color changed from silver to black.

ever offered up to this point and one of the best Corvette engines ever made. With an improved torque curve, the '62 Corvette could be a real runner, especially at the drag strip.

The 327 earned a great reputation in both passenger-car and high-performance applications, particularly when fuel injection was part of the equation. The numbers backed this view up. With a 0-to-30 time of just 2.5 seconds, a 5.9 second 0-to-60, a 13.5 second sprint from 0-to-100, a 14.5 second run through the traps and a top speed in the neighborhood of 150 mph, GM succeeded in doing what they had been doing ever since the Corvette was first introduced – the company took something good and made it better. A typical 327 with 3.70:1 gearing would do over 100 mph in 15 seconds. A new 3.08:1 rear axle was also added to the list for those who just wanted to cruise comfortably.

Even with vast improvements over the '61 model, particularly the new 327 engine, the '62 Corvette's base price was only marginally increased. No wonder the year turned out to be the Corvette's best sales season ever, with a total of 14,531 'Vettes leaving Chevrolet showrooms.

In 1962, a Corvette took first in class at the Daytona Continental. The "Flying Dentist"— Dr. Dick Thompson – took the SCCA Class A-Production title. Pennsylvania driver Don Yenko – who later gained fame for building muscular Camaros, Chevelles and Novas – became SCCA B-Production champ in his own Corvette.

The floor shift allowed the driver to race or cruise in style with the 1962 Corvette. *Tom Glatch*

1962 Corvette Status Guide	Basket Case		Average Driver		Rare, Unique or Completely Original		Restored
Condition of CORVETTE:	Production Status						
	Average	Rare/ Unique	N-O-M	O-M	Needs Work	Unrestored Low Mileage	Restored
Suggested Actions: Collect It							
Drive, Show and Enjoy							
Race, Autocross Competitively							
Store for a Future Project/Investment							
Candidate for Resto Rod							
Restore to Curb Appeal Condition							

1963 Corvette

The '63 Corvette Sting Ray was "majorly new." It evolved from a racing car called the Mitchell Sting Ray. Bill Mitchell had replaced Harley Earl as head of GM styling in 1958. He thought it was important to race the Corvette, so he persuaded Chevy's general manager Ed Cole to sell him the chassis of the '57 Corvette SS "mule" for $1. Mitchell then had designer Larry Shinoda create a body for the Sting Ray race car inspired by the sea creature of the same name.

For the first time, two distinct Corvette body styles were offered. The convertible returned and was available with an auxiliary hardtop for $236.75 extra. A unique new coupe had the look of a jet on wheels with a fastback roofline and a very aeronautical-looking two-piece rear window. Oohs and aahs went to this so-called "split-window" coupe. Larry Shinoda is credited with creating the "split-window," which Bill Mitchell loved. Zora Arkus-Duntov was against it because it limited the driver's rear vision. Duntov was into total functionality

The split-window was a one-year only design making it quite rare today. *Tom Glatch*

MIKE YAGER SAYS:	
CHEERS	Two completely new, timeless models with a completely new body design. Much was new including the interior, the independent rear suspension, air conditioning, the AM/FM radio, hidden headlights, the Saddle-colored leather interior and the knock-off aluminum wheels. There was an extra-rigid chassis and frame. Power steering and power brakes were available. New metallic paint colors were offered.
JEERS	Not many parts are easy to find for 1963 Corvettes. They are expensive to restore with many unique parts. Chrome and stainless moldings continue to be hard to find. The trunk was gone and the split-window coupe was a major blind spot for drivers. This is a tough car to restore to NCRS standards. Many unique features are difficult to find including the console, glove box door, body panels and seats. The fuel injection is very expensive to restore properly.
GAME PLAN	Look for an original and unrestored version, as much as possible. Many 1963 roadsters have been cut up to restore coupes—so look for a nice roadster! This is a car for the true enthusiast. Look for the Z0-6 and L-84 fuel injection options. Beware of cars with fake trim tags. This was the first year for documented color and trim tags. When you consider a coupe, look for rust and hidden problems. Inspect the window frame. Look carefully at the coupe's door fit. This is the car that made the Corvette hobby! From its introduction, Corvette has moved forward at a rapid pace and never looked back. Find a fuel roadster and hold on!

The '63 Corvette was sleek, powerful and available with many options. *Tom Glatch*

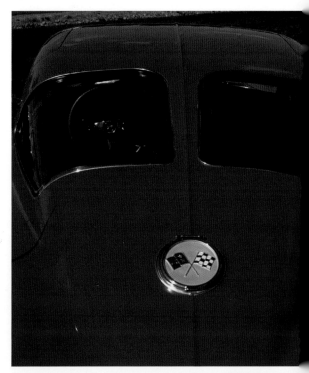

The split window – artistic and graceful but impractical for driving. *Tom Glatch*

1963 'VETTE FACTS	
VEHICLE IDENTIFICATION NUMBER	Corvette convertibles for 1963 were numbered 30867S100001 to 30867S121513. Corvette coupes for 1963 were numbered 30837S100001 to 30837S121513. The first symbol 3 = 1963. The second and third symbols 08 = Corvette. The fourth and fifth symbols 67 = convertible or 37 = coupe. The sixth symbol S = the St. Louis, Missouri, assembly plant. The last six symbols were digits representing the sequential production numbers.
ENGINE	**Type: V-8** Bore and stroke: 4.00 x 3.25 in. Displacement: 327 cid Brake hp: 250 at 4,400 rpm. Induction: Carter WCFB 4-barrel #3501S. **Options:** 327-cid/300-hp w/ 4-bbl. carb 327-cid/340-hp w/ 4-bbl. carb 327-cid/360 w/ Ram Jet fuel injection
VITAL STATS	**Convertible:** Original Price: $4,037 Production: 10,919 Wheelbase: 98 in. Length: 175.2 in. Tires: 6.70 x 15 **Coupe:** Original Price: $4,257 Production: 10,594 Wheelbase: 98 in. Length: 175.3 in. Tires: 6.70 x 15
COOL STUFF	Air conditioning was a rare Corvette option in 1963 because it was introduced late in the year. Larry Shinoda came up with the "split-window" coupe design, which Bill Mitchell loved although Zora Arkus-Duntov was against its vision-blocking look. The "split window" was offered only one year and has become a very collectible item. The fuel-injected '63 Corvette could go from 0-to-60 mph in 5.9 seconds and from 0-to-100 mph in 16.5 seconds. Corvette "firsts" for 1963 included optional knock-off wheels, air conditioning and leather upholstery. By March 1963, the stars of the "Route 66" TV show were feuding and George Maharis quit. Martin Milner continued to play the role of Tod who got a new sidekick named Lincoln Case (played by Glenn Corbett). The series continued for more than a year after the switch.

and the bar running down the center of the tiny window served no real function. The split-window style was offered for only one year and is very collectible now.

On both convertibles and coupes, the front fenders had two long non-functional louvers resembling brake cooling ducts. The rear deck resembled that of the 1962 model, but the rest of the car was totally new. Hideaway headlights were housed in an electrically-operated panel and enhanced the car's aerodynamics. The recessed fake hood louvers were decorative only.

The Corvette's sleek new interior had circular gauges with black faces. There was storage space under the seats of early models. Firsts for 1963 included optional knock-off wheels, air conditioning, power steering, power brakes and leather seats.

All four engines were based on the 327 offering 250, 300, 340 and 360 hp. The 360-

Drivers were greeted with a new gauge design among other amenities in 1963. *Tom Glatch*

The dramatic look of the 1963 Corvette Sting Ray was a sensation when it appeared. *Tom Glatch*

Semon "Bunkie" Knudsen had styling ideas expressed in this special '63 convertible. *Tom Glatch*

The styling exercise was carried out on the interior as well as the exterior of the car. *Tom Glatch*

The dramatic lake pipes are among the touches that marked the Knudsen Corvette. *Tom Glatch*

hp job carried the Rochester fuel-injection system.

Handling was greatly enhanced by the release of a independent rear suspension system. It was of three-link design with double-jointed open drive shafts on either end combined with control arms and trailing radius rods. A single transverse rear spring was mounted to the frame with rubber-cushioned struts. The differential was attached to the rear cross member. This gave improved 48 front and 52 rear weight distribution. Up front was a new re-circulating-ball steering gear and a three-link ball-joint front suspension.

As always, Duntov was intent on using what he learned at the track to improve the breed. His vision seemed to be paying off in increased sales and Corvette production totals increased year after year. On the Sting Ray's option list was a brand new Z06 package that included all sorts of race-bred goodies. Early in 1963, five historic Corvette Grand Sports were also constructed expressly for racing, before GM banned racing and canceled all factory support of race teams. The Grand Sports weighed 1,908 pounds. They were powered by a 377-cid version of the small-block Chevy V-8 equipped with an aluminum cylinder block and aluminum "hemi"-type cylinder heads. The Grand Sport Corvettes also featured a twin ignition system and port fuel-injection.

1963 Corvette Status Guide	Basket Case		Average Driver		Rare, Unique or Completely Original		Restored
Condition of CORVETTE:	Production Status						
	Average	Rare/ Unique	N–O–M	O–M	Needs Work	Unrestored Low Mileage	Restored
Suggested Actions: Collect It							
Drive, Show and Enjoy							
Race, Autocross Competitively							
Store for a Future Project/Investment							
Candidate for Resto Rod							
Restore to Curb Appeal Condition							

1964 Corvette

There are many similarities between the 1963 and 1964 Corvettes, but overall the styling was cleaned up a bit for 1964. On the aerodynamic coupe, the previous season's distinctive divided rear window was replaced by a solid piece of glass. The fake hood vents were eliminated and the rear quarter roof vents were restyled. These vents were now partly functional and allowed stale air to be extracted from inside the car.

Tan leather seating had been introduced in 1963, but this year, leather trim was available in all colors. A three-speed rear vent fan was available in the coupe to aid in ventilation. Also new outside were slotted standard wheel discs.

A quartet of 327-cid V-8s was offered again with the base 250-hp and the one-step-up 300-hp versions carried over. The solid-lifter four-barrel V-8 got a boost to 365 hp and the fuel-injection engine carried an even higher new 375-hp rating. This top engine option was fuel injected.

Zora Arkus-Duntov was behind a new CERV II (Chevrolet Engineering Research

This Corvette worked for a living as a test car at the GM Michigan Proving Grounds. *Tom Glatch*

MIKE YAGER SAYS:	
CHEERS	The split window from the coupe was gone and the coupe had better vision. The large fake hood grilles disappeared and there was a cleaner body design. Leather interiors were available in all colors. There were new metallic paints and two-tone interior colors. Knock-off aluminum wheels were readily available. Power steering, power brakes and back up lights were popular options.
JEERS	Like the 1963, the 1964 Corvette is expensive to restore and has many unique parts. It is very tough to restore to NCRS standards. There were many running changes during production. The hubcaps were unique. The drum brakes are a weak point in the 1964 Corvettes. Air conditioning and fuel injection are very hard to restore properly. Unique interior parts like the correct boot, automatic shifter, chrome and stainless molding and trim are all hard to find.
GAME PLAN	Many roadsters and coupes can be found. This is a great year to obtain a driver. It was a ho-hum year after the home run in 1963. Fully optioned cars with air conditioning, power steering, power brakes and Powerglide are favorite coupes. Look for high horsepower cars with the heavy duty brakes and heavy duty suspension, the N03 big tank and the L-84 fuel injection. Inspect the "bird cage" windows frame for rust and hidden problems and look carefully at the coupe's door fit. Note the early and late exterior door handle changes. Find a nice driver and join a Corvette club!

Leather trim was available in several colors on 1964 Corvette interiors. *Tom Glatch*

This Corvette once clocked 150 mph on the GM proving ground track. *Tom Glatch*

1964 'VETTE FACTS	
VEHICLE IDENTIFICATION NUMBER	Corvette convertibles for 1964 were numbered 40867S100001 to 40867S122229. Corvette coupes for 1964 were numbered 40837S100001 to 40837S122229. The first symbol 4 = 1964. The second and third symbols 08 = Corvette. The fourth and fifth symbols 67 = convertible or 37 = coupe. The sixth symbol S = the St. Louis, Missouri, assembly plant. The last six symbols were digits representing the sequential production numbers.
ENGINE	**Type: V-8** Bore and stroke: 4.00 x 3.25 in. Displacement: 327 cid Brake hp: 250 at 4,400 rpm. Induction: Carter WCFB 4-barrel #3501S. **Options:** 327-cid/300-hp w/ 4-bbl. carb 327-cid/365-hp w/ 4-bbl. carb 327-cid/375 w/ Ram Jet fuel injection
VITAL STATS	**Convertible:** Original Price: $4,037 Production: 13,925 Wheelbase: 98 in. Length: 175.2 in. Tires: 6.70 x 15 **Coupe:** Original Price: $4,252 Production: 8,304 Wheelbase: 98 in. Length: 175.3 in. Tires: 6.70 x 15
COOL STUFF	Most, 85.7 percent, were equipped with a four-speed manual transmission. An L84-powered 1964 Corvette could go from 0-to-60 mph in 6.3 seconds and from 0-to-100 mph in 14.7 seconds. It had a top speed of 138 mph. The "Route 66" TV show was cancelled in September 1964.

The 1964 convertible version of the new Corvette was as striking as the coupe. *Tom Glatch*

Vehicle II) experimental car that appeared this year. Designers Larry Shinoda and Tony Lapine worked on this prototype, which started off as a sports-racing-car concept. The engine was located behind the driver, with one torque converter in front and one at the rear. This car, along with the earlier CERV I made in 1959, went into the Briggs Cunningham Auto Museum in Costa Mesa, California to be preserved for many years. (Author Mike Yager now owns the CERV 1)

Another 1964 show car was the Sting Ray Shark. This was a mildly modified '64 Sting Ray roadster that was probably built for "Bunkie" Knudsen as a street-custom special. It has a white-painted hood blister and special four-outlet side exhaust system.

One of the most exciting special Corvettes is the bright red Styling Concept Car made for the New York World's Fair (also owned by Mike Yager). This car was designed by Bill Mitchell's styling studio and included door panel fitted with sequential flashing reflectors, stainless steel trim, disc brakes (not offered on production models in 1964), polished stainless steel grille inserts in the floorboards, high-back bucket seats with leather upholstery and trim custom dyed to match the iridescent brilliance of the exterior paint, which features a base coat of gold metallic under 15 coats of Candy Apple Red.

1964 Corvette Status Guide	Basket Case		Average Driver		Rare, Unique or Completely Original		Restored
Condition of CORVETTE:	Production Status						
	Average	Rare/ Unique	N–O–M	O–M	Needs Work	Unrestored Low Mileage	Restored
Suggested Actions: Collect It							
Drive, Show and Enjoy							
Race, Autocross Competitively							
Store for a Future Project/Investment							
Candidate for Resto Rod							
Restore to Curb Appeal Condition							

Stylish 1964 Corvette convertibles were as dramatic looking as the sleek coupes.

One memorable feature of the 1963 and '64 Corvettes was their hidden headlights.

Unique Corvette emblems decorate the car's deck lid and glove box door. Special functional side-outlet exhausts are fitted and a fuel-injected 327 hides under the hood. The car uses six Corvette taillights with the lenses reversed. The car also has special mirrors, a special hood cut out and unique, race-car-like, simulated brake-venting outlets in the top of its rear body. This was all complemented by a large one-piece cast nose grille.

GM's decision to honor the Automobile Manufacturers Association's ban on competition took open factory support of Corvette racing out of the picture in 1964, but with encouragement from Zora Arkus-Duntov and race-ready cars available right off the showroom floor, private competitors were having a field day driving Corvettes.

1965 Corvette

Three fully functional, vertical front, slanting louvers on the sides of the front fenders; a black anodized horizontal-bars grille and different rocker panel moldings were the main styling detail changes for 1965 Corvettes. A new hood without indentations was standard, but after midyear, Corvettes with a newly optional 396-cid "big-block" V-8 used a special hood with a funnel-shaped "power blister" air scoop. New additions to the optional equipment list included a side exhaust system and telescoping steering wheel. Knock-off style aluminum wheels were also optional.

Inside the car, the instruments were changed to a flat-dial, straight-needle

The sleek 1965 Corvette Sting Ray coupe continued to turn heads.   *Phil Kunz*

There is something about red that dresses up a Corvette, inside or outside. *Tom Glatch*

The Corvette interior, always fashionable in basic black, with 1965 trim. *Tom Glatch*

MIKE YAGER SAYS:	
CHEERS	It was the first year of the big block 396 with 425 hp for only an additional $292. There was a cleaner body design with new louvered side fenders and no more hood indentations. It was the first year for the superb, non-fading disc brakes and the only year for the fuel injection combination with disc brakes. There was a new teakwood steering wheel, a unique black grille, a transistorized ignition, new emblems, a new push-button automatic shifter and fresh looking interior. It was the first year for the side exhaust pipes. New metallic exterior colors as well as two-tone interior colors were available.
JEERS	The 1965 Corvette is among several that are expensive to restore, difficult to meet NCRS restoration standards and have difficult-to-find chrome and stainless trim and other pieces. The brakes tend to corrode internally, requiring replacement calipers. With a single brake system line on non-power steering cars, there are no brakes if the brake line is damaged. There tends to be corrosion in the lower radiator support and rusty frames at the rear "kick up" in front of the rear wheel. Big block engines have marginal cooling. The automatic shifters are very hard to find. The air conditioning and fuel injection systems are very hard to restore properly.
GAME PLAN	At first glance, the 1965 was a totally new car from the 1963 and '64 cars. It had a modern refinement that wasn't there on earlier models. This is another sleeper. This is the perfect year to obtain a driver, if you can find one. Fully optioned, air conditioned, coupes with power steering, power brakes and Powerglide are favorites. The new L-78 was the one to collect. Find a Goldwood Yellow roadster or coupe! Inspect the bird cage window frame for rust and hidden problems if you consider a coupe. Look carefully at the coupe's door fit. The fit of the molded door trim and panels was nice! Find a nice driver and head for a dairy bar on Saturday night!

The stylish knock-off wheels and fins offered style and suggested performance. *Tom Glatch*

1965 'VETTE FACTS	
VEHICLE IDENTIFICATION NUMBER	Corvette convertibles for 1965 were numbered 194675S100001 to 194675S123562. Corvette coupes for 1965 were numbered 194375S100001 to 194375S123562. The first symbol 1 indicated Chevrolet. The second and third symbols identified the body series 94 = Corvette. The fourth and fifth symbols indicated the body style number 67 = convertible and 37 = coupe. The sixth symbol indicated the model year 5 = 1965. The seventh symbol identified the assembly plant S = St. Louis, Missouri. The last six symbols indicated the sequential production numbers.
ENGINE	**Type: V-8** Bore and stroke: 4.00 x 3.25 in. Displacement: 327 cid Brake hp: 250 at 4,400 rpm. Induction: Carter WCFB 4-barrel #3501S. **Options:** 327-cid/300-hp w/ 4-bbl. carb 327-cid/350-hp w/ 4-bbl. carb 327-cid/365-hp w/ 4-bbl. carb 327-cid/375 w/ Ram Jet fuel injection (midyear) 396-cid/425 w/ Holley 4-bbl. carb
VITAL STATS	**Convertible:** Original Price: $4,106 Production: 15,376 Wheelbase: 98 in. Length: 175.2 in. Tires: 7.75 x 15 **Coupe:** Original Price: $4,321 Production: 8,186 Wheelbase: 98 in. Length: 175.3 in. Tires: 7.75 x 15
COOL STUFF	An L-78-powered 1965 Corvette could go from 0-to-60 mph in 5.7 seconds and from 0-to-100 mph in 13.4 seconds. Most 1965 Corvettes (89.6 percent) were sold with a four-speed manual transmission. General Motors introduced the use of a Protect-O-Plate this year as a system of keeping track of factory warranty work.

design with an aircraft-type influence. The seats had improved support and one-piece molded inside door panels were introduced. Standard equipment included: tachometer, safety belts, heater and defroster, windshield washer, outside rear view mirror, dual exhausts, electric clock, carpeting, manually-operated top (convertible) and sun visors.

A four-wheel disc-brake system was included as standard equipment on all 1965 Corvettes, although drum brakes could be substituted for a $64.50 credit, at least for a while during the model year. While the drum-brake delete-option didn't seem to make much sense, it may have turned out to be a blessing in disguise for Corvette buyers who ordered cars that way. The new disc-brake system turned out to be somewhat of a nightmare, as it used 16 pistons and they were prone to leaking. Eventually, aftermarket companies came up with a stainless steel brake setup that made the system last longer and work better.

Engines were a big part of the 1965 story.

The 250-hp 327 with a 10.5:1 compression ratio, hydraulic lifters and a single Carter WCFB four-barrel carburetor remained the base engine. Also carried over was the RPO L75 version of the 327 V-8 with the big change being a Carter AFB four-barrel and a 300-hp rating. For anyone wanting a hydraulic-lifter 327 with some more snort, there was the RPO L79 option. It used an 11.00:1 compression ratio, a high-lift camshaft and a Holley 4150 four-barrel to generate 350 hp at 5,800 rpm.

This was the muscle-car era and there were two additional 327-based choices to put under the hood. The RPO L76 V-8 had the same basics as the L-79, but used solid lifters instead of hydraulics. The result was 365 hp at 6,200 rpm. and 350 lbs.-ft. of torque at

4,000 rpm. There was also the last Rochester fuel-injected Corvette engine, the RPO L84 V-8 with 11.00:1 compression, solid lifters, a high-lift cam and Rochester fuel injection. It delivered 375 at 6,200 rpm and 350 lbs.-ft. of torque at 4,400 rpm.

In midyear, Chevy added the first big-block Corvette option based on the new 396-cid V-8 This was RPO L78 with 11.0:1 compression, solid lifters, a high-lift cam and a Holley four-barrel. With 425 hp at 6400 and 415 lbs.-ft. of torque at 4000 this was not an engine for the meek. To handle the extra power, the L-78s got stiffer front springs, a thicker front anti-sway bar, a new rear sway bar, a heavier clutch and a heavy-duty radiator.

1965 Corvette Status Guide	Basket Case		Average Driver		Rare, Unique or Completely Original		Restored
Condition of CORVETTE:	Production Status						
	Average	Rare/ Unique	N-0-M	0-M	Needs Work	Unrestored Low Mileage	Restored
Suggested Actions: Collect It							
Drive, Show and Enjoy							
Race, Autocross Competitively							
Store for a Future Project/Investment							
Candidate for Resto Rod							
Restore to Curb Appeal Condition							

1966 Corvette

Although the 1965 and 1966 Corvettes were near twins, there were many small changes, both at the start of the '66 model year and during the model run. A plated, cast-metal grille with an "eggcrate" insert was new. Ribbed rocker panel moldings, chrome-plated exhaust bezels, a vinyl covered headliner and the elimination of roof vents and the interior exhaust fan also helped set the 1966 Corvette apart from the previous year's model. The front fender sides again had three vertical air louvers.

Inside, a day/night rearview mirror became standard equipment, instead of part of a Comfort and Convenience package. The 1966 glove box door featured a neat-looking brushed aluminum finish inside a metal face plate that was painted black and trimmed with a thin chrome molding. The seats had an extra amount of pleats, a change that prevented the upholstery from splitting too easily. Early in the model year Corvettes used 1965 type seat belts, but cars built later on had a buckle with a tapered upper surface and a distinctive flat top to the taper. New seat belt retractors

The 1966 Corvette convertible showed subtle styling changes as illustrated by this big-block version. *Tom Glatch*

MIKE YAGER SAYS:	
CHEERS	The M22 "rock crusher" four-speed transmission is one of the strong points of the 1966 Corvette. This was the first year of the 427 "big block" initially rated at 450 hp. The fuel injection was gone. A telescopic steering column was added in 1966. Important additions were the F41 suspension, the unique cast egg crate grille, a shoulder harness and new seat belt retractors and knobs as well as new emblems. Optional headrests were offered. The "sail panel" on the coupe was cleaned up with no more vents. The highest number of Corvettes were produced in 1966 among the 1963 through '67 Corvettes.
JEERS	There are many unique parts that make the big block 427 engine hard to restore. The 1966 Corvette is another that is hard to restore to NCRS standards. The advent of smog equipment on California cars. The exhaust bezels were cast and were prone to corrosion. Vinyl-covered foam headliners were prone to deterioration and separated from the backing. Parts that are hard to find are the M22 "rock crusher" four-speed transmission, the AIR systems, the 36-gallon fuel tank and the telescopic steering column. The air conditioning system is expensive to restore properly.
GAME PLAN	Look for an example that is as original and untouched as possible. Production of 1966 roadsters was two to one with the coupes. Try to find a nice 427 coupe with air conditioning, power steering, power brakes and Powerglide. Once again, inspect coupes carefully for rust and hidden problems, look carefully at the door fit. Look for high horsepower cars with the extremely rare N03 big tank option, heavy duty brakes and suspension. Take your '66 on a tour of Route 66!

Inside were more pleats on the seats, a change that helped them last longer. *Tom Glatch*

1966 'VETTE FACTS	
VEHICLE IDENTIFICATION NUMBER	Corvette convertibles for 1966 were numbered 194676S100001 to 194676S127720. Corvette coupes for 1966 were numbered 194376S100001 to 194376S127720. The first symbol 1 indicated Chevrolet. The second and third symbols identified the body series 94 = Corvette. The fourth and fifth symbols indicated the body style number 67 = convertible and 37 = coupe. The sixth symbol indicated the model year 6 = 1966. The seventh symbol identified the assembly plant S = St. Louis, Missouri. The last six symbols indicated the sequential production numbers.
ENGINE	**Type: V-8** Bore and stroke: 4.00 x 3.25 in. Displacement: 327 cid Brake hp: 300 at 5,000 rpm. Induction: Holley 4-barrel. **Options:** 327-cid/350-hp w/ Holley 4-bbl. carb 427-cid/390-hp w/ Holley 4-bbl. carb 427-cid/425 w/ Holley 4-bbl. carb
VITAL STATS	**Convertible:** Original Price: $4,084 Production: 17,762 Wheelbase: 98 in. Length: 175.2 in. Tires: 7.75 x 15 redline or whitewall **Coupe:** Original Price: $4,295 Production: 9,958 Wheelbase: 98 in. Length: 175.3 in. Tires: 7.75 x 15 redline or whitewall
COOL STUFF	Starting in 1966, the finish quality of the Corvette Sting Ray body was greatly improved. With the increased emphasis on safety features, the 1966 Corvette got a new type of windshield wiper with duller, less reflective finish to cut down glare. An older style "tar top" battery was used in early 1966 Corvettes, while models built later in the year used a plastic-case battery. Shoulder harnesses were first used in 1966 models, but few cars were so-equipped. George Maharis never had much luck as an entertainer after "Route 66" was cancelled, but he released several record albums between 1962 and 1966

were used. A 60-psi oil gauge was used in cars with small-block V-8s. The 427-powered cars had an 80-psi oil gauge. A four-way hazard warning flasher system was introduced in 1966 and was required in a few states. A dealer-installation kit was available to add it to Corvettes not so equipped.

There was a quartet of four-barrel engine offerings for 1966, two based on the 327 and two based on a new 427-cid big-block V-8. The base L-75 small-block had 10.5:1 compression and hydraulic lifters. The L-79 small-block had 11.0:1 compression. Corvettes made for the California market (except for those with L-72 big-block V-8s) were required to have the GM Air Injection Reactor anti-pollution system installed.

The L-36 big-block had 10.26:1 compression, hydraulic lifters and a high-lift cam. The top L-72 engine had 11.0:1 compression, solid lifters and a special performance camshaft. Cars with this motor and 4.11:1 gearing could go from 0-to-60 mph in 4.8 seconds and had a 140-mph top speed. The 427s also included Chevy's F41 heavy-duty suspension, heavy-duty brakes and a positraction rear axle.

Cars with either version of the new 427-cid

It was unfair to other cars—but so much fun, the 1966 Corvette 427 convertible! *Phil Kunz*

1966 Corvette Status Guide	Basket Case		Average Driver		Rare, Unique or Completely Original		Restored
Condition of CORVETTE:	Production Status						
	Average	Rare/ Unique	N–O–M	O–M	Needs Work	Unrestored Low Mileage	Restored
Suggested Actions: Collect It							
Drive, Show and Enjoy							
Race, Autocross Competitively							
Store for a Future Project/Investment							
Candidate for Resto Rod							
Restore to Curb Appeal Condition							

In 1966, this L-72 Corvette had a 427 hp big block V-8 in the engine compartment. *Tom Glatch*

The interior of the 1966 L-72 Corvette was stylish and comfortable. *Tom Glatch*

V-8 came with a power-bulge hood. On these cars only, the hood support was moved to the driver's side of the car. A "Corvette" script with a "Sting Ray" plaque was seen on the left front corner of the hood on small-block-powered cars on both.

Small-block cars retained use of an aluminum radiator. Big-blocks used a copper core radiator with extra coolant capacity. Originally, Chevrolet had planned to offer a drum brake option again in 1966. However, this was rescinded in August 1965 and never installed on a production car.

In 1966 Corvette racing, Roger Penske's team finished 12th overall and first in the GT class at the Daytona Continental. In the Corvette styling studio, Frank Winchell's design team developed a rear-engined Corvette experimental car called the XP-819. Styled by Larry Shinoda—and based on his famous Monza SS – this car had hidden headlamps and a functional hood vent that allowed air that passed through the front-mounted radiator to escape.

1967 Corvette

The 1967 Corvette is considered the most refined of the original Sting Ray (written as two words) models of 1963 through 1967. Many marque enthusiasts consider the 1967 model to be the best looking of the Gen 1 Sting Rays. Its exterior styling was basically the same as seen on the 1966 Corvette, but was a bit cleaner.

The same egg crate style grille with Argent Silver finish was carried over from 1966. The same smooth hood was re-used. Cars using a big-block V-8 had a large front-opening air scoop over the hood center bulge, instead of the previous power blister. The crossed flags badge on the nose of the 1967 Corvette had a widened "V" at its top. On the sides of the front fenders were five vertical and functional air louvers that slanted towards the front of the car.

Minor changes were made to the Corvette's interior. The most noticeable revision was the relocation of the parking brake from under

Take a long look. There were only 16 of these L-89 coupes made in 1967. *Tom Glatch*

Under this hood scoop are aluminum heads and a monster 435 hp+ V-8   *Tom Glatch*

With so much power under the hood, drivers had to pay attention!   *Tom Glatch*

the dash to the center console. The new headliner was cushioned with foam and fiber material. Four-way flashers, directional signals with a lane-change function, larger interior vent ports and folding seat-back latches were all new. At the rear there were now dual round taillights on each side (instead of a taillight and optional back-up light). The twin back-up lights were now mounted in the center of the rear end panel, above the license plate holder.

Standard equipment for all Corvettes included: a new dual-chamber brake master cylinder, six-inch wide slotted rally wheels with trim rings, an odometer, a clock, carpeting and a tachometer. The optional finned aluminum wheels were changed in design and had a one-year-only, non-knock-off center.

The Corvette "427" with its own funnel-shaped, power bulge on the hood, returned in four versions for 1967. A 427-cid 435-hp 1967 Corvette convertible carried on 7.7 pounds per horsepower. It could hit 60 mph

MIKE YAGER SAYS:	
CHEERS	This was the first year of both the L-71 427 Tri Power and the L-88 427 engines. Only 20 of the L-88s were produced. The first 427-cid engines with aluminum heads. Rally wheels were standard with caps and rings. One-year-only bolt-on wheels were offered. Disc brakes were offered. Dual-circuit brakes were used on all Corvettes. The Corvettes had a new side gill fender design and a side pipe exhaust option. Last of the C2 Sting Ray series. Very refined with many unique, one-year-only features.
JEERS	The 1967 Corvettes are difficult to restore with many unique parts for the Big Block engines. They are a very tough car to bring to NCRS standards. The L-71, L-88 and L-89 Big Block engines all are hard to find as are the M-22 "rock crusher" four-speed transmissions, the AIR systems and the telescopic steering column. There were no more spinner and knock-off wheels. The emergency brake console between the seats was easily broken and the headlight motor had problems. The L-89 version is expensive to restore. Air conditioning systems also are difficult and expensive to restore. You may have a hard time finding chrome and stainless trim items.
GAME PLAN	Look for a nice 427 coupe! Try to find a fully optioned car with air conditioning, power brakes, power steering and Powerglide. The L-89 version was new this year and is a must have. Tuxedo black with a red stinger. Wow! Examine the coupe window frame for rust and hidden problems. Check the coupe's door fit. As always, beware of added options and fake trim tags. Consider ownership history and the car's provenance. Owning a 1967 will take you to Corvette heaven!

in 5.5 seconds and do the quarter-mile in 13.8 seconds. The regular L-36 was about the same. Next came the L-68, with 400 hp and then the Tri-Power L-71 with 435 hp. Extremely rare (only 20 built) — and off in a class by itself — was the aluminum-headed L-88. This powerhouse was officially rated at only 430 hp, but in fact developed nearly 600 hp!

Three four-speed manual gearboxes — wide-ratio, close-ratio and heavy-duty close-ratio — were optional on Corvettes. A desirable extra was side-mounted exhaust pipes.

Like other Gen 1 Sting Rays, the 1967 models had a full-length steel ladder type frame with five cross members. The independent front suspension featured unequal-length A-arms, coil springs, an anti-roll bar and tubular shocks. The Saginaw recirculating ball steering had a 17.6:1 ratio; 2.9 turns lock-to-lock and a turning circle 41.6 feet. The independent rear suspension utilized transverse leaf springs, transverse struts, half shafts with universal-joints, trailing arms and tubular shock absorbers. A semi-floating rear axle was used.

Hydraulic, vented four-wheel disc brakes with 1.75-inch diameter single calipers were fitted. The standard rear axle ratio was 3.36:1. Available rear axle gear ratios included 3.08:1, 3.55:1, 3.70:1, 4.11:1 and 4.56:1.

The fire-breathing, competition-ready L-88-powered Corvettes were winners in such diverse venues as NHRA and IHRA drag strips, road courses like Sebring, super speedways like Daytona, and even the Bonneville Salt Flats, where a '67 L-88 set the A Grand Touring record at 192.879 mph.

1967 'VETTE FACTS	
VEHICLE IDENTIFICATION NUMBER	Corvette convertibles for 1967 were numbered 194677S100001 to 194677S122940. Corvette coupes for 1966 were numbered 194377S100001 to 194377S122940. The first symbol 1 indicated Chevrolet. The second and third symbols identified the body series 94 = Corvette. The fourth and fifth symbols indicated the body style number 67 = convertible and 37 = coupe. The sixth symbol indicated the model year 7 = 1967. The seventh symbol identified the assembly plant S = St. Louis, Missouri. The last six symbols indicated the sequential production numbers.
ENGINE	**Type: V-8** Bore and stroke: 4.00 x 3.25 in. Displacement: 327 cid Brake hp: 300 at 5,000 rpm. Induction: Holley 4-barrel. **Options:** 327-cid/350-hp w/ Holley 4-bbl. carb 427-cid/390-hp w/ Holley 4-bbl. carb 427-cid/400 w/ Tri-Power 427-cid/435 w/ Tri-Power 427-cid/560 w/ Holley 4-bbl. carb
VITAL STATS	**Convertible:** Original Price: $4,141 Production: 14,436 Wheelbase: 98 in. Length: 175.2 in. Tires: 7.75 x 15 redline or whitewall **Coupe:** Original Price: $4,295 Production: 8,504 Wheelbase: 98 in. Length: 175.3 in. Tires: 7.75 x 15 redline or whitewall
COOL STUFF	Eighty-eight percent of 1967 Corvettes came with four-speed manual transmission. A 327-cid 300-hp V-8-powered Corvette of this vintage would go from 0-to-60 mph in 7.8 seconds and from 0-to-100 mph in 23.1 seconds. Not bad for a base model car. Big-block cars with air conditioning and Powerglide had the front license plate offset to the left to increase airflow through the grille. Most, but not all, big-block Corvettes had 4-2-7 numbers on both sides of the air scoop. A special "bat-wing" air cleaner was used on Tri-Power V-8s.

Did someone mention a rally? This 1967 427 Corvette coupe came in Rally Red. *Doug Mitchel*

The business end of the L-71 produced 435 hp with three two-barrel carburetors. *Tom Glatch*

1967 Corvette Status Guide	Basket Case		Average Driver		Rare, Unique or Completely Original		Restored
Condition of CORVETTE:	Production Status						
	Average	Rare/ Unique	N–O–M	O–M	Needs Work	Unrestored Low Mileage	Restored
Suggested Actions: Collect It							
Drive, Show and Enjoy							
Race, Autocross Competitively							
Store for a Future Project/Investment							
Candidate for Resto Rod							
Restore to Curb Appeal Condition							

The black "stinger" stripe and bulge meant it was the L-71 427 version in 1967. *Tom Glatch*

Marlboro Maroon was the name of the color on this '67 427 coupe. *Doug Mitchel*

1968 Corvette

The 1968 Corvette sported the marque's first major restyling since 1963. "Corvette '68... all different all over," said a sales brochure. The aerodynamic fastback of 1963 through 1967 was replaced by a tunneled-roof coupe. It featured a removable back window and a two-piece detachable roof section or T-top. The convertible was still available and could be had with an optional hardtop that had a glass rear window.

This was the start of the "designer" age and the Corvette's front end was smoother, more undulating and much more aerodynamic than those seen on previous Corvettes. As before, the headlights could be hidden when not in use. Now they were operated by vacuum, rather than by electricity. The windshield wipers also disappeared from view when turned off.

Except for the rocker panels, the sides of the Corvette were devoid of chrome. Conventional door handles were eliminated. Instead, there were push buttons. The blunt rear deck contained four round taillights

The 1968 Corvette had a smooth new shape and very little chrome. The look was a good blend of racing aggressiveness and understated refinement. *Mid America Motorworks*

with the word Corvette in chrome between each pair. The wraparound, wing-like rear bumper and license plate holder resembled that used on 1967 models.

Buyers who preferred a small-block V-8 had a choice of two 327s. The hotter one had a Rochester four-barrel, an 11.0:1 compression ratio and a high-performance cam. For the average driver, it was enough to "get into trouble."

Chevrolet's big-block 427-cid V-8 was available in the Corvette in four different muscular versions. The least powerful was RPO L36 with hydraulic valve lifters, a 10:25:1 compression ratio and a single Rochester four-barrel carburetor. Then came the L-68 with three Holley two-barrel carburetors.

Car and Driver tested an L-68 a four-speed manual gearbox and 3.70:1 rear axle in its May 1968 issue. It did 0-to-60 mph in 5.7 seconds and the standing-start quarter mile in 14.1 seconds at 102 mph. Its top speed was estimated to be 119 mph.

RPO L71 was a step up the performance ladder with its special-performance solid-lifter 427, three Holley two-barrels and an 11.0:1 compression ratio. An L-71 with a four-speed manual transmission and 3.55:1 rear axle was tested by Car Life in June 1968. It did the quarter mile in 13.41 seconds at 109.5 mph. Its top speed was 142 mph.

The ultimate option was the super-powerful RPO L88 aluminum-head V-8, a $947 option intended primarily for racing. The L-88 had

The tunneled roofline included a removable rear window. The rear deck carried the hint of a built-in spoiler.

Mid America Motorworks

MIKE YAGER SAYS:	
CHEERS	A beautiful new body design. The T-tops gave the convertible feel without the convertible top wind noise or deterioration. The 1968 Corvette had wider wheels and tires for that offered a better ride and handling. The 327 V-8, transmissions, suspension parts and replacement body panels are easy to find.
JEERS	There was less interior room and more cooling problems with the 427-cid V-8. The new T-tops often leaked, fiber optic cables often broke and there were wiper door and headlight problems due to vacuum leaks. Radiator supports and shrouds, the 427-cid V-8s, exterior and interior trim, P02 deluxe wheel covers, the shifter console, seats and steering column as well as seven-inch rally wheels all are hard to find. The side exhaust was no longer offered.
GAME PLAN	Look for as original and untouched car as possible. Don't overlook an old race car. Some rare cars have been found stowed away. Nice drivers can be found but beware the costly, one-year-only features.

Cordovan Maroon was the official name of the paint on this '68 L-89 coupe. *Tom Glatch*

mechanical valve lifters, a special-ultra-high-performance camshaft with .5365-in. intakes and a single Holley 850CFM four-barrel. With a 12.50:1 compression ratio it produced an advertised 430 hp. However, some said its actual output was 560 hp.

The L-88 package included a "power blister" hood and four heavy-duty options were required: RPO J56 heavy-duty brakes at $384.45; RPO F41 heavy-duty suspension

The new '68 interior was driver and passenger friendly as displayed here. *Tom Glatch*

1968 'VETTE FACTS

VEHICLE IDENTIFICATION NUMBER	Corvette convertibles for 1968 were numbered 194678S100001 to 194678S128566. Corvette coupes for 1968 were numbered 194378S100001 to 194378S128566. The first symbol 1 indicated Chevrolet. The second and third symbols identified the body series 94 = Corvette. The fourth and fifth symbols indicated the body style number 67 = convertible and 37 = coupe. The sixth symbol indicated the model year 8 = 1968. The seventh symbol identified the assembly plant S = St. Louis, Missouri. The last six symbols indicated the sequential production numbers.
ENGINE	**Type: V-8** Bore and stroke: 4.00 x 3.25 in. Displacement: 327 cid Brake hp: 300 at 5,000 rpm. Induction: Rochester Quadra Jet 4-barrel. **Options:** 327-cid/350-hp w/ Holley 4-bbl. carb 427-cid/390-hp w/ Holley 4-bbl. carb 427-cid/435 w/ Tri-Power 427-cid/430 w/ Holley 4-bbl. carb
VITAL STATS	**Convertible:** Original Price: $4,347 Production: 18,636 Wheelbase: 98 in. Length: 182.1 in. Tires: F70 x 15 **Coupe:** Original Price: $4,663 Production: 9,936 Wheelbase: 98 in. Length: 182.1 in. Tires: F70 x 15
COOL STUFF	The Sting Ray name was not used in 1968. Only the Corvette name was used until 1969. The glass rear window in the coupe was removable. This was the last year the 327-cid small-block V-8 was offered in the Corvette. The build quality of early '68 models was spotty and some of the cars spent as much time in the shop as they did on the road until new-model problems were sorted out.

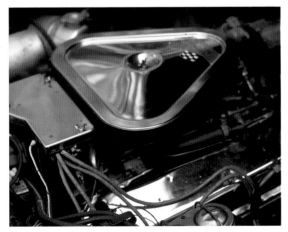

The L-88 version had aluminum heads on its V-8 engine, with speed in mind. *Tom Glatch*

Power to spare came inside the engine bay of this 1968 Corvette L-89 coupe. *Tom Glatch*

at $36.90; RPO K66 transistor ignition at $73.75 and RPO G81 positraction at $46.35. With a special high-performance Turbo Hydra-Matic transmission ($290.40 extra) the L-88 convertible sold for $6,562. "The tall gear (3.36:) in back made 13.56 seconds at 111 mph seem respectable," said *Hot Rod* of the 1968 L-88. "But we know it's about two seconds from where it should be."

The Oh-My-Heavens one. You release a few latches and those panels in the roof are ready for lift off. You release a few more and the rear window's ready for lift off. You flip the key in the ignition and you . . . and you . . . say, you're not listening. Hello, do you read us? What's the use. You're in a world all your own. **Corvette** Like a car, only better.

CHEVROLET

10 seconds to lift off.

GM

Sports Class winner of the Motor Trend 1968 Achievement Award, for which we thank them.

Chevrolet used language from the popular NASA space program in its heading to focus on its new removable top sections for the 1968 Corvette.

1968 Corvette Status Guide	Basket Case		Average Driver		Rare, Unique or Completely Original		Restored
Condition of CORVETTE:	Production Status						
	Average	Rare/ Unique	N–O–M	O–M	Needs Work	Unrestored Low Mileage	Restored
Suggested Actions: Collect It							
Drive, Show and Enjoy							
Race, Autocross Competitively							
Store for a Future Project/Investment							
Candidate for Resto Rod							
Restore to Curb Appeal Condition							

MID AMERICA MOTORWO

1969 Corvette

After a year's absence, the Corvette's name changed back to that of a delta-shaped sea creature, but it was now spelled as one word and "Stingray" badges name (now spelled as one word) re-appeared on the front fenders above the four slanting air vents. The back-up lights were now integrated into the center taillights, a steering-column-mounted ignition switch was used and the exterior door buttons used on 1968 models disappeared in favor of key locks.

There were other small changes such as the wheel rims growing from seven inches wide to eight inches and the steering wheel shrinking from 16 inches to 15. The interior door panels were mildly redesigned with a thicker upper section and a horizontally-mounted handle. Front and rear disc brakes, headlight washers, a center console, wheel trim rings, carpeting and all-vinyl upholstery were among standard equipment

The 350-cid V-8 became the base small-block offering this year starting with 300 hp in a mild hydraulic-lifter four-barrel format. RPO L46 was the hotter version with 11.0:1

A Corvette with the top down always seems to inspire dreams of the open road. *Tom Glatch*

MIKE YAGER SAYS:	
CHEERS	The advent of the 350-cid, 350-hp V-8, better cooling, better seats and seat releases, better exterior door handles, wider wheels and tires for handling and ride, a convenient map pocket and the handy tilt-telescoping steering column. The steering wheel was smaller and the side exhaust was back. Parts that are easy to find include the 350 engine, transmissions, suspension items, body panels, bumpers, trim rings and caps, emblems and hard tops.
JEERS	The trim on door panels warped and came loose. The long front end and high front fenders limited driver vision. The rear window leaked and the rear window tray rattled. The coupe's interior could be very hot without air conditioning. Difficult parts to find begin with the 427-cid V-8, the P02 deluxe wheel covers, the spare tire carrier, convertible top frames and the windshield washer motor with its multiple parts.
GAME PLAN	Look for as original and untouched car as possible, especially with low mileage and the big engine block. The 1968 and '69 Corvettes always have been an overlooked group of cars. Today they are coming of age. Look for this group to continue to rise in value. Pick out a nice 1969 today—the prices are rising!

Le Mans Blue was the color chosen for this 1969 Corvette convertible. *Jerry Heasley*

1969 'VETTE FACTS	
VEHICLE IDENTIFICATION NUMBER	Corvette convertibles for 1969 were numbered 194679S100001 to 194679S138762. Corvette coupes for 1969 were numbered 194379S100001 to 194379S138762. The first symbol 1 indicated Chevrolet. The second and third symbols identified the body series 94 = Corvette. The fourth and fifth symbols indicated the body style number 67 = convertible and 37 = coupe. The sixth symbol indicated the model year 9 = 1969. The seventh symbol identified the assembly plant S = St. Louis, Missouri. The last six symbols indicated the sequential production numbers.
ENGINE	**Type: V-8** Bore and stroke: 4.00 x 3.48 in. Displacement: 350 cid Brake hp: 300 at 4,800 rpm. Induction: Rochester 4-barrel. **Options:** 350-cid/350-hp w/ Rochester 4-bbl. carb 427-cid/390-hp w/ Rochester Quadra Jet 4-bbl. carb 427-cid/400-hp w/ three Holley 2-bbl 427-cid/435-hp w/ three Holley 2-bbl 427-cid/430-hp w/ Holley 4-bbl. carb* *Actually over 560 hp
VITAL STATS	**Convertible:** Original Price: $4,420 Production: 16,633 Wheelbase: 98 in. Length: 182.5 in. Tires: F70 x 15 **Coupe:** Original Price: $4,763 Production: 22,129 Wheelbase: 98 in. Length: 182.5 in. Tires: F70 x 15
COOL STUFF	After being dropped in 1968, a side-mount exhaust system was made optional again in 1969. RPO N14 sold for $147.45. The quality control on 1969 models was somewhat improved from 1968. Cars of both years took awhile to catch on with collectors, but in restored condition – with the factory problems solved – both years seem hot in the market the past two to three years. The Mako Shark II Corvette dream car was re-issued as the 1969 Manta Ray. A front spoiler was added, the grille got a little more protection and the external exhaust pipes were redesigned to be a bit rounder and more conventional than before. The body side emblems changed from a stylized shark to a stylized manta ray. Goodyear tires replaced the Firestones. The former Venetian blinds rear window treatment changed to a buttress style and the shape of the rear end was longer and more horizontal. The hood scoop carried ZL-1 engine call-outs. The Astro III was a two-passenger show car that featured a tricycle wheel arrangement. It was designed with gas turbine power in mind. Closed-circuit television provided rear vision. Flamboyant design chief Bill Mitchell customized two '69 Corvettes to his personal taste. The Sirocco had a periscope on the roof, cast alloy wheels with a laced-spokes pattern, a monochromatic color treatment, front and rear spoilers, a modified and rounder roof treatment and a 427-cid ZL-1 big-block V-8. The Aero Coupe had unique spoilers, cast alloy wheels with a laced-spokes pattern and much larger-diameter "segmented" side exhausts. Its one-piece roof hatch was hinged at the rear and swung up to make entering and exiting the car easier.

compression and one hp per cubic inch. Since this was getting into the heavy-duty-muscle era, there were no less than six 427s you could get in the Corvette, either as a regular or special option.

The 427-cid 390-hp RPO L36 V-8 was again the starting-point engine for muscle car enthusiasts. Then came RPO L68. It was the same 10.25:1 compression V-8 fitted with three two-barrel carburetors, which upped its output to 400 hp. The 427-cid 435-hp RPO L71 Tri-Power engine also returned in much the same form as 1968. Three ultra-high-performing options began with the RPO L88 V-8. Hot Rod tested an L-88 and described it as a "street machine with soul." This year the basic package required heavy-duty brakes and suspension,

transistor ignition and positraction. An L-88 convertible with a beefy Turbo Hydra-Matic and 3.36:1 rear axle did the quarter mile in 13.56 seconds at 111.10 mph.

There was also the RPO L89 V-8. This was a solid-lifter version of the 427 with aluminum heads on the L-71 block. It had a 12.0:1 compression ratio, a 435 hp at 5800 rpm rating and produced 460 foot-pounds of torque at 4,000 rpm.

Possibly the wildest performance muscle engine ever offered to the public, at least until modern times, was the ZL-1. This all-aluminum, 427-cid engine was installed in 69 Camaros and two production Corvettes. About 10 to 12 Corvette engineering test "mules" were also built with ZL-1s. They were used in magazines, engineering tests

Getting a Baldwin Motion product was all about performance, like this 1969 V-8. *Jerry Heasley*

The L-71 additions offered potency to the attractive 1969 Corvette convertible. *Tom Glatch*

The Baldwin Motion version of the 1969
Corvette coupe was truly solid gold. *Jerry Heasley*

and track evaluations and driven by the likes of Zora Arkus-Duntov and GM VPs. The evaluation vehicles were all destroyed. However, two Corvettes went out the door as ZL-1s – a Canary Yellow car with side pipes and a Can-Am white T-top coupe with black ZL-1 side stripes. At this writing, there is speculation that a <u>third</u> ZL-1 has been found and is undergoing authentication.

ZL-1 was technically an optional version of the L-88 engine, but it was some option with its thicker walls and main webbing and dry-sump lubrication provisions. The bottom end had four-bolt main bearings, a forged-steel crank, rods with 7/16-inch bolts, Spiralock washers and full floating pins. The pistons had a higher dome than the L-88

type and boosted compression to 12.5:1. The cylinder heads were also aluminum and featured open combustion chambers, round exhaust ports and 2.19-inch/1.88-inch valves. The aluminum dual plane intake was topped by an 850-cfm Holley "double-pumper" four-barrel carburetor featuring mechanical secondaries. The ZL-1's radical solid-lifter camshaft allowed the engine to stay together in the upper revs range.

It's hard to believe that there was a step above the L-88 Corvette in the muscle-car era, but the ZL-1 was such a machine. Today, it still ranks as one of the wildest RPO engine options ever offered to the public, although we have to admit things are getting pretty crazy again today.

1969 Corvette Status Guide	Basket Case		Average Driver		Rare, Unique or Completely Original		Restored
Condition of CORVETTE:	Production Status						
	Average	Rare/ Unique	N–O–M	O–M	Needs Work	Unrestored Low Mileage	Restored
Suggested Actions: Collect It							
Drive, Show and Enjoy							
Race, Autocross Competitively							
Store for a Future Project/Investment							
Candidate for Resto Rod							
Restore to Curb Appeal Condition							

1970 Corvette

The 1970 Corvette featured refinements on the basic styling used since 1968. There was a new ice-cube-tray grille and matching side fender louvers, rectangular clear front signal lights, fender flares and square exhausts. The bucket seats and safety belt retractor containers were improved. Standard equipment included: front and rear disc brakes, headlight washers, wheel trim rings, carpeting, center console and all-vinyl upholstery in a choice of black, blue, green, saddle or red. An array of 11 exterior colors was offered to buyers.

Marlboro Maroon was the color choice on this 1970 Corvette LT-1 coupe. *Tom Glatch*

The base ZQ-3 350-cid small-block V-8 was typical Corvette fare with the same 300-hp rating as last year. The 350-hp L-46 V-8 also returned. A new 454 LS-5 version of the big-block Chevy V-8 combined a relatively mild 10:25:1 compression ratio, a high-performance hydraulic lifter camshaft and a single Quadra-Jet carburetor for 390 hp at 4,800 rpm and 500 foot-pounds of torque at 3,400 rpm.

Hot foots had a neat new LT-1 offering, which was based on the 350-cid small-block V-8 with 11.0:1 compression, solid lifters and a Holley four-barrel on an aluminum intake. This was good for 370 hp at 6,000 rpm and 380 foot-pounds of torque at 4,000 rpm.

Even the Corvette wheel treatment was memorable and eye-appealing in 1970. *Tom Glatch*

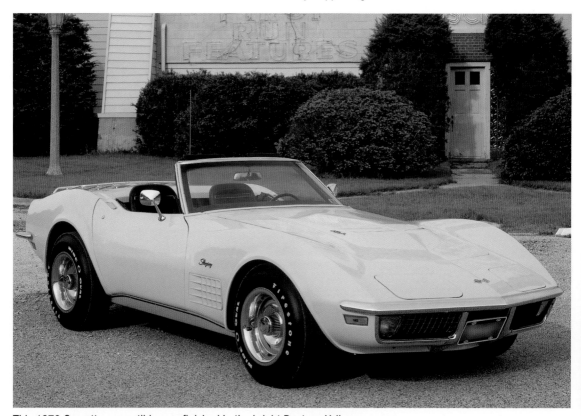

This 1970 Corvette convertible was finished in the bright Daytona Yellow. *Tom Glatch*

Corvettes seemed sleeker every year. This is the hood of the 1970 LS-5 convertible. *Tom Glatch*

This was the 1970 LS-5 V-8 with 454 cubic inches producing 390 hp. *Tom Glatch*

A new grille and side fender louvers were part of exterior changes on the '70 'Vette. *Tom Glatch*

MIKE YAGER SAYS:	
CHEERS	The new LT-1 350-cid V-8 and the return of the solid lifter small block. The first ZR-1 racing package was offered as an option and the first optional raised white letter tires. New egg crate fender grille treatment, new high back seats, an improved seat back release and cut pile carpeting with the deluxe leather interior option. The three-speed transmission was no longer offered. Low numbers were produced—only 17,316. The 350-cid engine blocks, transmissions, hard tops, seats, interior trim and eight-inch rally wheels all are easy parts to find.
JEERS	There was no more 427-cid V-8. There weren't any Tri-Power big blocks. Engine choices were reduced. There were weaker offerings including the lower powered 454 "Big Block" V-8. Parts that are difficult to find are the parking lamp grilles, air cleaners, smog equipment, NOS parts for the 1970 Corvettes, engine components and convertible tops and frames.
GAME PLAN	Look for an original, untouched example. Take your pick of the coupe or roadster, especially with the "Big Block." You can't go wrong! These cars are coming on strong—the collection builders of tomorrow.

The LT-1 Corvette engine coaxed 370 hp from the 350-cid small block V-8. *Tom Glatch*

The LT-1 logo on a Corvette meant the driver owned a vehicle that was quite special. *Tom Glatch*

1970 'VETTE FACTS	
VEHICLE IDENTIFICATION NUMBER	Corvette convertibles for 1970 were numbered 194670S100001 to 194670S117316. Corvette coupes for 1970 were numbered 194370S100001 to 194370S117316. The first symbol 1 indicated Chevrolet. The second symbol identified the body series 9 = Corvette. The third symbol indicated the type of engine with an even number like 4 that indicated a V-8 engine. The fourth and fifth symbols indicated the body style number 67 = convertible and 37 = coupe. The sixth symbol indicated the model year 0 = 1970. The seventh symbol identified the assembly plant S = St. Louis, Missouri. The last six symbols indicated the sequential production numbers.
ENGINE	**Type: V-8** Bore and stroke: 4.00 x 3.48 in. Displacement: 350 cid Brake hp: 300 at 4,800 rpm. Induction: Rochester 4-barrel. **Options:** 350-cid/350-hp w/ Rochester 4-bbl. carb 350-cid/370-hp w/ Holley 4-bbl. carb 454-cid/390-hp w/ Rochester 4-bbl. carb
VITAL STATS	**Convertible:** Original Price: $4,849 Production: 6,648 Wheelbase: 98 in. Length: 182.5 in. Tires: F70 x 15 Coupe: Original Price: $5,192 Production: 10,668 Wheelbase: 98 in. Length: 182.5 in. Tires: F70 x 15
COOL STUFF	A total of 1,287 buyers separately checked off the LT-1 engine option in 1970. In addition, 25 ZR-1 Corvettes carried the LT-1 engine. The ZL-1 package included the LT-1 engine, M22 heavy-duty four-speed manual transmission, J50/J56 dual-pin brakes with heavy-duty front pads and power assist and F41 suspension consisting of special 89 lb./in. ride rate front springs and 121 lb./in. ride rate rear springs, matching shock absorbers and a 0.75-inch front stabilizer bar. Starting in 1970, three-speed manual transmissions were no longer available in the Corvette. In terms of quality, the 1970 Corvette was a vast improvement over the 1968 and 1969 models. The Stingray name – again written as one word – appeared above the fender grilles on both sides of the Corvette

Car Life magazine said of the LT-1-powered Stingray, "It is, at this writing, the best of all possible Corvettes."

A proposed 454-cid big-block with 465 hp was listed in some early 1970 Corvette sales literature, but this "LS-7" V-8 never made it into the showroom. It had solid valve lifters, a high-performance camshaft and a Holley 800-CFM four-barrel carburetor. Only one car with the LS-7 engine was ever built.

Sports Car Graphic editor Paul Van Valkenburgh drove it 2,500 miles from a press conference at Riverside, California to Detroit, Michigan and raved about it. The car did the quarter mile in 13.8 seconds at 108 mph.

GM's policies against ultra-high-performance cars at this time led to the LS-7 option being dropped, but with the LT-1 around, Corvette lovers didn't miss it all that much. An LT-1-powered 1970 Corvette could do 0-to-30 mph in 2.5 seconds, 0-to-60 mph in 5.7 seconds and 0-to-100 mph in 13.5 seconds. It did the quarter mile in 14.17 seconds at 102.15 mph and had a top speed of 122 mph.

At least two "concept" Corvettes excited show goers and magazine readers in 1970. The first –the XP-882 – was actually slated for production as a 1973 model. Chevrolet general manager John Z. DeLorean viewed it as GM's answer to Ford's Pantera. It was powered by a transversely-mounted 400-cid V-8 mated to a Turbo-Hydra-Matic driving through an Oldsmobile Toronado transaxle. The rear window had a Venetian-blinds treatment like the Mako shark.

The XP-895 Reynolds Aluminum Corvette was built on an extra XP-882 chassis. It was designed by GM and built by an outside supplier for Reynolds Aluminum. The goal was to try to convince GM to make a production Corvette with an aluminum body. It had "roll-over" headlights, an all-coil-spring suspension and separate rear deck lids for the engine and luggage compartment.

In racing, the Corvette had, since 1968, continued the winning ways of its predecessors on track. In fact, Corvettes dominated the competition in the late 1960s and early 1970s. They won many SCCA national A- and B-Production titles and finished as high as third overall at Daytona and Sebring.

1970 Corvette Status Guide	Basket Case		Average Driver		Rare, Unique or Completely Original		Restored
Condition of CORVETTE:	Production Status						
	Average	Rare/Unique	N-O-M	O-M	Needs Work	Unrestored Low Mileage	Restored
Suggested Actions: Collect It							
Drive, Show and Enjoy							
Race, Autocross Competitively							
Store for a Future Project/Investment							
Candidate for Resto Rod							
Restore to Curb Appeal Condition							

1971 Corvette

The 1971 Corvette looked like a clone of the 1970 version. At a quick glance, the two models looked like the Doublemint Twins. Exterior-wise, they were essentially the same car. That made the 1971 a little easier to pick out in a crowd.

A new resin process was claimed to improve the Corvette's fiberglass body construction and probably did. Factory quality control was stepped up with additional tests for water leakage and body shaking. These were pushed through by Chevrolet general manager John Z. DeLorean. The fuel door was made easier to open and a new automatic transmission indicator lit up so it was easier to see what gear you were in when it was dark. The interior was redesigned a bit.

Leaded fuel was no longer required for a Corvette. The engines were de-tuned so the new no-lead fuel blends could be used and the "smog police" would be happy. Three Corvette engines used an 8.5:1 compression ratio and the LT-1 used a 9.0:1 ratio This robbed a little performance, but every other American car was going through the same thing at the time, so the Corvette remained one of the hottest machines around.

This 1971 LS-6 Corvette coupe was painted an eye-catching Ontario Orange.   *Tom Glatch*

MIKE YAGER SAYS:	
CHEERS	The coupe and roadster were both offered. There was new interior trim and enhancements with a deluxe interior and a wide choice of engine options. There also were new exterior colors available. There was a wider choice of engine options with the LS-6 being the final big horsepower engine. Parts that are found more easily include the 350-cid V-8, transmissions, wheel trim rings and reproduction "green numeral" gauges and clocks.
JEERS	There were few changes and it was "the same old car" in 1971. GM strikes limited production. The headlights and wiper doors were problematic once again. The fiber-optic material is hard to find and difficult to work with. Difficult parts to find include the 454-cid V-8 engines, convertible top frames, deluxe wheel covers, the spare tire carrier and the Corvette's jack and handle.
GAME PLAN	Look for as original and untouched version as you can find. Look for the LS-6, the ZR-1 small block or the ZR-2 performance packages. Give preference to a roadster and find an original with a vinyl hardtop. This car puts the top hat on this series. Look for this group of Corvettes to continue to rise in value. Choose a 1971 Corvette today. The cars are some of the finest examples of this series.

By 1971, Corvette owners could tailor options to their personal preferences. *Tom Glatch*

The 1971 Corvette LS-6 454-cid V-8 was intended for high performance uses. *Tom Glatch*

Standard equipment changed little, if at all. It was the final season for offering a fiber-optic light-monitoring system.

The de-tuned L-48 small-block engine was rated at 270 hp. High-performance engine options included the RPO LS5 V-8. This

454 also had an 8.5:1 compression ratio, hydraulic valve lifters, a high-performance cam and a Rochester 750CFM Quadra-Jet four-barrel carburetor. It was rated for 365 hp at 4,800 rpm and 465 foot-pounds of torque at 3,200 rpm.

1971 'VETTE FACTS

VEHICLE IDENTIFICATION NUMBER	Corvette convertibles for 1971 were numbered 194671S100001 to 194671S21801. Corvette coupes for 1971 were numbered 194371S100001 to 194371S121801. The first symbol 1 indicated Chevrolet. The second symbol identified the body series 9 = Corvette. The third symbol indicated the type of engine with an even number like 4 that indicated a V-8 engine. The fourth and fifth symbols indicated the body style number 67 = convertible and 37 = coupe. The sixth symbol indicated the model year 1 = 1971. The seventh symbol identified the assembly plant S = St. Louis, Missouri. The last six symbols indicated the sequential production numbers.
ENGINE	**Type: V-8** Bore and stroke: 4.00 x 3.48 in. Displacement: 350 cid Brake hp: 270 at 4,800 rpm. Induction: Rochester 4-barrel. **Options:** 454-cid/365-hp w/ Rochester 4-bbl. carb 454-cid/425-hp w/ Holley 4-bbl. carb 350-cid/330-hp w/ Holley 4-bbl. carb
VITAL STATS	**Convertible:** Original Price: $5,299 Production: 7,121 Wheelbase: 98 in. Length: 182.5 in. Tires: F70 x 15 **Coupe:** Original Price: $5,536 Production: 14,680 Wheelbase: 98 in. Length: 182.5 in. Tires: F70 x 15
COOL STUFF	This was the first year both Corvette body styles cracked the $5,000 barrier as far as base retail price. The ZL-1 package included the LT-1 engine, M22 heavy-duty four-speed manual transmission, J50/J56 dual-pin brakes with heavy-duty front pads and power assist and F41 suspension consisting of special 89 lb./in. ride rate front springs and 121 lb./in. ride rate rear springs, matching shock absorbers and a 0.75-inch front stabilizer bar.

Sleek, sophisticated, swoopy, sensational—just some of the adjectives for the '71 'Vette. *Tom Glatch*

Corvettes always looked great, coming or going. Many saw the 1971 only going away. *Tom Glatch*

1971 Corvette Status Guide	Basket Case		Average Driver		Rare, Unique or Completely Original		Restored
Condition of CORVETTE:	Production Status						
	Average	Rare/ Unique	N–O–M	O–M	Needs Work	Unrestored Low Mileage	Restored
Suggested Actions: Collect It							
Drive, Show and Enjoy							
Race, Autocross Competitively							
Store for a Future Project/Investment							
Candidate for Resto Rod							
Restore to Curb Appeal Condition							

Buyers willing to part with $1,221 could add the LS-6 big-block V-8. It also had hydraulic lifters, a high-performance cam, a lower compression and a four-barrel carburetor. However, the LS-6 carb was a big 880-cfm Holley model. The motor was rated 425 hp at 5,600 rpm and 475 foot-pounds of torque at 4,000 rpm.

Again offered to Corvette performance fans was the small-block-based LT-1 V-8. This 350-cid engine now had a 9.0:1 compression ratio. It was rated for 330 hp at 5,600 rpm and torque was 360 foot-pounds at 4,000 rpm. An LT-1-powered Corvette with the M-21 four-speed manual transmission and a 3.70:1 rear axle was rested by *Car and Driver* magazine in June

1971. It moved from 0-to-60 mph in 6.0 seconds and from 0-to-100 mph in 14.5 seconds. The same car did the quarter mile in 14.57 seconds at 100.55 mph and its top speed was 137 mph.

Production for 1971 increased to 14,680 Sport Coupes and 7,121 convertibles. A total of 1,949 buyers separately checked off the LT-1 engine option in 1971. In addition, eight ZR-1 Corvettes carried the LT-1 engine.

John Greenwood was winning races in a Corvette in 1971 and took the SCCA A-Production championship Allan Barker was winning other races in B-Production competition. Tony De Lorenzo and Don Yenko teamed up to take a first in class and a fourth overall at Daytona.

The 1971 Corvette LT-1 350-cid V-8 showed the beginnings of pollution controls. *Tom Glatch*

This interior shot of the 1971 Corvette LT-1 was inviting for drivers everywhere. *Tom Glatch*

1972 Corvette

The 1972 Corvette was basically the same as the 1971 version. Among its standard equipment was a positraction rear axle, outside rearview mirror, tinted glass, flo-thru ventilation system, front and rear disc brakes, electric clock, carpeting, wheel trim rings and all-vinyl upholstery. Also, an anti-theft alarm system was added to the list because so many Corvettes were being stolen. Chevy had to do something to give buyers a little extra security.

For the first time since 1956, only three V-8 engines were offered. If they seemed a little less powerful, part of the reason was that horsepower and torque ratings were now being quoted as SAE net figures. The base 350 carried a rating of just 200 hp at 4,400 rpm and generated only 300 lbs.-ft. of torque

The 1972 Corvette LT-1 version still was one of the top performers on the block. *Tom Glatch*

A telltale hood bulge meant the LT-1 V-8 was lurking in the 1972 engine bay. *Tom Glatch*

This was the final year for chrome bumpers front and rear on the Corvettes. *Tom Glatch*

MIKE YAGER SAYS:	
CHEERS	Some enhanced leather seat color choices were available this year. Both the LT-1 and LS-5 engines offered more performance choices. Fiber optics light monitors were gone and it was the final year for the removable rear window. It was the final year for the ZR-1 option and also the final year for front and rear chrome bumpers.
JEERS	This 1972 Corvette had few changes from the 1971. The new suppressed horsepower or "net" horsepower rating was applied. Watch for rust in the windshield/header area and the pillar posts. The pillars are hard to replace as the VIN tag is riveted on the left-side pillar. Convertible top frames as well as the LT-1 and 454-cid engines are very hard to find.
GAME PLAN	As with most years, look for original and untouched examples. For 1972, an LT-1 or "Big Block" convertible fits the bill. Look for the C3 group to continue rising in value. Go bold—lower production numbers are to be found in performance production cars. The '72 LT-1 with air conditioning was produced in fewer than 250 cars.

Many standard features and a host of options were available on the 1972 Corvettes. *Tom Glatch*

at 2,800 rpm. It had five main bearings, hydraulic valve lifters and a Rochester Quadra-Jet four-barrel carburetor. The 454-cid LS-5 V-8 added 70 hp and generated 390 lbs.-ft. of torque at 3,200 rpm. It teamed hydraulic lifters with a high-performance cam and a Rochester 750-cfm Quadra-Jet

carburetor. This motor was not available in cars bound for sale in California.

The LT-1 was again a hot small-block-based option, now carrying ratings of 255 hp at 5,600 rpm and 280 lbs.-ft. of torque at 4000 rpm. It had a 9.0:1 compression ratio, a forged steel crankshaft, solid valve lifters,

1972 'VETTE FACTS	
VEHICLE IDENTIFICATION NUMBER	Corvette convertibles for 1972 were numbered Z67K2S500001 to 1Z67K2S527004. Corvette coupes for 1972 were numbered 1Z37K2S500001 to 1Z37K2S527004. The first symbol 1 indicated Chevrolet. The second symbol identified the body series Z = Corvette. The third and fourth symbols indicated the body style number 67 = convertible and 37 = coupe. The fifth symbol indicated the engine: K = Base 350-cid V-8 and W = LS5 454-cid V-8 with dual exhausts. The sixth symbol indicated the model year 2 = 1972. The seventh symbol identified the assembly plant S = St. Louis, Missouri. The last six symbols indicated the sequential production numbers.
ENGINE	**Type: V-8** Bore and stroke: 4.00 x 3.48 in. Displacement: 350 cid Brake hp: 200 at 4,400 rpm. Induction: Rochester 4-barrel. **Options:** 454-cid/270 hp w/ Rochester 4-bbl. carb 350-cid/255-hp w/ Holley 4-bbl. carb
VITAL STATS	**Convertible:** Original Price: $5,296 Production: 6,508 Wheelbase: 98 in. Length: 182.5 in. Tires: F70 x 15 **Coupe:** Original Price: $5,533 Production: 20,496 Wheelbase: 98 in. Length: 182.5 in. Tires: F70 x 15
COOL STUFF	*Motor Trend* magazine tested a 1972 LT-1 coupe with the M-21 transmission and 3.70:1 axle in June 1972. The car did 0-to-30 mph in 2.9 seconds, 0-to-45 mph in 4.8 seconds, 0-to-60 mph in 6.9 seconds, 0-to-75 mph in 10.2 seconds and the quarter mile in 14.3 seconds at 92 mph. In its October/November 1971 edition, *Corvette News* said that "the engines in most cases still give about the same performance level in 1972 as they did in 1971."

The color wasn't merely red but racing inspired Mille Miglia Red in 1972. *KP Archives*

a high-performance cam, a Holley four-barrel carburetor, an aluminum intake manifold and a special 2.50-inch diameter dual exhaust system.

Very hard to find is a 1972 Corvette LT-1 with air conditioning. This combination was installed only this year. It was not a big favorite with Chevrolet service departments. The solid lifters could be revved higher than hydraulics and this led to many A/C belts flying off. Only about 240 cars ever got this setup. It is considered very desirable and rare among collectors.

There were a bunch of "lasts" for the 1972 Corvette. It was the last season the coupe was available with a removable rear window and was also the last year for chrome bumpers at both ends of the car. Also disappearing after 1972 were hidden windshield wiper doors, solid valve lifters and the use of an egg-crate grille.

Ex-drag racer John Greenwood took a pair of BFG-sponsored Corvettes to Le Mans in 1972. Two additional 'Vettes were entered by Henri Greder, of France. But it was another American entry – car No. 4 driven by Marietta Bob Johnson and Dave Heinz -- that hung in for 24 hours and finished the race in 15th position overall. The car was clocked at 212 mph on the Mulsanne Straight at Le Mans. Allan Barker again took the SCCA B-class title. At Daytona, Corvette pilots Tony De Lorenzo and Don Yenko finished fourth overall and first in GT class.

1972 Corvette Status Guide	Basket Case		Average Driver		Rare, Unique or Completely Original		Restored
Condition of CORVETTE:	Production Status						
	Average	Rare/ Unique	N–O–M	O–M	Needs Work	Unrestored Low Mileage	Restored
Suggested Actions: Collect It							
Drive, Show and Enjoy							
Race, Autocross Competitively							
Store for a Future Project/Investment							
Candidate for Resto Rod							
Restore to Curb Appeal Condition							

The No. 4 Heinz & Johnson Le Mans car actually started life as a wrecked and discarded 1968 roadster. It came to represent a true American grassroots motorsport's effort.

The car's original M-22 "Rock Crusher" four-speed gearbox and L-88 big-block V-8 were secretly supplied to Heinz and Johnson as part of Chevrolet's "back-door" racing involvement program. It featured a "distance kit" which included fixed headlight buckets, clear lens covers, large ZL-1 fender flares and wheel spacers.

After finishing 15th overall in the 1972 French Grand Prix at Le Mans, the car went on to a first place finish in the 12-hours of Sebring in 1973 and a second overall at the 1973 Daytona GTO-2.

Today the car belongs to author Mike Yager and is a featured attraction of his "My Garage Museum" in Effingham, Illinois.

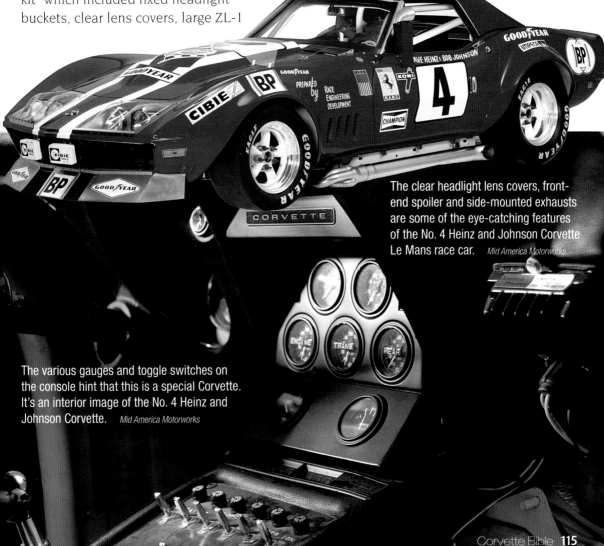

The clear headlight lens covers, front-end spoiler and side-mounted exhausts are some of the eye-catching features of the No. 4 Heinz and Johnson Corvette Le Mans race car. *Mid America Motorworks*

The various gauges and toggle switches on the console hint that this is a special Corvette. It's an interior image of the No. 4 Heinz and Johnson Corvette. *Mid America Motorworks*

1973 Corvette

There were predictions in the automotive press that Chevrolet would introduce a mid-engine Corvette in 1973, but nothing that radical came to be. Major changes for 1973 included a new domed hood, a body-color urethane plastic front bumper and a fixed rear window. The window redesign added a little more trunk space because a window storage tray was no longer required.

The 1973 'Vette was the only one that combined the new soft body-color front end with chrome rear bumpers. The late Larry Shinoda once said that the 1973 model was his favorite Stingray because its front and rear styling were closest to what designers had originally hoped for in this series.

Corvettes also had a new coolant-recovery system, new chassis mounts, and steel-guard-beam doors. The "eggcrate" front fender side vents of 1971-1972 models were replaced with non-trimmed air-duct types. Radial tires became standard and

The 1973 Corvette offered a new front end look with its integral bumper section. *Tom Glatch*

In an era of gas shortages, the 1973 Corvette interior offered a pleasant distraction. *Tom Glatch*

The new front end combined a hood bulge with a body colored urethane bumper. *Tom Glatch*

The LS 4 "big block" V-0 offered a combination of 454-cid with 275 horses. *Tom Glatch*

Designers were pleased with the final production of their visions in the '73 edition. *Tom Glatch*

MIKE YAGER SAYS:	
CHEERS	The front urethane body-color bumper was introduced in front and the rear chrome bumpers remained. The wiper door disappeared and a new side fender with an open cove was introduced. The LT-1 was gone but there were two engine options, including the first year of the L-82. The radial tires premiered and there were 10 color choices as well as side crash barriers in the doors. It was the first year for YJ-8 aluminum wheels. Easy parts to find today include hard tops, the 350 engine blocks, transmissions, gauges and seats.
JEERS	Horsepower output was suppressed and there were small performance selections. The four-speed transmission was losing ground to the automatic version. Rust developed around the windshield. Difficult parts to find include the original seat belts—now valued at $800 to $1,000 or more a set. Convertible top frames, 454-cid engines and smog equipment all are hard to find.
GAME PLAN	As always, a Corvette that is as original and untouched as possible is best. The '73 convertible had the lowest production numbers. The '73 Corvette is a nice driving car and there is great value to be found in a coupe.

an effort was made to reduce noise. It was largely effective, but *Road & Track* reported the 1973 was louder than a 1971 in certain circumstances.

The base ZQ-3 350-cid V-8 looked emasculated with a new 190-hp rating. The 454-cid LS-4 big-block used the same 8.5:1 compression ratio and hydraulic lifter combinations, but added a high-performance cam to generate 275 hp at 4,000 rpm. The L-82 was the high-performance 350 this year. It had a 9.0:1 compression ratio, a forged crank, a hi-po hydraulic-lifter cam and a rating of 250 hp at 5,200 rpm. A 1973 L-82-powered Corvette tested by *Car and Driver* magazine went from 0-to-40 mph in 3.5 seconds, from 0-to-60 mph in 6.7 seconds, from 0-to-80 mph in 10.8 seconds and from 0-to-100 mph in 17.1 seconds. It did the standing-start quarter mile in 15.1 seconds at 95.4 mph and had a top speed of 117 mph.

With designers considering major changes to the Corvette, it was not surprising that a pair of significant concept cars hit the show

In 1973, the L-82 V-8 was the most powerful engine option with 350 horsepower. *Tom Glatch*

The 1973 Corvette interior offered sports car feel with no lack of conveniences. *Tom Glatch*

1973 'VETTE FACTS	
VEHICLE IDENTIFICATION NUMBER	Corvette convertibles for 1973 were numbered 1Z67K3S400001 to 1Z67K3S434464. Corvette coupes for 1973 were numbered 1Z37K3S400001 to 1Z37K3S434464. The first symbol 1 indicated Chevrolet. The second symbol identified the body series Z = Corvette. The third and fourth symbols indicated the body style number 67 = convertible and 37 = coupe. The fifth symbol indicated the engine: K = Base 350-cid V-8, T = L82 350-cid V-8 with dual exhausts, X or W = LS4 454 V-8. The sixth symbol indicated the model year 3 = 1973. The seventh symbol identified the assembly plant S = St. Louis, Missouri. The last six symbols indicated the sequential production numbers.
ENGINE	**Type: V-8** Bore and stroke: 4.00 x 3.48 in. Displacement: 350 cid Brake hp: 190 at 4,400 rpm. Induction: Rochester 4-barrel. **Options:** 454-cid/275 hp w/ Rochester 4-bbl. carb 350-cid/250-hp w/ Rochester 4-bbl. carb
VITAL STATS	**Convertible:** Original Price: $5,685 Production: 4,943 Wheelbase: 98 in. Length: 182.5 in. Tires: F70 x 15 **Coupe:** Original Price: $5,921 Production: 25,520 Wheelbase: 98 in. Length: 182.5 in. Tires: F70 x 15
COOL STUFF	The majority of 1973 Corvettes, 70.8 percent, were sold with air conditioning. Only 41.2 percent of all '73 Corvettes had a four-speed manual gearbox. "Guardrail" type steel beams were added to the Corvette's doors in 1973.

The 1973 L-82 package was known for pure speed, as shown in this convertible version. *Tom Glatch*

circuit in 1973. The XP-897 GT Corvette – also known as the "2-Rotor" – was not originally promoted as a Corvette, since it had also been given consideration as a replacement for the German-built, Corvette-like, Opel GT. Horsepower was about 180. The "2-Rotor's" front-end treatment saw production on the Chevy Monza 2+2 in 1975.

Zora Arkus-Duntov decided he wanted a really fast Wankel-engined sports car, so he got Gib Hufstader to build a mid-engined, Wankel-powered vehicle utilizing a pair of the engines in the "2-Rotor." The result was a 350-hp car called the "4-Rotor" or Aerovette. It had the largest Wankel engine ever put in a car. Displacement would have been about 585 cid in a conventional engine. It also had double-folding gull-wing doors for entrance to the passenger compartment.

While it no longer dominated the streets (the Trans Am SD 455 was reportedly faster than the hottest production Corvette), Chevy's fiberglass sports car continued to dominate sports car racing, with Bill Jobe winning the SCCA B-Production title. In A-Production, veteran Corvette driver J. Marshall Robbins managed to outrun a pack of Cobras, but was later disqualified for using risers under his carburetor. Corvettes did sweep the first SCCA national autocross event. Of course, some of the cars raced in '73 were earlier model Corvettes.

1973 Corvette Status Guide	Basket Case		Average Driver		Rare, Unique or Completely Original		Restored
Condition of CORVETTE:	Production Status						
	Average	Rare/ Unique	N-O-M	O-M	Needs Work	Unrestored Low Mileage	Restored
Suggested Actions: Collect It							
Drive, Show and Enjoy							
Race, Autocross Competitively							
Store for a Future Project/Investment							
Candidate for Resto Rod							
Restore to Curb Appeal Condition							

1974 Corvette

By 1974, the Corvette was beginning to change in character. It had risen significantly in price and declined a bit when it came to outlandishly brutal performance. The car was still one of the hottest American rides in town, but it had gained a great deal of design sophistication and was more of a luxury cruiser than ever before. The popularity of the coupe over the convertible reflected this trend, as did a growing list of optional equipment.

While the basic design of the Stingray wasn't altered for 1974, the car had a completely restyled rear end. A sloping end piece replaced the once-favored "Kammback" look. The rear end panel tapered down to a strong, horizontal feature line. Two round taillights were "tunneled" into either end of the panel with the "Corvette" name spelled out in block letters between them. The use of a conventional rear bumper was entirely eliminated. A 5-mph, Federally-mandated

A 1974 Corvette 454-cid V-8 coupe spends a day at the beach. *Mike Mueller*

MIKE YAGER SAYS:	
CHEERS	Chrome was gone with the new urethane body-colored rear bumper. There were a number of "lasts" in 1974 including the mechanical tachometer drive, true dual exhausts, the points and distributor, the large rear gas cap and the smog-laden "Big Block" engine. Leather seats were no longer 100 percent leather. They had vinyl sides and backs. For the first time since 1962, there was no emblem on the fuel door. Parts that are found easily include the 350 engines, hard tops, seats and carburetors.
JEERS	The split rear bumpers had problems and the overall color matching on bumpers was poor. The bumpers also tended to get brittle. There was no rear emblem on the fuel door. Difficult parts to find include smog equipment, original brake calipers, the 454-cid V-8s, PO2 series wheel covers and the convertible top frames.
GAME PLAN	Look for as original and untouched a car as you can find. Choose a convertible, L-82 or 454-cid "Big Block." The convertible was the top choice in 1974.

The 454 V-8 was no shrinking violet as proven by its huge valve covers. *Mike Mueller*

The matching blue interior of the 1974 Corvette coupe. *Mike Mueller*

crash bumper was behind the body-colored urethane bumper, fully integrated into the lower rear panel. The new rear fascia was of two-piece design this year only. It met federal energy-absorbing standards, but it also added 30 pounds to the weight of the car. The weight boost was just about all at the rear of the body and necessitated minor suspension changes. Both the front and rear spring rates had to be revised. A optional new "gymkhana" suspension featured a 0.9375-inch diameter front stabilizer bar, heavier-duty front suspension bushings, beefier front springs with a 550 lb./in. rating and beefier

rear springs with a 304 lbs./in. rating.

The power steering system, seat belts and radiator were also improved. The alarm system activator was relocated. Tires were downgraded a bit, however. Previously they were speed-rated for 140 mph, but by 1974, 120 mph was considered good enough. Other options that once would have been considered "un-Corvette-like conduct" included electric window lifts, vacuum-assisted brakes, integrated air conditioning and a stereo tape deck. Leather trim seemed luxurious, too, but even the old British sports cars had used leather seats.

1974 'VETTE FACTS	
VEHICLE IDENTIFICATION NUMBER	Corvette convertibles for 1974 were numbered 1Z67| |4S400001 to 1Z67| |4S437502. Corvette coupes for 1974 were numbered 1Z37| |4S400001 to 1Z37| |4S437502. The first symbol 1 indicated Chevrolet. The second symbol identified the body series Z = Corvette. The third and fourth symbols indicated the body style number 67 = convertible and 37 = coupe. The fifth symbol |in blank| indicated the engine: J = 350-cid 195-hp four-barrel V-8, T = 350-cid 250-hp four-barrel V-8 and Z = LS4 454-cid 270-hp four-barrel V-8. The sixth symbol indicated the model year 4 = 1974. The seventh symbol identified the assembly plant S = St. Louis, Missouri. The last six symbols indicated the sequential production numbers.
ENGINE	**Type: V-8** Bore and stroke: 4.00 x 3.48 in. Displacement: 350 cid Brake hp: 195 at 4,400 rpm. Induction: Rochester 4-barrel. **Options:** 454-cid/270 hp w/ Rochester 4-bbl. carb 350-cid/250-hp w/ Rochester 4-bbl. carb
VITAL STATS	**Convertible:** Original Price: $5,766 Production: 5,472 Wheelbase: 98 in. Length: 185.5 in. Tires: GR70 X 15 **Coupe:** Original Price: $6,002 Production: 32,029 Wheelbase: 98 in. Length: 185.5 in. Tires: F70 x 15
COOL STUFF	The '74 was the last Corvette with a true dual exhaust system without catalytic converters. The '74 Corvette was also the last model to offer an optional 454-cid V-8. Most 1974 Corvettes, 95.6 percent, had power steering, 88.3 percent had power brakes, 63.1 percent had power windows, 72.9 percent had tilting steering wheel, 77.7 percent had air conditioning and 33.7 percent had a four-speed manual transmission.

There were again three engines on the Corvette order form. Base equipment was the V-8 of 350 cubic inches. It retained hydraulic lifters and a Quadrajet carburetor, but actually got its compression ratio boosted to 9.0:1 Chevy advertised 195 hp at 4,400 rpm and 275 lbs.-ft of torque at 2,800 rpm. The LS-4 option was the last 454 for the Corvette. It used a new 8.25:1 compression ratio, hydraulic lifters with a hi-po cam and a four-barrel. The advertised ratings were 270 hp at 4,400 rpm and 380 lbs.-ft. of torque at 2,800 rpm. The L-82 option also returned using the same essential setup – 9.0:1 compression,

forged steel crank, hydraulic lifters, hi-po cam and fat dual exhausts. It was rated for 250 hp at 5,200 rpm and 285 lbs.-ft. of torque at 4,000 rpm.

The hot 350 Corvette was no muscle car, but it still was good for a 0-to-60 mph run in 7.5 seconds and a top speed of 125 mph (watch those 120-mph tires close!)

In racing this year, J.M. Robbins took the SCCA A-Production Championship in a Corvette, Bill Jobe pulled a repeat performance on his B-Production title and Steve Eberman was the champ in B-Stock Solo II competition.

In sunny weather, the popular T-tops didn't stay on very long on 1974 Corvettes. *Phil Hall Collection*

1974 Corvette Status Guide	Basket Case		Average Driver		Rare, Unique or Completely Original		Restored
Condition of CORVETTE:	Production Status						
	Average	Rare/ Unique	N-O-M	O-M	Needs Work	Unrestored Low Mileage	Restored
Suggested Actions: Collect It							
Drive, Show and Enjoy							
Race, Autocross Competitively							
Store for a Future Project/Investment							
Candidate for Resto Rod							
Restore to Curb Appeal Condition							

One could keep the 1974 Corvette interior as sparse or as option laden as desired. *Phil Hall Collection*

There is something elegant about a Corvette convertible with its top down on the road. *Phil Hall Collection*

1975 Corvette

In January 1975, a milestone personnel change took place at Chevrolet Motor Division. Zora Arkus-Duntov reached the General Motors mandatory retirement age of 65 and had to step down as Corvette chief engineer. Zora had been the first to hold the title and kept it for over 20 years. Dave McLellan took his place. McLellan would hold the title for another 17 years and put his own personal trademark on the brand by developing the 1997 LS-1, 2005 LS-2, 1991 LS-6 and LT-5 engines, as well as the ZR-1 and C5 Corvettes.

Most of the changes on the Corvette for 1975 were hidden. The sloping rear end design was carried over, but a one-piece end cap replaced the two-piece type used in 1974. Two vertical "bumperettes" were now molded

Small vertical bumpers were one of the signs that this was a 1975 Corvette. *Tom Glatch*

The 1975 L-82 V-8 had a high-performance cam and developed 205 hp. *Tom Glatch*

A rear angle press image from 1975 shows the new vertical bumperettes that were stylishly added to the Corvette.

MIKE YAGER SAYS:	
CHEERS	It was the first year for HEI distributors, the catalytic convertor and the electronic tachometers. The L-82 was the performance engine of choice since the bigger engines were gone. New one-piece bumpers front and rear with bumper guards were new in 1975. Hard tops, seats, steering wheels, rally wheels, suspension parts and rear ends are easy to find.
JEERS	There was little that changed from the 1974 version. The "Big Block" was gone and horsepower ratings were suppressed. The catalytic convertor meant unleaded fuel had to be used. The coupe was lower than the convertible. The convertible was in its final year of production in this series. Original bumpers and convertible top frames are all hard to find.
GAME PLAN	This car is fun to drive with its gymkhana suspension system and a four-speed transmission! Look for one that is as original and untouched as possible. A L-82 version with a four-speed manual would make a fun-to-drive car. Try to find a '75 Corvette with the Z07 option—the L-82 engine, FE-7 suspension plus heavy duty power brakes front and rear.

into the bottom section of the fascia, one on each side. These were also added to the front of the car, on either side of the license plate recess. They made both ends of the Corvette look a little more streamlined.

On the inside, the speedometer included kilometers-per-hour for the first time. This was the last year for the Corvette C3 convertible, which still came with a simple manually-operated convertible top. An auxiliary hardtop was on the option list

and cost $267. You still couldn't order some upscale options like cruise control, but many Corvettes came "fully loaded" with the options buyers could get. Sales continued to climb higher each year and the options made the Corvette that much more profitable for GM every time a unit sold. No doubt about it, the '75 Corvettes were very successful products from the corporate point of view, if not from the enthusiast's view.

Under the hood was a new High-Energy

This 1975 Corvette convertible is shown with its hardtop in place. *Mike Mueller*

1975 'VETTE FACTS	
VEHICLE IDENTIFICATION NUMBER	Corvette convertibles for 1975 were numbered 1Z67||5S400001 to 1Z67||5S438465. Corvette coupes for 1975 were numbered 1Z37||5S400001 to 1Z37||5S438465. The first symbol 1 indicated Chevrolet. The second symbol identified the body series Z = Corvette. The third and fourth symbols indicated the body style number 67 = convertible and 37 = coupe. The fifth symbol |in blank| indicated engine: J = 350-cid 165-hp V-8 and T = 350-cid 205-hp V-8 The sixth symbol indicated the model year 5 = 1975. The seventh symbol identified the assembly plant S = St. Louis, Missouri. The last six symbols indicated the sequential production numbers.
ENGINE	**Type: V-8** Bore and stroke: 4.00 x 3.48 in. Displacement: 350 cid Brake hp: 165 at 3800 rpm. Induction: Rochester 4-barrel. **Options:** 350-cid/205-hp w/ Rochester 4-bbl. carb
VITAL STATS	**Convertible:** Original Price: $6,550 Production: 4,829 Wheelbase: 98 in. Length: 185.5 in. Tires: GR70 x 15 **Coupe:** Original Price: $6,810 Production: 33,836 Wheelbase: 98 in. Length: 185.5 in. Tires: F70 x 15
COOL STUFF	Zora Arkus-Duntov retired as the division's chief engineer. He was replaced by David R. McLellan. This was the last year the Corvette used GM's "Astro Ventilation" system. This was the last year for a Corvette convertible until 1986. This was the first year for use of a catalytic converter.

A rural location was chosen as background for this beautiful 1975 Corvette convertible. *Mike Mueller*

ignition system with the Corvette's first point-less distributor sparked the two remaining engines, both based on the 350-cid hydraulic-lifter small-block V-8. The base L-48 version had an 8.5:1 compression ratio and a Quadrajet carburetor. The factory rating on this puppy was 165 hp at 3,800 rpm and 255 lbs.-ft. of torque at 2,400 rpm. These were not numbers put forth at the drive-in for bragging rights. Part of the reason was the mandatory use of a catalytic converter. The Corvette's dual exhaust pipes went into a single catalytic converter, then exited in "split" fashion to the rear of the car.

The L-82 of course was the motor to buy. With its 9.0:1 compression and high-performance cam, it was good for 205 hp at 4,800 rpm and 255 lbs.-ft. at 3,600 rpm. *Car and Driver's* road test of a 1975 Corvette with the L-82 reported a 0-to-60 time of 7.7 seconds and a top speed of 129 mph.

Another first for 1975 was the addition of a fuel bladder to the fuel storage system to reduce the threat of a fire breaking out after a rear-impact collision. The basics for this innovation dated back to Duntov's CERV 1 experimental car of the late '50s, which is housed in Mid America Motorwork's "My Garage" Museum today.

Racing driver John Greenwood competed with a Corvette in the popular Trans-Am racing series and took first place overall. Frank Fahey drove his Corvette to the SCCA A-Production Championship.

1975 Corvette Status Guide	Basket Case		Average Driver		Rare, Unique or Completely Original		Restored
Condition of CORVETTE:	Production Status						
	Average	Rare/ Unique	N-O-M	O-M	Needs Work	Unrestored Low Mileage	Restored
Suggested Actions: Collect It							
Drive, Show and Enjoy							
Race, Autocross Competitively							
Store for a Future Project/Investment							
Candidate for Resto Rod							
Restore to Curb Appeal Condition							

1976 Corvette

Unlike some companies, Chevrolet was accurate in advertising the fiberglass-bodied Corvette as "America's only true production sports car."

The big-block V-8 had disappeared after 1974, leaving a 350-cid (5.7-liter) small-block as the power plant for all Corvettes. Two versions were offered this year, both with a four-barrel carburetor. The base L-48 version now developed 180 hp (15 more than in 1975). An optional L-82 V-8 produced 210 hp. The L-82 had special heads with larger valves, impact-extruded pistons and finned aluminum rocker covers.

The standard V-8 drove a new, slightly lighter weight automatic transmission: the Turbo Hydra-Matic 350, which was supposed to improve shifting at wide-open throttle. The optional engine kept the prior Turbo Hydra-Matic 400, but with a revised torque converter. A wide-range four-speed manual gearbox (with 2.64:1 first gear ratio) was standard and a close-ratio version was available at no extra cost. A new Carburetor Outside Air Induction system moved intake from the cowl to above the radiator.

No longer offered this season was a Corvette convertible. It had been dropped

A page from 1976 Corvette literature shows Orange Flame and Silver Corvettes. *Phil Hall Collection*

MIKE YAGER SAYS:	
CHEERS	There were no more rear deck vents in 1976. The L-82 option was the only performance engine choice. Parts that are easy to find include the 350 engines, the transmission, rear ends, suspension parts and the seats.
JEERS	Once again there were few changes from the 1974 model. The Big Block and convertible were both gone and horsepower outputs were suppressed. With the second-year catalytic convertor, the Corvette now had a single exhaust with dual mufflers. Rust was common in the windshield header and the pillar posts. Difficult 1976 parts to find include the smog equipment, good original YJ-8 wheels, an original jack and handle, the spare tire carrier, one-year-only steering wheels in good condition, the one-year-only steering column, rocker moldings, plus original exhausts and mufflers.
GAME PLAN	These are the "drivers' series" Corvettes. If you're looking for a weekend cruiser, these are the cars for you. Not much excitement was available in terms of performance.

In 1976, many Corvette owners were choosing automatic transmissions.   *Mike Mueller*

1976 'VETTE FACTS	
VEHICLE IDENTIFICATION NUMBER	Corvette coupes for 1976 were numbered 1Z37| |6S400001 to 1Z37| |6S446558. The first symbol 1 indicated Chevrolet. The second symbol identified the body series Z = Corvette. The third and fourth symbols indicated the body style number 37 = coupe. The fifth symbol |in blank| indicated the engine: L = 350-cid 180-hp V-8 and X = 350-cid 210-hp V-8. The sixth symbol indicated the model year 6 = 1976. The seventh symbol identified the assembly plant S = St. Louis, Missouri. The last six symbols indicated the sequential production numbers.
ENGINE	**Type: V-8** Bore and stroke: 4.00 x 3.48 in. Displacement: 350 cid Brake hp: 180 at 4,000 rpm. Induction: Rochester 4-barrel. **Options:** 350-cid/210-hp w/ Rochester 4-bbl. carb
VITAL STATS	**Coupe:** Original Price: $7,605 Production: 46,558 Wheelbase: 98 in. Length: 185.2 in. Tires: GR70-15
COOL STUFF	Though largely a carryover from 1975, the new Corvette set an all-time sales record. The suggested retail price for the base Corvette coupe cracked the $7,000 barrier for the first time – and the $7,500 barrier, too. *Car and Driver* (April 1976) tested an L-82 Corvette with the M-40 transmission and 3.36:1 rear axle. It went from 0-to-30 mph in 2.8 seconds, 0-to-60 mph in 7.1 seconds and 0-to-100 mph in 1995 seconds. It did the standing start quarter mile in 15.3 seconds at 91.9 mph. It had a top speed of 124.5 mph. A sealed battery was standard for the first time this year. Kelsey-Hayes aluminum wheels were reintroduced on the 1976 Corvette. They looked like the aluminum wheels used on earlier models, but carried "Made in Mexico" stampings on their interior surface.

An impression of the 1976 Corvette coupe in black and white.   *K. Scott Teeters*

at the end of 1975. Only the Stingray coupe remained. It had twin removable roof panels. A partial steel underbody replaced the customary fiberglass, to add strength and improve shielding from exhaust system heat. This can be a problem for restorers, as the underbody can rust. Mid America Motorworks now offers reproductions.

A new one-piece-bar Corvette nameplate was seen on the rear of the car, between the twin-unit taillights (which were inset in the bumper cover). Of the 10 body colors, eight were Corvette exclusives. Corvettes had side marker lights with reflectors, parking lamps that went on with headlights, lane-change turn signals and two-speed wiper/washers. Inside was a new, smaller-diameter four-spoke sports steering wheel with crossed-flags medallion. This wheel actually came from the Chevrolet Vega subcompact. Not everyone appreciated its lowly origin, so it lasted only this year. A grained vinyl-trimmed instrument panel (with stitched seams) held a 160-mph speedometer with trip odometer and 7,000-rpm electronic tachometer. A key lock in the left front fender set the anti-theft alarm.

Corvettes had fully-independent suspension and four-wheel disc brakes. Wide GR-70 SBR tires rode 15 x 8-inch wheels. A total of 5,368 Corvettes had the FE-7 Gymkhana suspension installed, 5,720 came with the L-82 V-8 and 2,088 had the M-21 four-speed close-ratio manual gearbox.

1976 Corvette Status Guide	Basket Case		Average Driver		Rare, Unique or Completely Original		Restored
Condition of CORVETTE:	Production Status						
	Average	Rare/Unique	N–O–M	O–M	Needs Work	Unrestored Low Mileage	Restored
Suggested Actions: Collect It							
Drive, Show and Enjoy							
Race, Autocross Competitively							
Store for a Future Project/Investment							
Candidate for Resto Rod							
Restore to Curb Appeal Condition							

An Orange Flame decorated 1976 Corvette brightens a wooded rural scene. *Mike Mueller*

Corvettes, like this 1976 coupe always seem to look good from any angle. *Mike Mueller*

Cast-aluminum wheels were a new option, installed on 6,253 cars. Standard equipment included bumper guards, flush retracting headlights, Soft-Ray tinted glass, Hide-A-Way wipers, wide-view day/night mirror and a center console with lighter and ashtray. Behind the seat backs were three carpeted storage compartments. The Corvette bucket seats had Wallaby-grain -vinyl upholstery and deep-pleated saddle-stitched seat panels.

This year's factory show car was the 1976 Corvette Mulsanne. It was a customized update of the Aero Coupe with stationary headlights under transparent covers. It had twin NASA-style hood scoops on either side of the power blister in the center of the hood, a ZL-1 V-8, external side exhausts with ribbed covers, a periscope-style roof treatment and dual high-mounted rear-view mirrors. The hood was finished with stylized frames and the car was photographed wearing Michigan Bicentennial license plates.

Corvettes again dominated sports car racing events. Gene Bothello took the A-Production title, Howard Park took the B-Production honors and Orin Butterick was the B-Stock Solo II champion.

1977 Corvette

For 1977, the Stingray was gone… but the Corvette looked much the same as before. It's just that Chevrolet removed the Stingray nameplates on the front fender. Sometimes marketing experts make funny decisions. It's interesting to note that Corvette sales rose steadily until the year after they did the model-name change. Sometimes it pays to leave what's working alone!

Although Chevrolet's fiberglass sports car technically no longer had a secondary moniker, real changes were fairly modest this year. Many improvements, like a steel hood reinforcement, were hidden. One obvious revision was the new crossed-flags emblems between the headlights and on the fuel filler door. A thinner pillar with blackout style finish made the windshield and side

A 1977 Corvette coupe with T-top was on display at Cypress Gardens, Florida. *KP Archives*

A look inside the 1977 Corvette using the open-sky T-top angle. *Phil Hall Collection*

glass look more integrated into the overall body styling.

There were other changes inside the cockpit. The center convenience console was restyled. It looked more like the gauge cluster in an airplane with individual gauges. A voltmeter replaced the former ammeter and the old "Door ajar" and "headlamp up" warning lights disappeared. New heater and air conditioning controls were seen and there was an ashtray and a lighter on the horizontal surface. A recessed pocket was added behind the gearshift lever.

The power window switches were relocated into the redesigned console.

Cars with manual transmission had a gear shift lever that was about an inch higher than before, but it traveled a shorter distance between gears. A pointer was added to the automatic transmission lever and both manual and automatic shifters added a new black leather boot. The steering column was shortened and a "Euro-style" multi-function control lever hung off it. This lever operated the windshield wiper/washer system and the headlight dimmer switch.

MIKE YAGER SAYS:	
CHEERS	It was the final year of the inset rear window. The L-82 engine was the only performance choice. The interiors were a blend of old and new but a leather-wrapped brushed steering wheel was available. A new eight-track player and T-top carrier were offered. Cruise control was offered on cars with automatic transmission. Parts that are easy to find include the engines and transmissions as well as the suspension, seats and T-tops. Dual sport mirrors changed the look of the car. The left-hand chrome mirror was gone.
JEERS	There was no convertible in 1977. The Corvette had few changes from 1974. The "Big Block" engines were gone and the horsepower outputs were suppressed. Difficult parts to find today include the smog equipment—it was often discarded—as well as original interior trim that often turned brittle with age. Also such parts as functional AC and heater controls, the original door panels—used only in 1977 and the original luggage rack with the T-top carrier.
GAME PLAN	Not much performance excitement available so grab an L-82! This was a transition period for Corvette as new features were on the horizon. The 1977 Corvette is a "sleeper" with many nondescript cars—but if you choose wisely, it is a great car to own. Low mileage examples exist with interesting color combinations that add to the collector value. A year that flies under the radar. Choose an early model and watch for that early brushed horn button!

Coming at you, the 1977 Corvette! This was an original angle used for publicity. *KP Archives*

1977 'VETTE FACTS	
VEHICLE IDENTIFICATION NUMBER	Corvette coupes for 1977 were numbered 1Z37| |7S400001 to 1Z37| |7S449213. The first symbol 1 indicated Chevrolet. The second symbol identified the body series Z = Corvette. The third and fourth symbols indicated the body style number 37 = coupe. The fifth symbol |in blank| indicated the engine: L = 350-cid 180-hp V-8 and X = 350-cid 210-hp V-8. The sixth symbol indicated the model year 7 = 1977. The seventh symbol identified the assembly plant S = St. Louis. The last six symbols indicated the sequential production numbers.
ENGINE	**Type: V-8** Bore and stroke: 4.00 x 3.48 in. Displacement: 350 cid Brake hp: 180 at 4,000 rpm. Induction: Rochester 4-barrel. **Options:** 350-cid/210-hp w/ Rochester 4-bbl. carb
VITAL STATS	**Coupe:** Original Price: $8,648 Production: 49,213 Wheelbase: 98 in. Length: 185.2 in. Tires: GR70-15
COOL STUFF	Optional glass roof panels were announced as a $349 option, but were then delayed for another year. Prices rose more than $1,000 and brought the MSRP for the lowest-priced Corvette to more than $8,600. Yikes! The marketing of automotive sound systems became big business in the late 1970s and one reason for the 1977 Corvette's redesigned console was that it could fit any Delco radio. Some of the changes made in the 1977 Corvette gave enthusiasts an "early warning" of what to expect in the 1978 "Silver Anniversary" Corvette.

The black and white vision of the 1977 Corvette coupe was a graceful sight. *K. Scott Teeters*

The 1977 steering wheel also had a Euro-style leather-wrapped rim.

The Custom interior, which was previously an extra-cost option, was now made the standard trim in Corvettes. It had cloth upholstery – a first in a Corvette. The Dynasty cloth material came with horizontal ribbing and the cloth sections were framed in leather. As an option, buyers could have the customary all-leather seat panels. The leather came in 10 colors and the Dynasty cloth came in six colors. The interior door panel inserts were finished in Satin Black instead of the wood grain pattern used in 1976. Both the instrument panel and door trim panels lost their embossed stitch lines. New padded sunshades could swivel to side windows. Passenger-side roof pillars held a soft vinyl coat hook.

Power trains were the same as in 1976. The 180-hp L-48 was the base 350-cid V-8 with 8.5:1 compression, hydraulic lifters and a Quadrajet carburetor. The optional L-82 version had a bit more compression and again produced 210 hp. A total of 6,148 Chevrolets came with the special L-82 V-8 engine under the hood. Only 5,743 Corvettes had the M-20 four-speed manual gearbox and 2,060 used the M-26 close-ratio four-speed.

Remember in the early days when you could not get power brakes or power steering in a Corvette? Now both features were standard equipment. The optional Gymkhana suspension was relatively popular with 7,269 installs, but a trailering equipment package – which seemed like a strange option for a sports car – was ordered by a mere 289 buyers. New-for-1977 options included an AM/FM stereo radio with tape player, cruise control (for cars with automatic transmission only) and a luggage carrier that could hold the roof panels.

1977 Corvette Status Guide	Basket Case		Average Driver		Rare, Unique or Completely Original		Restored
Condition of CORVETTE:	Production Status						
	Average	Rare/ Unique	N–O–M	O–M	Needs Work	Unrestored Low Mileage	Restored
Suggested Actions: Collect It							
Drive, Show and Enjoy							
Race, Autocross Competitively							
Store for a Future Project/Investment							
Candidate for Resto Rod							
Restore to Curb Appeal Condition							

1978 Corvette

To mark Corvette's 25th anniversary, the 1978 model got a major aerodynamic restyling with large wraparound back window and a fastback roofline. This was the Corvette's first restyling since 1968. Two special editions were produced, one well known as a collector car and the other little more than a nice-looking optional paint job. New tinted glass lift-out roof panels were wired into the standard anti-theft system. A 24-gallon fuel cell replaced the former 17-gallon tank, filling space made available by a new temporary spare tire.

Inside was a restyled, padded instrument panel with face-mounted round instruments and a new locking glove box that replaced the former map pocket. The restyled interior had more accessible rear storage area with a roll shade to hide luggage. The wiper-washer control was moved from the steering column back to the instrument panel, but turn signal and headlight-dimmer controls remained on the steering column. Door trim was now of a cut-and-sew design with soft expanded vinyl or cloth. As in 1977, the seats had leather side bolsters, with either leather or cloth seating areas in a fine rib pattern.

It was the 25th anniversary of the Corvette in 1978 marked by this special coupe. *Tom Glatch*

MIKE YAGER SAYS:	
CHEERS	There were three coupe models. The 25th anniversary and Indy 500 Pace Car Corvettes were special with two-tone paint, decals and more. Enhanced leather color choices were available along with new seats and special upholstery in the Pace Car. There were several new features including the "green house" rear window, glass T-tops, the power antenna, aluminum wheels and front and rear spoilers on the Pace Car. The L-82 option still was available! Rally wheels, seats, suspension parts, the engines and transmissions all are easy parts to find.
JEERS	The rear spoiler dimples and sags badly with age. Difficult parts to find include original decal kits, the outside trim on the rear windows, the jack and handle, the spare tire carrier, original style Goodyear tires, a glass top with the original tint, 140 mph speedometers and an original power antenna that is operating.
GAME PLAN	Start the 1978 Corvette collecting craze! Look for as original and untouched an example as you can find. An L-82 four-speed Indy Pace Car with low mileage would be good. A 25th Anniversary car with red interior and cloth seats would be another. Some unusual, low-production cars started to appear during the 1978 production run with low production runs of colors and accessories. Look for these to continue to rise in value! Be careful with the Silver Anniversary cars. There is nothing on the VIN to authenticate an original.

The engine of the 25th anniversary Corvette was as memorable as the exterior. *Tom Glatch*

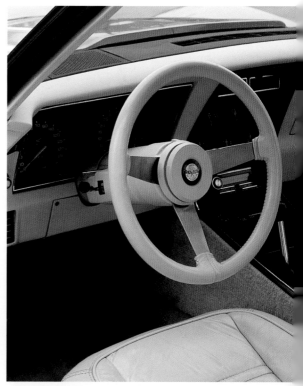

The 1978 Corvette's interior included a restyled dash with new padding. *Tom Glatch*

1978 'VETTE FACTS

VEHICLE IDENTIFICATION NUMBER	Corvette coupes for 1978 were numbered 1Z87| |8S400001 to 1Z87| |8S440274. Corvette Indy Pace Cars were numbered 1Z87| |8S900001 to 1Z87| |8S906502. The first symbol 1 indicated Chevrolet. The second symbol identified the body series Z = Corvette. The third and fourth symbols indicated the body style number 87 = coupe. The fifth symbol |in blank| indicated engine: L = 350-cid 175-hp or 185-hp V-8 and H = 350-cid 220-hp V-8 The sixth symbol indicated the model year 8 = 1978. The seventh symbol identified the assembly plant S = St. Louis, Missouri. The last six symbols indicated the sequential production number.
ENGINE	**Federal:** Type: V-8 Bore and stroke: 4.00 x 3.48 in. Displacement: 350 cid Brake hp: 185 at 4,000 rpm. Induction: Rochester 4-barrel. **California Emissions:** Type: V-8 Bore and stroke: 4.00 x 3.48 in. Displacement: 350 cid Brake hp: 175 at 4,000 rpm. Induction: Rochester 4-barrel. **Options:** 350-cid/220-hp w/ Rochester 4-bbl. carb
VITAL STATS	**Coupe:** Original Price: $9,446 Production: 40,274 Wheelbase: 98 in. Length: 185.2 in. Tires: P225/70R-15 SBR **Indy Pace Car Coupe:** Original Price: $13,653 Production: 6,502 Wheelbase: 98 in. Length: 185.2 in. Tires: P225/70R-15 SBR
COOL STUFF	The limited-edition Pace Car replica was created to commemorate the selection of Corvette as Pace Car for the 62nd Indy 500 race on May 28, 1978. A production run of 2,500 was planned, but so many potential buyers who saw it at the New York Auto Show in February wanted one that Chevy decided to build at least one for every Chevy dealer. (6,502) The mirrored glass roof panels introduced on the Indy Pace Car later became a $349 option for other 1978 Corvettes. Before long, the original $13,653 list price of the Indy Pace Car meant little, as speculators eagerly paid double that amount and more. Asking prices in the $60,000 range were seen at the time. Even though so many were built, the Indy Pace Car remains a collectible model today.

The Corvette's optional L82 high-performance 350-cid V-8 reached 220 hp as a result of a new dual-snorkel cold-air intake system, larger-diameter exhaust and tailpipes and lower-restriction mufflers. The automatic transmission used with the optional V-8 lost weight and had a low-inertia, high-stall torque converter. The base 350-cid engine used a Borg Warner four-speed manual gear box with higher first-second gear ratio than before. The performance V-8 used a close-ratio Borg-Warner gearbox.

The axle ratios used in cars sold in California and high-altitude counties were switched from 3.08:1 to 3.55:1. A total of

Corvette literature celebrated the 25th anniversary in 1978 on its brochure cover. *Tom Glatch*

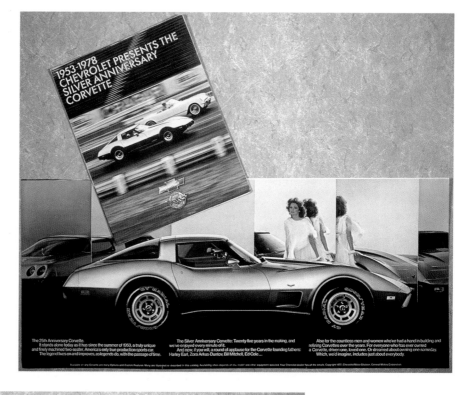

The many generations of Corvette were depicted in the 1978 literature. *Tom Glatch*

12,739 optional L-82 engines were installed, while 3,385 Corvettes had the M-21 four-speed close-ratio gear box and 38,614 had automatic transmission.

Glass roof panels, which had been promised earlier, actually became available this year. What Chevrolet described as "aggressive" 60-series white-letter tires also joined the option list for the first time. An optional AM/FM-CB stereo radio used a tri-band power antenna on the rear deck. Each of this year's Corvettes would have Silver Anniversary emblems on the nose and rear deck. A total of 15,283 cars displayed the $399 special two-tone "Silver Anniversary" paint combination with silver metallic on top and charcoal silver on the lower body. Pinstripes accentuated the fenders' upper profiles, wheel openings, front fender vents, hood and rear license cavity. Interiors were Black, Red or Oyster White. Various other options were required on Silver Anniversary models, including aluminum wheels.

For a considerably higher price, buyers could have the Limited Edition replica of the Indy Pace Car with distinctive black-over-silver paint and red accent striping. Equipment in this "Indy Package" (RPO code Z78) included a special silver interior with new lightweight high-back seats, special front and rear spoilers. P255/60-R15 white-letter tires required the factory to trim the leading edge of the wheel well for tire clearance. The Indy Pace Car package's content included nearly all Corvette options, plus special decals. Upholstery was silver leather or

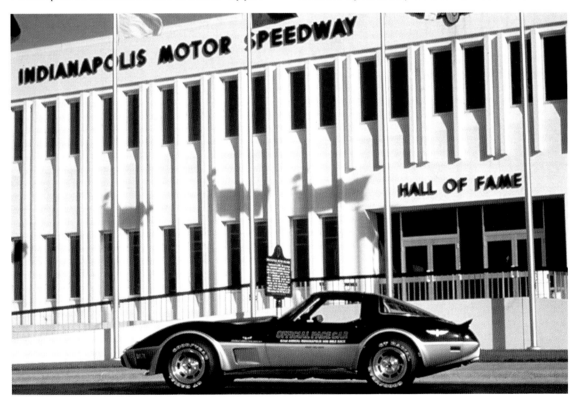

The 1978 Indianapolis 500 Pace Car Corvette was part of that year's 25th anniversary celebration. *KP Archives*

In case anyone needed reminding, Corvette used a 25th anniversary badge in 1978. *Tom Glatch*

endure a selection of "forced RPOs" (items installed at the factory whether wanted or not). The mandatory extras included power windows, air conditioning, sport mirrors, a tilt-telescope steering wheel, a rear defogger, an AM/FM stereo with either an 8-track tape player or CB radio, plus power door locks and a heavy-duty battery.

In racing, Greg Pickett's Corvette was the overall winner in the Trans-Am Series. Elliott Forbes-Robinson was SCCA A-Production champ, Andy Porterfield took the B-Production title and David M. Wright was the B-Stock Solo II Champion. John J. Seiler took B-Prepared Solo II honors and Sandra Schneider, another Corvette pilot, was champion in B-Stock Ladies Solo II racing.

leather with smoke gray cloth inserts.

A production run of 2,500 Indy Pace Cars had been planned, but so many people wanted one that the production target quickly grew to 6,502 units. Buyers had to

1978 Corvette Status Guide	Basket Case		Average Driver		Rare, Unique or Completely Original		Restored
Condition of CORVETTE:	Production Status						
	Average	Rare/Unique	N–O–M	O–M	Needs Work	Unrestored Low Mileage	Restored
Suggested Actions: Collect It							
Drive, Show and Enjoy							
Race, Autocross Competitively							
Store for a Future Project/Investment							
Candidate for Resto Rod							
Restore to Curb Appeal Condition							

1979 Corvette

"The Corvette evolution continues," declared a 1979 Corvette sales catalog. Not much of that evolution was visible, however, after the prior year's massive styling changes.

Under the Corvette's hood, the base engine got the dual-snorkel air intake that first appeared on 1978 models with the higher-performing L-82 V-8. The air cleaner by itself added 10 extra horsepower. This year's L-82 V-8 had a higher-lift camshaft, special cylinder heads with larger valves and higher compression, impact-extruded pistons, a forged steel crankshaft and finned aluminum rocker covers. The "Y" pipe exhaust system had new open-flow mufflers, while the automatic transmission got a higher numerical (3.55:1) rear axle ratio.

All Corvettes now had the high-back bucket seats that were introduced on the 1978 limited-edition Indy Pace Car. A high pivot point let the seat backrest fold flat on the passenger side, level with the luggage area floor. A Delco AM/FM radio was now standard equipment. Corvettes had black roof panel moldings and black window moldings. Bolt-on front and rear spoilers (also adapted from the Indy Pace Car)

It couldn't fly but many thought the 1979 Corvette looked natural near runways.   *Mike Mueller*

MIKE YAGER SAYS:	
CHEERS	A new seat design was used based on the 1978 Indy Pace Car Corvette. It was the only year for the front and rear spoiler option. Power windows and AC all were standard. Reproduction door panels (available from Mid America Motorworks), 350-cid engines, automatic transmissions, seats and seat foam, interior trim and suspension parts are all easy to get.
JEERS	Same style with few changes from 1978. The old style "pellet" catalytic converters produced a great deal of interior heat and tended to clog up. The interiors used a lot of plastic trim pieces. Horsepower outputs were again suppressed. Seat clam shells in good condition, correct date M-21 transmissions, the spare tire carrier, the optional differential ratios and heater/AC controls all are hard parts to find.
GAME PLAN	Look for the most original and untouched example you can find. A few 1979 Corvettes were produced for promotional purposes and were finished in a Red Oxide primer. Trim tags are marked "Primer." Watch for these rare cars! The 1979 Corvettes were great driving cars and had good interior room.

No fancy names in 1979, the color was named Yellow for this beautiful Corvette. *KP Archives*

became available. Corvette buyers who didn't want to go for the full Gymkhana suspension could now order heavy-duty shocks alone.

The standard equipment list for 1979 included the L-48 V-8 with four-barrel carburetor, a choice of either an automatic transmission or a four-speed manual gearbox (a close-ratio version was optionally available), power four-wheel disc brakes and a limited-slip differential. Other standard items included tinted glass, a front stabilizer bar, concealed windshield wipers and washers, a day/night inside mirror, a wide outside mirror, an anti-theft alarm system, a three-spoke sport steering wheel, an electric clock, a trip

The tightly packed 1979 L-82 V-8 offered high performance engine goodies. *Mike Mueller*

1979 'VETTE FACTS	
VEHICLE IDENTIFICATION NUMBER	Corvette coupes for 1979 were numbered 1Z87| |9S400001 to 1Z87| |9S453807. The first symbol 1 indicated Chevrolet. The second symbol identified the body series Z = Corvette. The third and fourth symbols indicated the body style number 87 = coupe. The fifth symbol |in blank| indicated the engine: 8 = 350-cid 195-hp V-8 and 4 = 350-cid 225-hp V-8. The sixth symbol indicated the model year 9 = 1979. The seventh symbol identified the assembly plant S = St. Louis, Missouri. The last six symbols indicated the sequential production number.
ENGINE	**Type: V-8** Bore and stroke: 4.00 x 3.48 in. Displacement: 350 cid Brake hp: 195 at 4,000 rpm. Induction: Rochester 4-barrel. **Options:** 350-cid/225-hp w/ Rochester 4-bbl. carb
VITAL STATS	**Coupe:** Original Price: $10,220 Production: 53,807 Wheelbase: 98 in. Length: 185.2 in. Tires: P225/70R-15 SBR
COOL STUFF	Production of over 53,000 Corvettes was an all-time record. So was the $10,000+ price for the base model. Bolt-on front and rear spoilers like those on the '78 Indy Pace Car became optional on the 1979 Corvette. The emblems used on the 1979 Corvette body were the same ones used on 1977 models.

The interior of this 1979 Corvette shows that it is equipped with a four-speed transnmission. *Mike Mueller*

odometer, a heater and defroster, bumper guards and a luggage security shade. The standard tires were now P225/70-R15 steel-belted radials with black sidewalls on 15 x 8-inch wheels.

The Corvettes continued with a four-wheel independent suspension. Inside, the bucket seats came with a choice of cloth or leather trim. The aircraft-type convenience console held a 7,000-rpm tachometer, a voltmeter and oil-pressure, temperature and fuel gauges. Seat inserts could have either leather or cloth facings.

In racing, another Corvette driver – Gene Bothello – became the overall winner in the Trans-Am Series. Andy Porterfield repeated his B-Production title and Steve Eberman was the B-Stock Solo II Champion. Corvette driver Larry Park took B-Prepared Solo II honors and Janet Saxton was champion in B-Stock Ladies Solo II racing. At Riverside, California the first vintage auto race was held and one of the highlights of the event was an appearance of the No. 003 Corvette Grand Sport owned and drive by Bob Paterson.

A pair of Turbo Corvette show cars was put together. One had hood vents and one did not. The cars were basically modified versions of the factory type Corvette, but they used a turbocharged V-6 for power. The reason was the energy crunch and a desire for fuel mileage improvements at this time. The Turbo Corvettes' graphics resembled those of the production-style 1982 Collector Edition Corvette.

1979 Corvette Status Guide	Basket Case		Average Driver		Rare, Unique or Completely Original		Restored
Condition of CORVETTE:	Production Status						
	Average	Rare/Unique	N-O-M	O-M	Needs Work	Unrestored Low Mileage	Restored
Suggested Actions: Collect It							
Drive, Show and Enjoy							
Race, Autocross Competitively							
Store for a Future Project/Investment							
Candidate for Resto Rod							
Restore to Curb Appeal Condition							

Corvette

Chevrolet

1979

This is the aerodynamic nose section of the 1979 Corvette from official literature.   *KP Archives*

1980 Corvette

"How many other cars can you name at a single glance?" asked the 1980 Corvette sales catalog. "That should tell you something about the uniqueness of the Corvette." The copywriters said the Corvette was "the most recognizable car on the road today."

The Corvette legend lived on in 1980 with a car that was more aerodynamic and lost close to 250 pounds. The hood had a lower profile and the doors were lighter with thinner door glass. The aerodynamically-designed front bumper cover featured an

The Corvette was lighter and even more aerodynamic in 1980. *Tom Glatch*

The 1980 L-82 Corvette engine had a high-lift cam, special heads and more. *Tom Glatch*

Inside were changes like power windows and a tilt/telescopic steering wheel. *Tom Glatch*

MIKE YAGER SAYS:	
CHEERS	The 1980 Corvette was a lighter car with an aluminum rear housing and a fiberglass rear spring on cars with automatic transmission. New items included the side fender treatment, emblems, an aluminum intake manifold, front and rear fascias and an 85-mph speedometer. It was the final year for the L-82 option. The Corvette could be equipped with polished aluminum wheels in 1980. Reproduction YJ-8 wheels and center caps are available. Automatic transmissions and rear differentials are easy to find as are door panels and interior parts.
JEERS	There was little changed since 1978 and the horsepower output continued to be suppressed. Difficult to come by today are original exhaust systems, original smog pumps and tubing, the original Goodyear tires, an original 85-mph speedo—many were changed—and the correct and dated MM-4 four-speed transmission. Roof carrier parts also are hard to find.
GAME PLAN	Look for as original and untouched example as possible and look forward to driving a very roadworthy car. If the 85 mph speedo has been changed, the mileage may not be accurate.

The 1980 Corvette cut through the wind and turned heads on highways. *Tom Glatch*

Even the 1980 wheel and fender view shows the Corvette was something special. *Tom Glatch*

The L-82 badge let all viewers know that this '80 Corvette was power-laden. *Tom Glatch*

1980 'VETTE FACTS	
VEHICLE IDENTIFICATION NUMBER	Corvette coupes for 1980 were numbered 1Z87| |AS400001 to 1Z87| |AS440614. The first symbol 1 indicated Chevrolet. The second symbol identified the body series Z = Corvette. The third and fourth symbols indicated the body style number 87 = coupe. The fifth symbol |in blank| indicated the engine: 8 = L-48 350-cid 190-hp V-8, H = California L-48 350-cid 180-hp V-8 and 6 = L-82 350-cid 230-hp V-8. The sixth symbol indicated the model year A = 1980. The seventh symbol identified the assembly plant S = St. Louis, Missouri. The last six symbols indicated the sequential production number.
ENGINE	**Type: V-8** Bore and stroke: 4.00 x 3.48 in. Displacement: 350 cid Brake hp: 190 at 4,200 rpm. Induction: Rochester 4-barrel. **Options:** 350-cid/230-hp w/ Rochester 4-bbl. carb
VITAL STATS	**Coupe:** Original Price: $13,140 Production: 40,614 Wheelbase: 98 in. Length: 185.3 in. Tires: P225/70R-15/B SBR
COOL STUFF	Production continued at the St. Louis plant, but a new GMAD operation at Bowling Green, Kentucky, was planned to begin production of the next-generation Corvettes. Chevrolet engineers released a TurboVette that used a Garrette AiResearch turbocharger and fuel injection, but press people who drove it discovered performance more sluggish than a regular L-82 V-8 could dish out. This was the first year for a distinct "California" engine designed to meet the stricter emissions standards of the "Golden State." Only 5,069 Corvettes made in 1980 carried the special L-82 high-performance engine. Nearly all 1980 Corvettes were equipped with automatic transmission.

integral air dam and a deeply-recessed grille and parking lights. Functional air exhaust louvers, finished in black, were added to the front fender air vents.

A new rear bumper cover incorporated an integral spoiler. There were new cross-flags emblems, new rear lights and cornering lights. The cornering lights were illuminated by the turn signals when the headlights were on and turned off when the signal was cancelled.

Inside was a new rich, ribbed pattern cloth interior and a sliding sun visor for the driver to help cut down on side sun. A Special Custom trim featured a choice of cloth or leather seating surfaces. Also found inside the 'Vette was a day/night rearview mirror,

a sport-styled three-spoke steering wheel, an aircraft-style center console, a 7,000-rpm tachometer, an electric clock, full array of gauges, a separate trip odometer, a console-mounted parking brake handle, cut-pile carpeting, color-keyed seat belts, folding seat back latches, a roof courtesy light with door-mounted switches and an under floor stowage compartment.

The 1980 type lift-off roof panels were made of lightweight, low-density microscopic glass beads. The body panels were urethane-coated. Weight cuts also hit the power train. The differential housing and supports were made of aluminum.

The base L-48 350-cid V-8 had a new aluminum intake manifold, hydraulic lifters, a Quadrajet carburetor and an 8.2:1 compression ratio to produce 190 hp at 4,200 rpm. In California cars, however, a 305-cid 180-hp LG-4 V-8 was standard. It used an 8.5:1 compression ratio. The performance-option L-82 had a 9.0:1 compression ratio and generated 230 hp at 5,200 rpm. It also incorporated a higher-lift hydraulic cam, special heads with impact-extruded pistons, a forged steel crank, four-bolt main bearing caps and heat-dissipating aluminum rocker arm covers. New emblems included special engine identifiers for the L-82.

The dashboard carried a new 85-mph speedometer. Only two storage bins stood behind the seat, where three used to be.

The Corvette's optional Turbo Hydra-Matic transmission added a lock-up torque converter that engaged at about 30 mph, while the four-speed manual transmission got new gear ratios. In California cars the 305 was the sole engine choice and came only with automatic transmission.

New standard equipment this year included formerly-optional power windows, a tilt-telescopic steering wheel, dual Sport mirrors, a convenience group (with time-delay dome and courtesy lights and intermittent windshield wipers) and Four Season air conditioning. Rally wheels held P225/70-R15 black sidewall steel belted radial (SBR) tires with trim rings and center caps.

1980 Corvette Status Guide	Basket Case		Average Driver		Rare, Unique or Completely Original		Restored
Condition of CORVETTE:	Production Status						
	Average	Rare/ Unique	N-O-M	O-M	Needs Work	Unrestored Low Mileage	Restored
Suggested Actions: Collect It							
Drive, Show and Enjoy							
Race, Autocross Competitively							
Store for a Future Project/Investment							
Candidate for Resto Rod							
Restore to Curb Appeal Condition							

1981 Corvette

"No other American car looks like or stirs the spirit like a Corvette," said Chevrolet's 1981 sales brochure for its fiberglass-bodied sports-luxury model. The theme was essentially the same one used in 1980 and it was working. Although the auto industry was in a tailspin at this time, the Corvette was a bright column on the sales charts.

The catalog described the 1981 Corvette as being "lean, responsive and roadable." It suggested that it had the aerodynamics and engineering to meet the demands of sophisticated sports car enthusiasts along with a tradition that dated back to 1953. "All the style that makes Corvette instantly recognizable anywhere," is how Chevy stated it.

Probably the most significant change for 1981 was one that was hidden from

This Beige-on-Dark Bronze Corvette T-top must have been resplendent looking in 1981. *Mike Mueller*

MIKE YAGER SAYS:	
CHEERS	In 1981, the St. Louis production was moved to Bowling Green, Kentucky where new quality control standards were put in place. The Bowling Green-made cars had enamel paint rather than the lacquer paint used at St. Louis. It was the first year for the Computer Command Control, just one engine option was available, a digital radio was available and fiberglass springs now were standard. Two-tone exterior colors in 22 different combinations were available—most of those painted at Bowling Green. It was the final year for the carburetor. Easy to find in the parts bin are engines, automatic transmissions, YJ-8 wheels, emblems and rear differentials.
JEERS	The narrow seat design was a problem in 1981. There were problems with the carburetors. Cracked glass T-tops, original Goodyear tires, roof panel carriers and a functioning Electronic Tuned Reciever stereo with an eight-track player are among the difficult items to find.
GAME PLAN	In addition to finding the most original and untouched example possible, look for a four-speed Corvette from 1981. Some low production colors to note are Bright Blue Metallic, Dark Blue Metallic, Dark Bronze and Dark Claret Metallic.

A stunning example of the 1981 Corvette coupe.   *Mike Mueller*

1981 'VETTE FACTS	
VEHICLE IDENTIFICATION NUMBER	Corvette coupes for 1981 were numbered: |St. Louis Assembly Plant| 1G1AY87 | |4BS400001 to 1G1AY87| |4BS431611. |Bowling Green Assembly Plant| 1G1AY87 | |4B5100001 to 1G1AY87| |4B5108995. The first symbol 1 indicated U.S. built. The second symbol G indicated a General Motors product. The third symbol 1 indicated a Chevrolet Motor Division vehicle. The fourth symbol A indicated the type of non-passive passenger restraint system used. The fifth symbol Y indicated the car line or series, in this case Corvette. The sixth and seventh symbols indicated the body style number 87 = two-door plain back special coupe. The eighth symbol |in blank| indicated the engine: | | = L81 350-cid (5.7-liter) 190-hp Chevrolet V-8. The ninth symbol was a check digit that varied. The 10th symbol indicated the model year B = 1981. The 11th symbol indicated the assembly plant S = St. Louis, Missouri and 5 = Bowling Green, Kentucky. The last six symbols indicated the sequential production numbers starting with 100001 at each factory.
ENGINE	**Type: V-8** Bore and stroke: 4.00 x 3.48 in. Displacement: 350 cid Brake hp: 190 at 4,200 rpm. Induction: Rochester 4-barrel.
VITAL STATS	**Coupe:** Original Price: $15,248 Production: 40,606 Wheelbase: 98 in. Length: 185.3 in. Tires: P225/70-R15/B SBR
COOL STUFF	The Corvette factory in St. Louis, Mo., built its last Corvette on June 1, 1981. Of the total output this model year, 8,995 Corvettes came out of the new plant at Bowling Green, Kentucky, which began production in June 1981. This was the first year the Corvette offered a power-adjustable driver's seat as an option. Despite some weak years in the industry, Corvette sales remained strong through this period. Two-tone Corvettes were available from the Bowling Green plant.

The 1981 Corvette was powered by a V-8 engine, as pictured here. *Mike Mueller*

view. Corvettes with Turbo Hydra-Matic transmission had a new fiberglass-reinforced monoleaf rear spring that weighed just eight pounds (33 pounds less than the multi-leaf steel spring it replaced). The new spring eliminated interleaf friction. Manual-shift models kept the old spring, as did those with optional Gymkhana suspension.

The Corvette's side door glass was made even thinner again, in a further attempt to cut overall car weight. A new L-81 version of the 350-cid V-8 arrived this year. It was rated for 190 hp and had lightweight magnesium rocker arm covers and stainless-steel free-flowing exhaust manifolds that weighed 14 pounds less than the previous cast-iron manifolds.

1981 Corvette Status Guide	Basket Case		Average Driver		Rare, Unique or Completely Original		Restored
Condition of CORVETTE:	Production Status						
	Average	Rare/ Unique	N–O–M	O–M	Needs Work	Unrestored Low Mileage	Restored
Suggested Actions: Collect It							
Drive, Show and Enjoy							
Race, Autocross Competitively							
Store for a Future Project/Investment							
Candidate for Resto Rod							
Restore to Curb Appeal Condition							

The bright red Corvette instrument panel was inviting to potential drivers. *Phil Hall Collection*

A new thermostatically-controlled auxiliary electric fan boosted cooling and allowed use of a smaller main fan. The engine air cleaner had a new, chromed cover. A new Computer Command Control system controlled fuel metering, as well as the torque converter lock-up clutch that operated in second and third gears. The four-speed fully synchronized manual transmission was available in all 50 states. It was the first time in several years that buyers of Corvettes sold in California could order a stick shift and also the last year for a four-speed.

A quartz crystal clock was now standard inside. The Corvette's standard anti-theft alarm added a starter-interrupt device. Joining the option list was a driver's side only six-way power seat. Electronic-tuning radios could have built-in cassette or 8-track tape players or a CB transceiver. The ample standard equipment list also included four-wheel power disc brakes, a limited-slip differential, power steering, tinted glass all around, twin remote-control sport mirrors and concealed two-speed windshield wipers. Also standard were halogen high-beam retractable headlights, air conditioning, power windows, a tilt-telescope leather-wrapped steering wheel, a tachometer, an AM/FM radio, a trip odometer, courtesy lights and a luggage compartment security shade. Corvette buyers had a choice of cloth or leather-and-vinyl upholstery at no difference in price.

Even though the base Corvette was a fairly "loaded" automobile by this time, there still were options available. A new one was electrically-operated twin remote-control sport mirrors. Other options popular with collectors now include aluminum wheels, automatic speed control with resume, various Delco sound systems (including CB radios, 8-track players and cassette players) and a 6-way power driver's seat. The optional Gymkhana suspension (price $54) was also included with the trailer-towing package.

1982 Corvette

The 1982 model was the last Corvette to employ the same basic body introduced in 1968. Its chassis dated back to even five years before that. No doubt, some buyers preferred to wait for the next generation to arrive. Still, this was the end of the big Corvette era: "An enthusiast's kind of Corvette. A most civilized one," said the factory sales catalog. *Road & Track* called it "truly the last of its series," though one with an all-new drive train."

For the first time since 1955, no stick shift Corvettes were produced. Every Corvette had a new type of four-speed automatic transmission with lock-up function in every gear except first. Under the hood was a new kind of 350-cid V-8 with Cross-fire fuel injection. Twin throttle-body injectors with computerized metering helped boost horsepower to 200 (10 more than in 1981) and cut emissions at the same time. This

The lines and curves of the 1982 Corvette are still considered among the most aesthetically pleasing. *Tom Glatch*

After this year, the Corvettes would be changed inside and out. *Tom Glatch*

The Cross-fire injection V-8 engine offered 350 cubic inches and 200 hp for drivers in 1982. *Tom Glatch*

The Cross-fire insignia showed what kind of engine had been chosen for this Corvette. *Tom Glatch*

MIKE YAGER SAYS:	
CHEERS	The new automatic transmission. The Cross-fire fuel injection system was new. There were unique emblems and there was a Collector Edition with special paint and unique interior trim. It was the final year of the C3 series. There was more focus on quality control at the Bowling Green plant.
JEERS	It was the first time the Corvette price rose above $20,000. Narrow seating continued to be a problem and the four-speed manual transmission was not available. Problem parts to find are the Bronze Collector Edition dash and gauges, the 85-mph speedo, a Cross-fire air cleaner in good condition, bronze glass T-tops and an ETR stereo with an eight-track player.
GAME PLAN	In addition to finding the most untouched car in as original condition as possible, be sure to enjoy this great driving car. The 1982 was the culmination of the C3 series and a fitting end to the "shark" body design. The new assembly plant was on line with great quality control for the 1982 model year.

was the first fuel-injected Corvette in nearly two decades. It had a much different type of fuel-injection system, since mini-computerization had arrived. In the gas tank was a new electric fuel pump. Externally, the final version of the "big" (1968 Stingray-style) Corvette changed little, but a special "Collector Edition" model displayed quite a few custom features, highlighted by a frameless glass lift-up hatch in place of the customary fixed backlight. The Collector Edition Corvette's unique Silver-Beige metallic paint was accented by pin stripes and a "fading shadow" treatment on the

The glass hatchback door was depicted in the 1982 Corvette sales literature.   *KP Archives*

1982 'VETTE FACTS	
VEHICLE IDENTIFICATION NUMBER	Corvette coupes for 1982 were numbered: 1G1AY8786C5100001 to 1G1AY8786C512408. The first symbol 1 indicated U.S. built. The second symbol G indicated a General Motors product. The third symbol 1 indicated a Chevrolet Motor Division vehicle. The fourth symbol A indicated non-passive manual seat belts. The fifth symbol Y indicated the car line or series: Y = Chevrolet Corvette. The sixth and seventh symbols indicated the body style number 87 = two-door plain back special coupe and 07 = Collector Edition two-door hatchback coupe. The eighth symbol indicated the engine: 8 = 5.7-liter Cross-fire Injection (CFI) Chevrolet V-8. The ninth symbol was a check digit that varied. The 10th symbol indicated the model year C = 1982. The 11th symbol indicated the assembly plant: 5 = Bowling Green, Kentucky. The last six symbols indicated the sequential production numbers starting with 100001 at each factory.
ENGINE	**Type: V-8** Bore and stroke: 4.00 x 3.48 in. Displacement: 350 cid Brake hp: 200 at 4200 rpm. Induction: Twin throttle-body injectors
VITAL STATS	**Coupe:** Original Price: $18,290 Production: 18,648 Wheelbase: 98 in. Length: 185.3 in. Tires: P225/70-R15/B SBR **Collector Edition:** Original Price: $22,538 Production: 6,759 Wheelbase: 98 in. Length: 185.3 in. Tires: P255/60-R15
COOL STUFF	Introduced: Dec. 12, 1981. Model-year production: 25,407. Calendar-year production: 22,838. Model-year sales by U.S. dealers: 22,086. All Corvettes now came from the factory at Bowling Green, Kentucky. Production fell dramatically this year, reaching the lowest total since 1967. Cross-fire Injection was introduced on the '82 'Vette. It used a pair of single throttle bodies mounted on opposite ends of a special manifold. The Chevy-developed system was for high-performance cars featuring throttle body injection (TBI). Before Tuned Port Injection (TPI) arrived, engineers had to use Cross-fire Injection on hot cars. Cross-fire Injection had its problems. The system was prone to wetting the manifold and poor fuel distribution. The throttle body bores also iced up under certain conditions. In addition, a leaky air intake seal often created havoc. There are ways to make Cross-fire Injected Corvettes run reliably and perform better. Enthusiasts have worked out modifications to get more power. Information can be found on a variety of websites. Use your favorite search engine and enter "Cross-fire injection."

hood, fenders and doors . . . plus distinctive cloisonné emblems. It had special finned wheels similar to the cast-aluminum wheels that dated back to 1967.

The Collector Edition's removable glass roof panels had special bronze coloring and solar screening. The model's crossed-flags emblems read "Corvette Collector Edition" around the rim. Inside was a matching Silver-Beige metallic interior with multi-tone leather seats and door trim. Even the Collector Edition's hand-sewn leather-wrapped steering wheel kept the theme color and its leather-covered horn button had a cloisonné emblem. The tires were P255/60-R15 Goodyear SBR WLT Eagle GT.

The Collector Edition earned the dubious distinction of being the first Corvette to cost more than $20,000. Collector Edition cars were built to order, rather than according to a predetermined schedule. They carried a special VIN code with a "0" in the sixth position (Body Code 07), but did not have a separate serial number sequence. The special VIN plates were used to prevent swindlers from turning an ordinary Corvette into a Collector Edition (which had happened all too often with 1978 Indy Pace Car replicas). The Indy Pace Cars also had unique VIN numbers that the Silver Anniversary models did not have.

Standard equipment for other Corvettes included power brakes and steering, P225/70-R15/B SBR tires on steel wheels with center hub and trim rings, cornering lamps, front fender louvers, halogen high-beam retractable headlamps, dual remote sport mirrors and tinted glass. The body-color front bumper had a built-in air dam. Also standard: luggage security shade, air conditioning, push-button AM/FM radio, concealed wipers, power windows, time-delay dome/courtesy lamps, headlamp-on reminder, a lighted visor vanity mirror, a leather wrapped tilt/telescoping steering wheel, a 7,000-rpm tachometer, an analog quartz clock with sweep second hand, a day/night mirror, a lighter and a trip odometer. Bucket seats could be trimmed in all-cloth or leather options.

1982 Corvette Status Guide	Basket Case		Average Driver		Rare, Unique or Completely Original		Restored
Condition of CORVETTE:	Production Status						
	Average	Rare/ Unique	N-O-M	O-M	Needs Work	Unrestored Low Mileage	Restored
Suggested Actions: Collect It							
Drive, Show and Enjoy							
Race, Autocross Competitively							
Store for a Future Project/Investment							
Candidate for Resto Rod							
Restore to Curb Appeal Condition							

Another view of the always-inviting Corvette interior, 1982 version. *KP Archives*

1984 Corvette

The eagerly-awaited fourth-generation Corvette for the 1980s missed the 1983 model year completely, but arrived in spring 1983 in an all-new form. An aerodynamic exterior featuring an "acute" windshield rake (64 degrees) covered a series of engineering improvements. A one-piece, full-width fiberglass roof (no T-bar) was removable. The solid-painted top was standard. The removable transparent roof panel was optional. At the rear of the new Corvette body was a frameless glass back window or hatch above four round taillights. Hidden headlights were featured, along with clear,

Here's a picture of a 1984 Corvette that went racing—new style and all. *Bob Harrington*

It was a new generation in 1984, like this white Corvette. *Mike Mueller*

Basic black always made a Corvette look great, including this 1984 version. *Mike Mueller*

MIKE YAGER SAYS:	
CHEERS	The 1984 Corvette was the first passenger car to excel on the skid pad pulling 1 g. This Corvette began to make extensive use of electronic sensors for the engine and drive train. The modern C4 design offered better performance and fuel economy. The new style included the first use of a large one-piece glass top. Both interior and exterior parts are available as well as chassis items for restoration.
JEERS	The Cross-fire injection system was retained from 1982. The digital dash was rather fault prone and the overdrive often failed. It could not withstand hard driving. There were performance limitations on the L-83. The Z-51 option offered a bone-jarring ride. There were paint problems on red cars. Some brake and engine management/fuel delivery parts are hard to find. The transmission parts are hard to find and quite expensive. The Delco-Bose stereo system wasn't compatible with most aftermarket components and its speakers often failed.
GAME PLAN	Low mileage, original, pristine cars are the order of the day. Collect a 4 + 3 with some interesting options, a future winner in the Corvette C4 series. This car will grow in value as each day passes.

A new instrument panel greeted drivers of the new generation 1984 Corvettes. *KP Archives*

1984 'VETTE FACTS	
VEHICLE IDENTIFICATION NUMBER	Corvette coupes for 1984 were numbered: 1G1AY0782E5100001 to 1G1AY0782E5151547. The first symbol 1 indicated U.S. built. The second symbol G indicated a General Motors product. The third symbol 1 indicated a Chevrolet Motor Division vehicle. The fourth symbol A indicated non-passive manual seat belts. The fifth symbol Y indicated the car line or series: Y = Chevrolet Corvette. The sixth and seventh symbols indicated the body style number 07 = two-door hatchback coupe. The eighth symbol indicated the engine: 8 = 5.7-liter Cross-Fire Injection (CFI) Chevrolet V-8. The ninth symbol was a check digit that varied. The 10th symbol indicated the model year E = 1984. The 11th symbol indicated the assembly plant: 5 = Bowling Green, Kentucky. The last six symbols indicated the sequential production numbers starting with 100001 at each factory.
ENGINE	**Type: V-8** Bore and stroke: 4.00 x 3.48 in. Displacement: 350 cid Brake hp: 205 at 4,200 rpm. Induction: CFI.
VITAL STATS	**Coupe:** Original Price: $21,800 Production: 51,547 Wheelbase: 96.2 in. Length: 176.5 in. Tires: P215/65-R15
COOL STUFF	*Motor Trend* described it as "the best-handling production car in the world, regardless of price." Heady praise indeed. *Car and Driver* called the new Corvette "the most advanced production car on the planet." The new Corvette body offered the lowest drag coefficient of any Corvette: just 0.341. Testing at GM's Proving Grounds revealed 0.95G lateral acceleration - the highest ever for a production car. Of the total production, 240 Corvettes were modified for use with leaded gasoline (for export).

integrated halogen fog lamps and front cornering lamps. The dual sport mirrors were electrically remote controlled. The unit body (with partial front frame) used a front-hinged "clam shell" hood with integral twin-duct air intake.

The sole 1984 V-8 was L-83 350-cid (5.7-liter) V-8 with Cross-fire injection. Stainless steel headers led into its exhaust system. The air cleaner and the valve train had cast magnesium covers. A four-speed automatic returned as the standard Corvette transmission. Although it was not offered until January 1984, a four-plus-three-speed manual transmission with computer-activate overdrive in every gear except first, was offered at no extra cost. It used an

hydraulic clutch. Overdrive was locked out during rigorous acceleration above specified speeds and when a console switch was activated.

Under the chassis was an aluminum drive shaft, forged-aluminum suspension arms and a fiberglass transverse leaf springs front and rear. Power rack-and-pinion steering and power four-wheel disc brakes were standard. Optional Goodyear 50-series "unidirectional" tires were designed for mounting on a specific wheel. Inside, an electronic instrument panel featured both analog and digital LCD readouts in either English or metric measure. A Driver Information System between the speedometer and tachometer gave a selection of switch-chosen readings. At the driver's left was the parking brake.

The 1984 Corvette's long standard equipment list included an advanced (and very necessary) theft-prevention system with starter-interrupt. Other standard equipment: air conditioning, power windows, electronic-tuning seek/scan AM/FM stereo radio with digital clock, reclining bucket seats, leather-wrapped tilt/telescope steering wheel, luggage security shade, and side window defoggers.

At least two sleek, modern Corvette show cars were built by the Bertone design studio of Italy. Called "Ramarros," they had doors that swung a little out and slid alongside the front fenders. Inside, a unique seat was used. It was slung like a saddle over the center console.

Racing at this time were Corvettes of a different nature than in the past. Labeled "Showroom Stock," they were as close to a street-driven production cars as imaginable. When chief engineer Dave McLellan rolled out the C4 (or fourth-generation) Corvette, it was all over for the racetrack competition. Things quickly reached the point where the question wasn't which car would win, but which Corvette would win. The Corvette won every SCCA Showroom Stock Series race until the fiberglass Chevy race cars were simply legislated out of the series after 1987.

1984 Corvette Status Guide	Basket Case		Average Driver		Rare, Unique or Completely Original	
Condition of CORVETTE:	Production Status					
	Average	Rare/Unique	N-O-M	O-M	Needs Work	Unrestored Low Mileage
Suggested Actions: Collect It						
Drive, Show and Enjoy						
Race, Autocross Competitively						
Store for a Future Project/Investment						
Candidate for Resto Rod						
Restore to Curb Appeal Condition						

THE EXOTIC AMERICAN.

The new Corvette is born.
And it will take you
places you've never been
before.

This all-American Corvette was not only exotic, it had brand new styling in 1984. *KP Archives*

1985 Corvette

A very elaborate 44-page sales booklet was used to tell the story of "America's own sports car" to potential Corvette buyers in 1985. Photos in the catalog depicted Corvettes in European settings from a piazza in Italy to a sports car race with a Volkswagen, Mercedes-Benz and Porsche in the back of the pack of six Corvettes.

"Europe has been, and remains, many peoples and places separated by discreet boundaries, languages and customs," said the catalog copy. "America is many things,

too, but underneath it is a unity born of individual freedom. Corvette was born to suit the experience that is America – and let Europe take what view it would. Literally, and figuratively, for 33 years, that view has been primarily of the taillights."

Two details marked the 1985 Corvette as being different from its newly restyled 1984 predecessor. At the rear, it was not the taillights, but the straight tail pipes The other detail was a new "Tuned Port Injection" plaque on the front fender molding. It meant

This beautiful 1985 Corvette may have been driven to the track, then entered in racing.   *Bob Harrington*

Red and black combined to offer a stunning looking interior on the 1985 Corvette. *Mike Mueller*

A dramatic way to portray a Corvette is to show the front from a dramatic low angle. *Mike Mueller*

MIKE YAGER SAYS:	
CHEERS	The 1985 Corvette offered tuned port injection. It was America's fastest car at 150 mph. New suspension tuning offered a better ride and there were improved brakes and rear axle options plus good exterior color choices and wheel options. The automatic transmission, suspension, wheels and interior trim parts all are easy to find.
JEERS	Weak points in 1985 include the rough shifts of the 700R automatic transmission. The 4 + 3 manual transmission also had problems. The fuel management system was a weakness. The car offered a rough ride with the Z-51 option. The car has low collectible value currently. Among the scarce goodies in the parts bin are good 4 + 3 transmissions, headlight motors, original glass tops without crazing and the original style Goodyear tires.
GAME PLAN	This is another year that is becoming extremely hard to find in pristine condition. Many of the '85 Corvettes were modified and customized. Many were daily drivers. The car does offer great value as a driver.

The 1985 Corvette instrument panel was very modern looking and included digital read-out gauges. *Phil Hall Collection*

1985 'VETTE FACTS	
VEHICLE IDENTIFICATION NUMBER	Corvette coupes for 1985 were numbered 1G1YY0787F5100001 to 1G1YY0787F5139729. The first symbol 1 indicated U.S. built. The second symbol G indicated a General Motors product. The third symbol 1 indicated a Chevrolet Motor Division vehicle. The fourth symbol Y indicated the type of restraint system. The fifth symbol Y indicated the car line or series: Y = Chevrolet Corvette. The sixth and seventh symbols indicated the body style number 07 = two-door hatchback coupe. The eighth symbol indicated the engine: 8 = 5.7-liter Tuned Port Injection (TPI) Chevrolet V-8. The ninth symbol was a check digit that varied. The 10th symbol indicated the model year F = 1985. The 11th symbol indicated the assembly plant: 5 = Bowling Green, Kentucky. The last six symbols indicated the sequential production number starting with 100001 at each factory.
ENGINE	**Type: V-8** Bore and stroke: 4.00 x 3.48 in. Displacement: 350 cid Brake hp: 230 at 4,000 rpm. Induction: TPI
VITAL STATS	**Coupe:** Original Price: $24,873 Production: 39,729 Wheelbase: 96.2 in. Length: 176.5 in. Tires: P255/50-VR16 SBR
COOL STUFF	Chevrolet claimed a 17 percent reduction in 0 to 60 mph times with the TPI power plant. To save weight, Corvettes used not only the fiberglass leaf springs front and rear, but over 400 pounds of aluminum parts (including steering, suspension components and frame members). Only 16 Corvettes are listed as having a CB radio, and only 82 were sold with an economy rear axle ratio. A total of 14,802 Corvettes had the Z-51 performance handling package installed. It added $470 to the car's price.

there was a new 5.7-liter (350-cid) V-8 under the hood. This engine had tuned-port-fuel-injection (TPI) and 230 hp. In addition to adding power, it increased the 'Vette's fuel economy ratings. Experts might also have noticed higher-intensity Bright Red and Silver Metallic exterior body colors.

The Corvette's smoothly-sloped nose was adorned by nothing other than a circular emblem and held retracting halogen headlights. Wide parking and signal lamps nearly filled the space between license plate and outer body edge. Wide horizontal side marker lenses were just ahead of the front wheels.

Below the hood the large 1984 air cleaner was replaced by an elongated plenum chamber with eight curved aluminum runners. Mounted ahead of the radiator, it ducted incoming air into the plenum through a Bosch hot-wire mass-airflow sensor. Those tuned runners were meant to boost power at low to medium rpms, following a principle similar to that used for the tall intake stacks in racing engines. Electronic Spark Control (ESC) sensed knocking and adjusted timing to fit fuel octane.

Under the chassis, the 1985 carried a reworked suspension that softened the ride without reducing control. An optional Z-51 handling package now included 9.5-inch wheels all around, along with Delco-Bilstein gas-charged shock absorbers and a heavy-duty cooling system. The stabilizer bars in the Z-51 package were thicker and spring rates on both suspensions were reduced. The cast-aluminum wheels held P255/50-VR16 Eagle GT tires.

There were many technical improvements. The brake master cylinder used a new large-capacity plastic booster. Manual gearboxes drove rear axles with 8.5-inch ring gears. The Corvette's instrument-cluster graphics had a bolder look and its roof panels added more solar screening. An optional leather-trimmed sport seat arrived at midyear.

Corvette standard equipment included an electronic information center, air conditioning, limited-slip differential, power four-wheel disc brakes, power steering, cornering lamps and a seek-and-scan AM/FM stereo radio with four speakers and automatic power antenna. Also standard were a cigarette lighter, a digital clock, a tachometer, intermittent windshield wipers, halogen fog lamps and side window defoggers. Corvettes had contour high-back cloth bucket seats, power windows, a trip odometer, a theft-deterrent system with starter interrupt, a compact spare tire, dual electric remote-control sport mirrors and tinted glass. The bodies were protected by black belt line moldings, windshield and body side moldings, plus color-keyed rocker panel moldings. A four-speed overdrive automatic transmission was standard, with a four-speed manual (with overdrive in three gears) available at no extra cost.

1985 Corvette Status Guide	Basket Case		Average Driver		Rare, Unique or Completely Original	
Condition of CORVETTE:	Production Status					
	Average	Rare/ Unique	N-O-M	O-M	Needs Work	Unrestored Low Mileage
Suggested Actions: Collect It						
Drive, Show and Enjoy						
Race, Autocross Competitively						
Store for a Future Project/Investment						
Candidate for Resto Rod						
Restore to Curb Appeal Condition						

1986 Corvette

One new body style and an important engineering development were the Corvette highlights of 1986. A new convertible was added during the model year. It was the first Corvette ragtop since 1975.

A computerized anti-lock braking system (ABS) was made standard equipment. This system was based on a Bosch ABS II design. During hard braking, the system detected any wheel that was about to lock up, then altered braking pressure, in a pulsating action, to prevent lock up from happening. Drivers could feel the pulses in the pedal. This safety innovation helped the driver to maintain traction and keep the car under directional control without skidding, even on slick and slippery surfaces.

The engine used in the Corvette was the same 5.7-liter 230-hp tuned-port-injected V-8 as 1985, but it now featured centrally-positioned copper-core spark plugs. New aluminum cylinder heads had sintered

The 1986 Corvette convertible drew attention as the Indy Pace Car. *Tom Glatch*

MIKE YAGER SAYS:	
CHEERS	Both the coupe and convertible were offered in 1986 models. All 1986 Corvette convertibles were Indy Pace Cars. There was an improved fuel management system, a third brake light, new ABS brakes, tuned suspension, a VATS security system and adjustable spring ratios. Aluminum cylinder heads had limited availability. Glass tops now came in various colors. Parts that are easy to find include the interior trim, suspension components, engines and automatic transmission.
JEERS	The automatic transmission performance was weak and the 4 + 3 transmission still had problems with its shifter in performance applications. Plastic interior trim was annoying and the ABS brakes caused problems. Scarce in the parts bin are original body decal kits, the original, correct tires, a factory exhaust system, anti-lock brake system pieces and the dashboard.
GAME PLAN	In addition to finding that 1986 Corvette in as original and untouched version as you can, watch for a convertible Indy 500 Pace Car that has original decals.

Another way the 1986 Indy Pace Car convertible was highlighted was badging. *Tom Glatch*

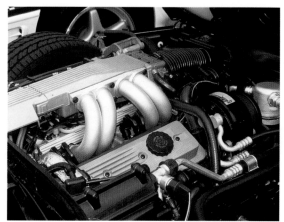

The engine used in this Indy Pace Car Corvette was the L-98 350-cid V-8. *Tom Glatch*

This '86 Corvette interior wasn't Spartan inside. *Tom Glatch*

1986 'VETTE FACTS

VEHICLE IDENTIFICATION NUMBER	Corvette coupes for 1986 were numbered 1G1YY0789G5100001 to 1G1YY0789G5127794. The 1986 Corvette convertibles were numbered 1G1YY6789G5900001 to 1G1YY6789G5907315. The first symbol 1 indicated U.S. built. The second symbol G indicated a General Motors product. The third symbol 1 indicated a Chevrolet Motor Division vehicle. The fourth and fifth symbols indicated the car line and series: YY = Corvette. The sixth and seventh symbols indicated the body style number 07 = two-door hatchback coupe and 67 = convertible. The eighth symbol indicated the engine: 8 = 5.7-liter Tuned-Port-Injection (TPI) Chevrolet V-8. The ninth symbol was a check digit that varied. The 10th symbol indicated the model year G = 1986. The 11th symbol indicated the assembly plant: 5 = Bowling Green, Kentucky. The last six symbols indicated the sequential production numbers starting with 100001 at each factory for coupes; 900001 for convertibles.
ENGINE	**Type: V-8** Bore and stroke: 4.00 x 3.48 in. Displacement: 350 cid Brake hp: 230 at 4,000 rpm. Induction: TPI
VITAL STATS	**Coupe:** Original Price: $27,027 Production: 27,794 Wheelbase: 96.2 in. Length: 176.5 in. Tires: P245/50-VR16 or P255/50-VR16 SBR **Convertible:** Original Price: $32,032 Production: 7,315 Wheelbase: 96.2 in. Length: 176.5 in. Tires: P245/50-VR16 or P255/50-VR16 SBR
COOL STUFF	Problems with cracking of the new aluminum cylinder heads meant the first 1986 models had old cast-iron heads. The difficulties were soon remedied. It was estimated that the new anti-theft system would require half an hour's work to overcome, which would dissuade thieves who are typically in a hurry. Only 6,835 Corvettes carried the MM4 four-speed manual transmission.

metal valve seats and increased intake port flow, plus higher (9.5:1) compression. The engine had an aluminum intake manifold with tuned runners, magnesium rocker covers and an outside-air induction system.

Both four-plus-three manual and four-speed overdrive automatic transmissions were available, now with an up shift indicator light on the instrument cluster. Three monolith catalytic converters in a new dual-exhaust system kept emissions down during warm up. Cast alloy wheels gained a new raised hub emblem and a brushed-aluminum look.

Inside the car, the instrument cluster was tilted to cut glare. Electronic air conditioning, announced earlier, arrived as a late option. Otherwise, standard equipment was similar to 1985. A new electronic Vehicle Anti-Theft System (VATS) was also made standard. A small electrically-coded pellet was embedded in the ignition key, while a decoder was hidden in the car. When the key was placed in the ignition, its resistance code was "read." Unless that code was compatible, the starter relay wouldn't close and the Electronic Control Module wouldn't activate the fuel injectors.

At the rear of the Corvette were four round, recessed taillight lenses with "Corvette" spelled out between them in block letters. The license plate sat in a recessed housing. Cloth seats had lateral support and back-angle adjustments. Size 16 x 8-1/2 in. cast-alloy aluminum wheels held unidirectional P255/50-VR16 Goodyear Eagle GT SBR tires.

Styled like the Corvette "roadster" that would serve as the 1986 Indy Pace Car, the new open model – technically a roll-up-window convertible – went on sale late in the model year. Instead of being a conversion done by an outside company (like most 1980s ragtops) the Corvette open model was built by Chevrolet alongside the coupes. It had a manual top with a velour inner liner. The yellow console button opened a fiberglass panel behind the seats to reveal the fabric top's storage area.

The actual Indy Pace Car was Yellow. It differed from showroom models only in the addition of special strobe lights for track use. Chevrolet considered "Indy Pace Car" to be synonymous with "open top," so all 1986 convertibles were considered to be Indy Pace Car models. Special decals were packed in the car, but not installed at the factory. The Corvette was the only street-legal vehicle to pace the Indy race since the 1978 Corvette Indy Pace Car.

1986 Corvette Status Guide	Basket Case		Average Driver		Rare, Unique or Completely Original	
Condition of CORVETTE:	Production Status					
	Average	Rare/ Unique	N-O-M	O-M	Needs Work	Unrestored Low Mileage
Suggested Actions: Collect It						
Drive, Show and Enjoy						
Race, Autocross Competitively						
Store for a Future Project/Investment						
Candidate for Resto Rod						
Restore to Curb Appeal Condition						

Early development
work on what would
ultimately become the
ZR1 was well underway
in 1986. *Tom Glatch*

This experimental Corvette was saved from the crusher at the Lotus Ltd. plant in England. *Tom Glatch*

1987 Corvette

The pride of Bowling Green, Kentucky – the Chevrolet Corvette – wasn't a new car for 1987, but it was a better one with some of its rough edges honed a bit.

The already-world-class suspension system was augmented by an optional new Z-52 Sport Handling package that was available on even the standard suspension.

1987 Corvette, refined open air excitement.

CORVETTE

 THE HEARTBEAT OF AMERICA. TODAY'S CHEVROLET.

It was the era of the "Heartbeat of America" as displayed in 1987 Corvette literature. *KP Archives*

MIKE YAGER SAYS:	
CHEERS	In 1987, performance improvements were on the rise and they included the RPO Z52 sport handling package, The Callaway Corvette was available as a performance alternative. Climate control HVAC and heated mirrors were both introduced. Easy pickings are found with interior and exterior trim, suspension parts and emblems. This was a fine riding car and showed that Corvette still was a world-class sports car.
JEERS	The 4 + 3 transmission was still offered. The same car as previous years still had the same old interior and wheels. Challenging parts to come by include wheels, the sport seats, controls and internal parts, the Delco-Bose stereo components, console parts and an original exhaust system.
GAME PLAN	An original as possible and untouched example is preferable. The 1987 was a much better car to drive—a real highway cruiser. The roadster is perfect for a country picnic outing. Watch out for modified bodies,and the extensive use of ground effects kits and other modifications.

The content included Bilstein shock absorbers, a 13.0:1 ratio steering gear, 9.5-inch wide wheels and a 3.07:1 ring and pinion gear.

Under the hood, the spark plugs were repositioned so that they fired better. The addition of roller hydraulic lifters to the Corvette's 350-cid (5.7-liter) V-8 reduced internal friction and made the motor smoother and quieter. Horsepower also got a boost to 240 at 4,000 rpm thanks to the new friction-cutting roller-type valve lifters. The 1987 Corvette also had a higher fuel-economy rating: 16 mpg for city driving.

Joining the option list was an electronic tire-pressure monitor that signaled a dashboard light to warn of low pressure in any tire. Two four-speed transmissions were available: manual or automatic.

Standard equipment included power steering, power four-wheel disc brakes (with anti-locking), air conditioning, a theft-deterrent system, tinted glass, twin remote-control mirrors, power windows, intermittent wipers, tilt/telescope steering column and an AM/FM seek/scan radio. Both the centers and slots of the wheels (unpainted in 1986) were now finished in argent gray. A new piece of optional equipment was a 6-way power seat for Corvette passengers.

Chevrolet added a new option code in 1987, but this one – B2K – was far different than a power passenger seat or a more exotic sound system. B2K identified performance modifications carried out by Reeves Callaway's company in Old Lyme, Connecticut. Callaway Engineering was formed in the same mold as a European sports car tuning shop such as Morris

1987 'VETTE FACTS	
VEHICLE IDENTIFICATION NUMBER	Corvettes for 1987 were numbered 1G1YY|2/3|182H5100001 to 1G1YY|2/3|182H5130632. (On coupes the sixth symbol was a 2, on convertibles the sixth symbol was a 3). The first symbol 1 indicated U.S. built. The second symbol G indicated a General Motors product. The third symbol 1 indicated a Chevrolet Motor Division vehicle. The fourth and fifth symbols indicated the body type and series: YY = Corvette. The sixth symbol indicated the body style: 2 = Two-door hatchback, GM styles 07, 08, 77, 87and 3 = Two-door convertible, GM style 67. The seventh symbol indicated the restraint code: 1 = Manual belts and 2 = Automatic belts. The eighth symbol indicated the engine: 8 = 5.7-liter Tuned-Port-Injection (TPI) Chevrolet/GM of Canada V-8. The ninth symbol was a check digit that varied. The 10th symbol indicated the model year H = 1987. The 11th symbol indicated the assembly plant: 5 = Bowling Green, Kentucky. The last six symbols indicated the sequential production numbers starting with 100001 at each factory for coupes and convertibles.
ENGINE	**Type: V-8** Bore and stroke: 4.00 x 3.48 in. Displacement: 350 cid Brake hp: 240 at 4,000 rpm. Induction: TPI
VITAL STATS	**Coupe:** Original Price: $27,999 Production: 20,007 Wheelbase: 96.2 in. Length: 176.5 in. Tires: P245/60-VR16 Goodyear Eagle GT **Convertible:** Original Price: $33,172 Production: 10,625 Wheelbase: 96.2 in. Length: 176.5 in. Tires: P245/60-VR16 Goodyear Eagle GT
COOL STUFF	A $19,995 Callaway Twin-Turbo engine package could be ordered through specific Chevrolet dealers as RPO B2K. Cars that received the Twin-Turbo package were sent from Bowling Green to the Callaway factory in Old Lyme, Connecticut, to receive engine modifications and other upgrades. A total of 184 Callaway Twin-Turbos were built (21 coupes and 63 convertibles.) The 1987 Callaways had 345 hp and 465 lbs.-ft. of torque. All had manual transmissions and were not certified for sale in the state of California. For 1987 Callaway Twin-Turbo Corvettes a different engine-coding system was used. Callaway engines were stamped with the first two symbols indicating model year, followed by three symbols indicating order in the Callaway production sequence, followed by four symbols matching the last four digits of the Chevrolet VIN.

Garages (MG) or Carroll Shelby's "Good Old (American) Boy" Cobra operation. Buyers ordered the car from a Chevrolet dealer and it was then shipped to Callaway for some very special upgrades.

The '87 Callaway model had improvements that boosted horsepower to 435 and generated 465 lbs.-ft. of torque. The Callaway modified/tuned Corvette was good for a top speed of 177.9 mph. At this point, body panel changes were very minor and modest and most of the Callaway "tweaks" occurred under the hood.

After the C4 Corvette was introduced in 1984, Corvettes began to totally dominate SCCA Showroom Stock competition. They took nearly every checkered flag (19 wins in a row) and four consecutive national titles. They seemed to get better each time they raced. In the corners, the Corvettes were approaching the same G-force levels as Formula 1 racing cars.

After the 1987, season, the other SCCA competitors like Porsche threatened to withdraw from Showroom Stock racing if the Corvettes were allowed to keep winning. Corvette fans were upset when it happened, but the SCCA gave into the pressure and banned Corvettes from the popular series. This turned out to be a blessing in disguise, since it led to the creation of the Corvette Challenge racing series of 1988 and 1989.

1987 Corvette Status Guide	Basket Case		Average Driver		Rare, Unique or Completely Original	
Condition of CORVETTE:	Production Status					
Suggested Actions:	Average	Rare/Unique	N–O–M	O–M	Needs Work	Unrestored Low Mileage
Collect It		■			■	■
Drive, Show and Enjoy			■	■	■	■
Race, Autocross Competitively	■			■		
Store for a Future Project/Investment			■	■	■	■
Candidate for Resto Rod	■		■			
Restore to Curb Appeal Condition	■		■	■		

1988 Corvette

By 1988, approximately 900,000 Corvettes had been produced in the 35 years since America's sports car had been introduced in 1953. "It is not surprising that the critics have called Corvette one of the world's best sports cars," said the year's classy-looking, 30-page sales booklet. "Nor would it be surprising, once you have experienced the '88 edition, for you to agree with them."

Little changed in the Corvette's basic appearance this year, except for a change to styled six-slot wheels. The optional 17-inch wheels looked similar to the standard 16-inch wheels, but held massive P275/40-ZR17 Goodyear Eagle GT tires. Suspension modifications were intended to improve control during hard braking, while brake components were toughened, including the use of thicker rotors.

A rare 1988 Corvette was the Z-51 optioned GTO model that incorporated a special ground effects package and a unique rear deck lid spoiler. This package was merchandised as a Special Production Option (SPO) rather than a Regular Production Option (RPO). It had to be specially ordered and very few buyers went through the trouble of doing so.

Under the hood, the standard 350-cid (5.7-liter) V-8 could breathe more easily with a pair of modified aluminum cylinder heads. Performance also got a boost via a new camshaft, though horsepower only rose by five units. As in 1987, two body styles – a convertible and a hatchback coupe – were offered.

The Chevy design studio was busy cranking out concept car versions of the Corvette for

In 1988, Corvette marked a milestone with its 35th anniversary cars. *Mike Mueller*

MIKE YAGER SAYS:	
CHEERS	The 35th anniversary edition was very special. The Zero Scrub Suspension made for a new car. The Callaway option was available and 50 cars were converted to Challenge Racing Corvettes. Dual power seats and the Z-52 top option were available and new aluminum 17-inch wheels also were offered. Easy parts to find include the 17-inch wheels, suspension parts, engines and automatic transmissions and the interior and exterior trim.
JEERS	The interior was unchanged and the 4 + 3 still was offered. Difficult parts to come by include 16-inch wheels in good condition, the 4 + 3 transmission, original equipment glass tops, sport seat controls, internal parts, electronic air conditioning controls and Delco-Bose components.
GAME PLAN	Look for some fine collectibles in this series including a 35th Anniversary Corvette, a Challenge Car or a Callaway. Those are the top acquisitions. I have several 1988 Corvettes and they are great cars to own! Enjoy!

A shot of the stunning white and black 35th anniversary 1988 Corvette interior. *Mike Mueller*

Here's the engine used for the 35th anniversary edition revealed by a lift-up nose section. *Mike Mueller*

1988 'VETTE FACTS	
VEHICLE IDENTIFICATION NUMBER	Corvettes for 1988 were numbered 1G1YY[2/3]182J5100001 to 1G1YY[2/3]182J5122789. (On coupes the sixth symbol was a 2, on convertibles the sixth symbol was a 3). The first symbol 1 indicated U.S. built. The second symbol G indicated a General Motors product. The third symbol 1 indicated a Chevrolet Motor Division vehicle. The fourth and fifth symbols indicated body type and series: YY = Corvette. The sixth symbol indicated the body style: 2 = Two-door hatchback, GM styles 07, 08, 77, 87and 3 = Two-door convertible, GM style 67. The seventh symbol indicated the restraint code: 1 = Manual belts and 2 = Automatic belts. The eighth symbol indicated the engine: 8 = 5.7-liter Tuned-Port-Injection (TPI) Chevrolet/GM of Canada V-8. The ninth symbol was a check digit that varied. The 10th symbol indicated the model year H = 1987. The 11th symbol indicated the assembly plant: 5 = Bowling Green, Kentucky. The last six symbols indicated the sequential production numbers starting with 100001 at each factory for coupes and convertibles.
ENGINE	**Type: V-8** Bore and stroke: 4.00 x 3.48 in. Displacement: 350 cid Brake hp: 240/245 at 4,000 rpm.* Induction: TPI *Engine rating is 245-hp for hatchbacks using 3.07:1 rear axle due to use of low-restriction mufflers with this option combination only.
VITAL STATS	**Coupe:** Original Price: $29,480 Production: 15,382 Wheelbase: 96.2 in. Length: 176.5 in. Tires: P255/50-ZR16 Goodyear Eagle GT **Convertible:** Original Price: $34,820 Production: 7,407 Wheelbase: 96.2 in. Length: 176.5 in. Tires: P255/50-ZR16 Goodyear Eagle GT
COOL STUFF	The above production figures include a total of 2,050 special 35th Anniversary Edition Corvette hatchback coupes, each with a specific build sequence number and special badging. The 35th Anniversary Edition option listed for $4,795. The 35th Anniversary Edition Corvettes featured a custom two-tone paint scheme consisting of a white body color, painted white wheels and black roof bow with transparent black roof panels. The white scheme was carried out through the interior trim, which included 35th Anniversary badges embroidered on the seat backs. A $25,895 Callaway Twin-Turbo engine package could be ordered through specific Chevrolet dealers as RPO B2K. Cars that received this package were sent from Bowling Green to the Callaway factory in Old Lyme, Connecticut to receive engine modifications and other upgrades. The 1988 Callaways had 382 hp and 562 lbs.-ft. of torque. Callaway modified a Chevrolet truck-type Turbo Hydra-Matic transmission as a $6,500 option for Callaways. A total of 125 were built.

1988. The Corvette Indy was one of these. In the mid-1980s, GM vice president of design Chuck Jordan commissioned Cecomp of Italy to build a full-size clay model of a futuristic-looking mid-engined show car with a prototype 225-cid Indy Car type racing engine. In 1988, a functional version of the Corvette Indy was showcased, but it had a 380-hp LT-5 engine that was an early version of the special ZR-1 V-8. This car caused quite a stir on the show circuit.

GM Corporate Engineering actually produced the third car in the series of CERV (Chevrolet Engineering Research Vehicle) experimental cars that started way back in 1959. The concept behind the CERV III of 1988 was to take the Corvette Indy design and make it roadworthy. CERV III also used a version of the ZR-1's LT-5 V-8 rated at 650 hp. This concept car actually inspired the roof styling used on the fifth-generation or C5 Corvette.

The 1988 Geneve was a smoothened-up Corvette convertible with a built-in front spoiler, flush round taillights, an integral rear spoiler and revised body side vents. It was the work of American Sunroof Corp., of Southgate, Michigan, a company that hoped to sell GM on making it so ASC could supply the needed customizing components.

Undaunted by being outlawed from showroom stock racing the year earlier, Chevrolet launched its own race series in 1988. It was called the Sports Car Club of America's (SCCA) Corvette Challenge racing series The Corvette Challenge (also run in 1989) was open to C4 Corvettes with some of the world's best drivers aboard. They competed for million-dollar purses and produced some of the most thrilling showroom stock racing ever.

For 1988, Chevrolet built 56 Corvette Challenge race cars. These "street-legal" track cars all had stock engines specially built at the Flint, Michigan Engine plant. They were matched for power and sealed to insure that all of the cars were as identical as possible in a technical sense. Protofab, an aftermarket race car builder in Wixom, Michigan, installed all of the race-car modifications and roll bars.

1988 Corvette Status Guide	Basket Case		Average Driver		Rare, Unique or Completely Original	
Condition of CORVETTE:	Production Status					
	Average	Rare/ Unique	N-O-M	O-M	Needs Work	Unrestored Low Mileage
Suggested Actions: Collect It						
Drive, Show and Enjoy						
Race, Autocross Competitively						
Store for a Future Project/Investment						
Candidate for Resto Rod						
Restore to Curb Appeal Condition						

1988 CORVETTE

The year 1988 marked the 35th anniversary of the Corvette (in calendar years that is, since there was no 1983 model) and this milestone was celebrated by the release of a Special Edition package for coupes only. This RPO Z01 35th Anniversary Special Edition package retailed for $4,795. It included the following content: A two-tone white exterior with a black roof, white leather seats, a white leather steering wheel, special exterior and interior accents, a console-mounted anniversary plaque, special emblems and white-finished wheels.

Author Mike Yager includes a very rare example of this package in his "My Garage" Corvette Museum in Effingham, Illinois. Mike's car is one of only two Callaway Twin-Turbo Corvettes known to have been ordered with the 35th Anniversary package. This car had a $61,495 window sticker when it was new in 1988. In reality, the car is still "new" today, as it shows just 346 original miles. Wow!

This stunning 1988 Callaway Twin-Turbo 35th Anniversary Corvette is owned by Mike Yager.

Mid America Motorworks

Mike's car is one of only two Callaway Twin-Turbo Corvettes known to have been ordered with the 35th Anniversary package. *Mid America Motorworks*

1989 Corvette

Most of the publicity efforts focused on the 1989 Corvette were centered on the eagerly-awaited ZR-1 "super" model, which Chevrolet Motor Division claimed would become the world's fastest production automobile once it arrived in the showroom. After several early announcements of the car proved to be premature, the ZR-1's introduction was delayed until the 1990 model year.

For model year 1989, the "ordinary" Corvette added a new ZF six-speed manual gearbox with two overdrive ratios. To meet increasingly tightening fuel-economy standards, the ingenious ZF transmission was designed to incorporate a computer that sent a signal to prevent shifts from first to second gear unless the gas pedal hit the floor. Instead, a blocking pin forced the shifter directly into fourth gear for improved fuel economy during light-throttle operation.

A new addition to the 1989 Corvette options list was a high-tech FX-3 Delco-Bilstein Selective Ride Control system with a switch to select the desired degree of shock-absorber damping for touring, sport or competition driving. Only hatchback coupes with a manual transmission and the Z-51 Performance Handling package could get the ride-control option.

For the first time since 1975, a removable fiberglass hardtop became available for

A dramatic looking white ZR-1 edition of the 1989 Corvette. *Mike Mueller*

Like all fast Corvettes, many viewers saw the 1989 version from the rear angle. *Mike Mueller*

This experimental Corvette ZR-2 prototype used a 454 V-8, a Chevrolet truck engine. *Tom Glatch*

MIKE YAGER SAYS:

CHEERS	There was a new ZF manual transmission in 1989. The FX-3 was an adjustable suspension. The hardtop returned to the Corvette lineup. The Callaway was still available and there were 60 Challenges Series Corvettes built. Exterior color choices were limited. There was a new low tire pressure system and restyled seats. Transmissions, engines, wheels, suspension parts plus interior and exterior trim all is easy to find.
JEERS	The same old interior was offered and there were no performance engine options. The stereos were not compatible with the aftermarket products offered. Scarce parts include original equipment glass top without crazing, Delco-Bose stereo components and dash/gauge sets.
GAME PLAN	The 1989 Corvette was the final flat-dash car. Snag a Challenge Series Corvette for your collection. With the racing heritage and the low production numbers, it's a winning combination!

This Corvette ZR-2 prototype could not pass stringent CAFE standards. *Tom Glatch*

This mighty 454-powered Corvette was called the ZR-2. *Tom Glatch*

1989 'VETTE FACTS	
VEHICLE IDENTIFICATION NUMBER	Corvettes for 1989 were numbered | 1G1YY[2/3]186K5100001 to 1G1YY[2/3]186K5126328. (On coupes the sixth symbol was a 2, on convertibles the sixth symbol was a 3). The first symbol 1 indicated U.S. built. The second symbol G indicated a General Motors product. The third symbol 1 indicated a Chevrolet Motor Division vehicle. The fourth and fifth symbols indicated the body type and series: YY = Corvette. (Note: Code YZ was planned for use on ZR-1s and appears on GM passenger-car VIN system cards.) The sixth symbol indicated the body style: 2 = Two-door hatchback or liftback, GM styles 07, 08, 77, 87 and 3 = Two-door convertible, GM style 67. The seventh symbol indicated the restraint code: 1 = Manual belts, 3 = Manual belts with driver-inflatable restraint system and 4 = Automatic belts. The eighth symbol indicated the engine: 8 = 5.7-liter Tuned-Port-Injection (TPI) Chevrolet/GM of Canada V-8. The ninth symbol was a check digit that varied. The 10th symbol indicated the model year K = 1989. The 11th symbol indicated the assembly plant: 5 = Bowling Green, Kentucky. The last six symbols indicated the sequential production numbers starting with 100001 at each factory for coupes and convertibles.
ENGINE	**Type: V-8** Bore and stroke: 4.00 x 3.48 in. Displacement: 350 cid Brake hp: 240/245 at 4,000 rpm.* Induction: TPI *Engine rating is 245-hp for hatchbacks using 3.07:1 rear axle due to use of low-restriction mufflers with this option combination only.
VITAL STATS	**Hatchback Coupe:** Original Price: $31,545 Production: 16,663 Wheelbase: 96.2 in. Length: 176.5 in. Tires: P275/40-VR17 Goodyear Eagle GT **Convertible:** Original Price: $36,785 Production: 9,749 Wheelbase: 96.2 in. Length: 176.5 in. Tires: P275/40-VR17 Goodyear Eagle GT
COOL STUFF	For 1989, Callaway Twin-Turbo Corvettes used a different engine-coding system. Callaway engines were stamped with the first two symbols indicating model year, followed by three symbols indicating order in the Callaway production sequence, followed by four symbols matching the last four digits of the Chevrolet VIN. A neat '89 Corvette collectible is Chevrolet sales folder No. 4843, July 1988, that includes write ups on the Camaro, Corsica, Celebrity, Caprice, Beretta and Cavalier. When opened up and flipped over, the folder becomes an 8-panel poster showing the profile of a white 1989 Corvette Hatchback. There is no copy describing the 'Vette – only the beautiful photo.

the convertible, but it did not arrive until late in the model year. Corvettes came in a choice of eight different exterior colors this year. Chevrolet also painted 35 cars in two non-standard colors. Eight were done in Yellow and 27 were done in Arctic Pearl. Interior trims came in five different choices. A removable body-color roof panel for hatchback coupes was standard equipment, along with cloth upholstery.

The $25,895 Callaway Twin-Turbo engine package could again be ordered through specific Chevrolet dealers as regular production option B2K. Cars that received this package were sent from Bowling Green, Kentucky, to the Callaway factory in Old Lyme, Connecticut, to receive engine modifications and other upgrades. The 1988

Callaways had 382 hp and 562 lbs.-ft. of torque.

Chevrolet built 60 Corvette Challenge cars with standard engines in 1989. Thirty of these were shipped to Powell Development of America to receive race-modified engines and other competition modifications for the 1989 Sports Car Club of America (SCCA) Corvette Challenge racing series. At the end of the year, many of these cars had their original factory-numbered engines re-installed.

In his book *Corvettes: The Cars That Created the Legend*, author Dennis Adler states, "Since 1989, only a few Challenge Cars have changed hands, with each successive transaction raising the ownership stakes" Adler pointed out that the late Chip Miller, of Carlisle Productions, owned the No. 7 car which retained its L-98 competition engine. Miller owned five of the cars including the '89 backup car that was never raced. Chip and I also enjoyed joint ownership in a sixth Corvette Challenge Car. My company, Mid America Motorworks (then known as Mid America Designs) was also a primary sponsor of the 1988-1989 Corvette Challenge race Series.

Chevrolet also built 84 ZR-1 type 1989 Corvettes for testing, plus a ZR-2 but then said on April 19 that the ZR-1's introduction would be delayed until 1990.

1989 Corvette Status Guide	Basket Case		Average Driver		Rare, Unique or Completely Original	
Condition of CORVETTE:	Production Status					
	Average	Rare/ Unique	N-O-M	O-M	Needs Work	Unrestored Low Mileage
Suggested Actions: Collect It						
Drive, Show and Enjoy						
Race, Autocross Competitively						
Store for a Future Project/Investment						
Candidate for Resto Rod						
Restore to Curb Appeal Condition						

1990 Corvette

"Corvette for 1990 is the exotic American with world-class technology, incomparable style and V-8 performance that has humbled some of Europe's finest," said the 1990 Chevrolet sales folder. "The 1990 Corvette is available as a coupe, a convertible or the ultimate – the limited production ZR-1, which features an ultra-high-performance 32-valve quad-cam V-8."

That's right! Finally, after months of hoopla and a few false starts, the super-performance ZR-1 Corvette arrived in Chevrolet dealerships. Intended for production in small numbers, with a price tag higher than any General Motors product, the ZR-1 became a collectible long before anyone ever saw one "in the flesh."

ZR-1 customers seemed eager to pay far above the suggested retail price for the few

Corvette's new instrument panel combines advanced ergonomics with futuristic style.

The 1990 Corvette convertible was one of three models available that year. *KP Archives*

A 1990 Corvette ZR-1 in racing action. *Bob Harrington*

examples that became available at first. Who could blame them? Under the ZR-1's hood was a Lotus-designed 32-valve, dual-overhead-cam, 5.7-liter V-8 built by Mercury Marine in Oklahoma. Although the engine's displacement was identical to that of the standard Corvette V-8, this was an all-new power plant with different bore-and-stroke dimensions.

Wider at the rear than a standard model, partly to contain huge 315/35-ZR17 rear tires, the ZR-1 was easy to spot because of its convex rear end and rectangular taillights. Regular Corvette coupes and convertibles continued to display a concave rear end with round taillights. Standard ZR-1 equipment included an FX-3 Selective Ride adjustable suspension (which was also available on standard Corvettes with the six-speed manual gearbox).

In regular Corvettes, a four-speed overdrive automatic transmission was available at no cost. Added to the standard equipment list was an engine oil cooler, 17-inch alloy wheels and improved ABS II-S anti-lock brakes. The Corvette convertible added a new backlight made of flexible "Ultrashield" for improved scratch resistance and visibility. An air bag was installed in the new steering wheel on all Corvettes and a revised dashboard mixed digital and analog instruments.

Corvettes came in a choice of 10 colors with five interior color options available. Also standard was a removable body-color roof panel for hatchbacks or a convertible top (which came in a choice of colors, depending on body color). Also standard was cloth upholstery. "Whichever configuration you choose, however equipped, you will enjoy a world-class performance car with a uniquely American personality," said the Chevrolet copywriters.

At least two "dreamy" versions of the

Corvette Coupe.

Corvette Convertible.

Corvette ZR-1

The limited production ZR-1 joined the coupe and convertible as 1990 models. *KP Archives*

Corvette were publicized this year. Both cars were produced by aftermarket firms, one in Italy and one nearer Chevrolet headquarters in Michigan. The Nivola was a Bertone-designed mid-engine Corvette roadster featuring a removable hardtop. A foam model preceded construction of a running metal prototype. The Nivola had a

MIKE YAGER SAYS:	
CHEERS	In 1990, Corvette offered a new aircraft-style cockpit. Other interior changes abounded. The new dash and the return of the glove box! Several special interest cars appeared in 1990 including the "King of the Hill" ZR-1, 23 Limited R9-G World Challenge cars and Indy Festival Track Corvettes in Turquoise and Yellow. The LT-5 Lotus developmental engine debuted. There were new aluminum wheels and it was the first year the air bag appeared on the Corvette's steering wheel. Plentiful choices in the parts bin include wheels, transmissions, suspension pieces plus interior and exterior trim.
JEERS	Narrow seating continued to be a problem with Corvettes. Parts as scarce as hen's teeth include sport seat parts, ABS brake parts, body belt-line trim and air conditioning controls.
GAME PLAN	Start, as always, with as original and untouched a Corvette as you can find. An Indy Festival Corvette would be something grand to own. Chevrolet built approximately 80 special edition Indianapolis Festival Corvettes to complement the Beretta Indy 500 Pace Cars in 1990. Fifty of the Corvettes in turquoise were used by the Festival committee while 30 were yellow and used by the race track officials. But a lack of a back seat meant the cars weren't used—Camaro Z-24s were substituted. The 80 Corvettes were sold by dealers as used cars. The 1990 Corvette is a stunning blend of raw performance and luxury, a fitting introduction for the "King of the Hill." There were 23 R9G World Challenge Corvettes made.

Five interior color options were available to match 10 exterior colors on the 1990 Corvettes. *KP Archives*

1990 'VETTE FACTS

VEHICLE IDENTIFICATION NUMBER	Base Corvettes for 1990 were numbered 1G1YY|2/3|380L5100001 to 1G1YY|2/3|380L5120597. ZR-1 Corvettes for 1990 were numbered 1G1YZ2|3|6L5800001 to 1G1YZ23|6L5803049. (On base coupes the sixth symbol was a 2, on base convertibles the sixth symbol was a 3). The first symbol 1 indicated U.S. built. The second symbol G indicated a General Motors product. The third symbol 1 indicated a Chevrolet Motor Division vehicle. The fourth and fifth symbols were YY (Base Corvette) or YZ (Corvette ZR-1). The sixth symbol indicated the body style: 2 = two-door hatchback or liftback GM styles, 07, 08, 77, 87 and 3 = two-door convertible, GM style 67. The seventh symbol indicated the restraint code: 1 = Manual belts, 3 = Manual belts with driver-inflatable restraint system and 4 = Automatic belts. The eighth symbol indicated the engine: 8 = RPO L98 5.7-liter Tuned-Port-Injection (TPI) Chevrolet/GM of Canada V-8 and J = RPO LT5 5.7-liter TPI V-8. The ninth symbol was a check digit that varied. The 10th symbol indicated the model year L = 1990. The 11th symbol indicated the assembly plant: 5 = Bowling Green, Kentucky. The last six symbols indicated the sequential production numbers starting with 100001 at each factory for base coupes and convertibles and 800001 for ZR-1s.
ENGINE	**Base TPI V-8 (L-98):** Type: V-8 Bore and stroke: 4.00 x 3.48 in. Displacement: 350 cid Brake hp: 240/245 at 4,000 rpm.* Induction: TPI *Engine rating is 245-hp for hatchbacks using 3.07:1 rear axle due to use of low-restriction mufflers with this option combination only. **ZR-1 V-8 (LT-5):** Type: V-8 Bore and stroke: 3.90 x 3.66 in. Displacement: 350 cid Brake hp: 375 at 5,800 rpm. Induction: TPI
VITAL STATS	**Hatchback Coupe:** Original Price: $31,979 Production: 16,016 Wheelbase: 96.2 in. Length: 176.5 in. Tires: P275/40-ZR17 Goodyear Eagle GT **Convertible:** Original Price: $37,264 Production: 7,630 Wheelbase: 96.2 in. Length: 176.5 in. Tires: P275/40-ZR17 Goodyear Eagle GT **ZR-1:*** Original Price: $58,995 Production: 3,049 Wheelbase: 96.2 in. Length: 176.5 in. Tires: (Front) P275/40-ZR17 Goodyear Eagle GT (Rear) P315/35-ZR17 Goodyear Eagle GT *ZR-1 option quantity included in hatchback coupe production of 16,016.
COOL STUFF	The $26,895 Callaway Twin-Turbo engine package could again be ordered through specific Chevrolet dealers as RPO B2K. For a limited time an RPO R9G option was offered through Chevrolet dealers for competition-minded Corvette buyers who wanted to participate in the new World Challenge racing series. Only 23 cars were built. In 1990, Corvette chief engineer Dave McLellan was the annual recipient of the Society of Automotive Engineers' Edward N. Cole Award for automotive engineering innovation. McLellan was specifically recognized for his work on the ZR-1 package. The new ZR-1 super-high-performance option gave Corvette's so-equipped a new nickname – "King of the Hill."

hydra-pneumatic suspension that adjusted to different loads. The hardtop roof could be stored above the engine compartment. The cars doors were a foot thick and had built-in storage bins.

The 1990 ASC ZR-1 Spyder was a creation of Dick Chrysler's American Sunroof Corp. (ASC), which did sun roof installations and convertible conversions, Hoping to get more work from GM on the Corvette ZR-1, ASC crafted this beautiful ragtop. It had a racing-type windscreen, unique body side vents and a Porsche-Speedster-style roof. This job led to ASC getting a contract for the manufacture of a hardtop for the Corvette convertible.

On March 2, 1990, ZR-1 fired a shot heard round the world. Long-time endurance racer Tommy Morrison took a bone-stock ZR-1, and a small group of Corvette-experienced drivers (including three Corvette engineers), to Firestone's test track in Fort Stockton, Texas.

Mid America Motorworks, then Mid America Designs, supplied the special wide Dymag wheels for those world record runs. Steve Wiedman of Mid America personally shipped them to Tommy Morrison.

There, the ZR-1 proceeded to shatter three world records, one of which had been on the books for almost 50 years. Morrison's ZR-1 set new speed and endurance records for 24-hours, 5,000 miles and 5,000 kilometers. A stunning achievement for what was then a brand-new car, and another notch in Corvette's motorsports belt.

1990 Corvette Status Guide	Basket Case		Average Driver		Rare, Unique or Completely Original	
Condition of CORVETTE:	Production Status					
	Average	Rare/ Unique	N-O-M	O-M	Needs Work	Unrestored Low Mileage
Suggested Actions: Collect It		▓				▓
Drive, Show and Enjoy			▓	▓		▓
Race, Autocross Competitively	▓		▓			
Store for a Future Project/Investment		▓			▓	
Candidate for Resto Rod	▓		▓			
Restore to Curb Appeal Condition	▓		▓		▓	

1991 Corvette

The 1991 model-year was not a time of massive changes. After the launch of the ZR-1 the previous year, Chevrolet was ready to relax and enjoy the fruits of its labor. However, the regular Corvette coupe and convertible needed some extra pizzazz to keep them selling well and they were treated to a very noticeable makeover at one end.

The base models were heavily restyled at the rear to make them more closely resemble the ZR-1. This entailed designing a convex rear fascia with two rectangular taillights on either side of the car. A new front end with wrap-around style fog lamps and turn signal lights was used on both regular and ZR-1 models. Also seen on both types of Corvettes were new side-panel louvers with a more horizontal look and wider body-color body

The new-for-1990 ZR-1 was back in the Corvette lineup for the 1991 model year. *Tom Glatch*

MIKE YAGER SAYS:	
CHEERS	In 1991, Corvette had a new front and rear fascia in keeping with the ZR-1. There also were more Callaway options as well as a new color beltline trim available. The Z07 suspension system was new and a blue glass top was added during the production run. Easier to find parts from 1991 include the base engines, transmissions, suspension pieces, lights and lenses, plus interior and exterior trim.
JEERS	The appearance of the wheels was softened. Parts as difficult to come by as water in the Sahara Desert include the ZR-1 engine and body parts, ZR-1 wheels, some dash components and gauges, the air conditioning controls, headlight motors and the Delco-Bose stereo components.
GAME PLAN	The "King of the Hill" was on a roll. You might look in your mirror and then look again—only to find that red flash blowing your doors off. This was a scenario often repeated at the time and credited to the "King." A ZR-1 is a fine car but engine parts as well as maintenance items are becoming harder to find. Look for a nice, low-mileage example, then hold on as the price will soar.

The 1991 ZR-1 retained the same wide-body stance. *Tom Glatch*

1991 'VETTE FACTS	
VEHICLE IDENTIFICATION NUMBER	Base Corvettes for 1991 were numbered 1G1YY|2/3|386M5100001 to 1G1YY|2/3|386M5118595. ZR1 Corvettes for 1991 were numbered 1G1YZ23J6M5800001 to 1G1YZ23J6M5802044. (On base coupes the sixth symbol was a 2 and on base convertibles the sixth symbol was a 3). The first symbol 1 indicated U.S. built. The second symbol G indicated a General Motors product. The third symbol 1 indicated a Chevrolet Motor Division vehicle. The fourth and fifth symbols were YY (Base Corvette) or YZ (Corvette ZR-1). The sixth symbol indicated the body style: 2 = two-door hatchback or liftback, GM styles 07, 08, 77, 87 and 3 = two-door convertible, GM style 67. The seventh symbol indicated the restraint code: 1 = Active manual belts, 3 = Active manual belts with driver-inflatable restraint system and 4 = Passive automatic belts. The eighth symbol indicated the engine: 8 = RPO L98 5.7-liter Tuned-Port-Injection (TPI) Chevrolet/GM of Canada V-8 and J = RPO LT5 5.7-liter TPI V-8. The ninth symbol was a check digit that varied. The 10th symbol indicated the model year M = 1991. The 11th symbol indicated the assembly plant: 5 = Bowling Green, Kentucky. The last six symbols indicated the sequential production number starting with 100001 at each factory for base coupes and convertibles and 800001 for ZR-1s.
ENGINE	**Base TPI V-8 (L-98):** Type: V-8 Bore and stroke: 4.00 x 3.48 in. Displacement: 350 cid Brake hp: 245/250 at 4,000 rpm.* Induction: TPI *Engine rating is 250-hp for hatchbacks using 3.07:1 rear axle due to use of low-restriction mufflers with this option combination only. **ZR-1 V-8 (LT-5):** Type: V-8 Bore and stroke: 3.90 x 3.66 in. Displacement: 350 cid Brake hp: 375 at 5,800 rpm. Induction: TPI
VITAL STATS	**Hatchback Coupe:** Original Price: $32,455 Production: 14,967 Wheelbase: 96.2 in. Length: 178.6 in. Tires: P275/40-ZR17 Goodyear Eagle GT **Convertible:** Original Price: $38,770 Production: 5,672 Wheelbase: 96.2 in. Length: 178.6 in. Tires: P275/40-ZR17 Goodyear Eagle GT **ZR-1:*** Original Price: $64,138 Production: 2,055 Wheelbase: 96.2 in. Length: 178.5 in. Tires: (Front) P275/40-ZR17 Goodyear Eagle GT (Rear) P315/35-ZR17 Goodyear Eagle GT *ZR-1 option quantity included in hatchback coupe production of 14,967.
COOL STUFF	Corvette buyers who wanted to participate in World Challenge Series racing had to buy a stock Corvette from Chevrolet and handle race-prep work themselves. Black, Saddle, Red, White and (late in the year) Blue top colors were available on convertibles, but the choices were determined by body paint color. Some of the more expensive 1991 Corvette options were: RPO AQ9 Leather sports seats ($1,050). RPO B2K Callaway Twin Turbo installed by Callaway Engineering ($33,000). RPO FX3 Electronic Selective Ride & Handling system ($1,695). RPO U1F Delco-Bose stereo system with compact disc changer ($1,219). RPO ZR1 Special Performance package for coupe ($31,683).

side moldings. All Corvette wheels were also changed over to a painted aluminum finish.

Although it was now more similar to the regular Corvette in a visual sense, the "King of the Hill" ZR-1 again had different doors and a wider rear to accommodate its 11-inch wide rear wheels and fat tires. Also, on the ZR-1 the high-mounted stop lamp was placed on the roof instead of on the rear fascia, where it was on the standard Corvette. All models were again equipped with ABS II-S anti-lock braking and a driver's side airbag, as well as an anti-theft system.

The ZR-1 was again powered by the 32-valve double overhead cam 5.7-liter LT-5 V-8, which was mated to a six-speed tranmission.

Regular Corvette models used a totally different 5.7-liter V-8 that also had tuned port fuel injection. It was mated to a four-speed overdrive automatic transmission or the optional six-speed manual transmission.

Three different suspension systems were offered for 1991 'Vettes. The base system was good, while the FX-3 Electronic Selective Ride & Handling system – a $1,695 option — was even better for everyday use. The third choice was the new Z-07 suspension package for the hatchback coupe. It was released for those who wanted to take their cars racing and rallying. This $2,045 "competition" suspension was akin to the

1991 Corvette Status Guide	Basket Case		Average Driver		Rare, Unique or Completely Original	
Condition of CORVETTE:	Production Status					
	Average	Rare/ Unique	N-O-M	O-M	Needs Work	Unrestored Low Mileage
Suggested Actions: Collect It		▨				▨
Drive, Show and Enjoy			▨	▨		▨
Race, Autocross Competitively	▨					
Store for a Future Project/Investment					▨	
Candidate for Resto Rod	▨					
Restore to Curb Appeal Condition	▨			▨		

Unique to the ZR-1 in 1991 was the 32-valve, overhead cam LT-5 V-8 engine. *Tom Glatch*

Inside the Corvette was much like 1990 and still carried six interior color choices. *Tom Glatch*

well-liked Z-51 Performance & Handling package, which had become part of the Selective Ride Control option after 1990.

Corvette exterior color choices for 1991 rose to 10, but interior color selections stayed at five. Other trim features were basically the same as in 1990.

The optional Callaway Twin-Turbo engine package – now priced at $33,000 – could again be ordered through specific Chevrolet dealers as RPO B2K. As in the past, cars to be modified were sent from Bowling Green to the Callaway factory in Connecticut for their transformation. The rework involved mainly

high-performance engine modifications, but other upgrades were added, too. Callaway built its 500th conversion on September 26, 1991. Callaway Twin-Turbos made after that date were called "Callaway 500" editions. They had special features and a $600 higher price tag.

C4 Corvettes, including the ZR-1, posted many racing wins during the 1990s and were a staple at SCCA and other race series events throughout their existence. As was true from the beginning, the Corvette continued to be a car that weekend and professional racers alike could win with.

1992 Corvette

The 1,000,000th Corvette was produced on July 2, 1992. It was a 1992 Corvette convertible and was posed for a factory publicity photograph alongside a first-year 1953 Corvette. Although the 1992 had few cosmetic changes from the model that immediately preceded it, the car incorporated considerable technical changes that truly brought the regular-production Corvette into the realm of "world-class" sports cars.

With the introduction of new LT-1 base V-8, the introduction of an Acceleration Slip Regulation (ASR) traction-control system as standard equipment and the standard use of Goodyear Eagle GS-C high-performance tires with directional and asymmetrical tread design, Chevrolet Motor Division could advertise that "The all-around performance of the Corvette has been raised to the highest point in the car's 39-year history."

Eight major factors contributed to the increased power of the LT-1 engine: 1) A reverse-flow cooling system; 2) Computer-controlled ignition timing; 3) A low-restriction exhaust system incorporating a two-piece converter and exhaust-runner assembly for easier service access; 4) The use of high-

The 1992 Corvette coupe was stunning in its coat of quite bright Yellow paint.   *Tom Glatch*

The Corvette LT-1 V-8 displaced 350 cubic inches and produced 300 hp in 1992. *Tom Glatch*

A new digital speedometer was among the interior changes found on the 1992 Corvette. *Tom Glatch*

MIKE YAGER SAYS:	
CHEERS	The one-millionth Corvette was built in 1992. It was the year of anagrams for Corvette with the ECM, GSC and ASR. The ECM was a computer that controlled fuel injection. The GSC was a new Goodyear tire series. The ASR was Acceleration Slip Regulation—what most of us would call traction control. The LT-1 was introduced, a completely new small block engine. Corvette introduced reverse flow cooling and Optic spark ignition. Mobil 1 set the standard as a Corvette lubricant. There were new interior enhancements and improved door seals. Easy-to-find parts include the base engines, the transmissions, most suspension pieces, interior and exterior trim and wheels.
JEERS	All C4 Corvettes have large, high sills so "up and over" is the only exit strategy. The new Optic-spark ignition system had problems. Scarce parts include components of the adjustable suspension, some gauges, Delco-Bose stereo components, sport seat parts and bladders, the ZR-1 engine and ZR-1 body parts and ZR-1 windshields.
GAME PLAN	Start with as untouched and original example as you can find. In 1992, you could buy options to create a ZR-1-like car without the expensive engine options. The 1992 Corvette is a fantastic car for cruising, autocross or driving to work.

compression-ratio pistons; 5) The use of a new camshaft profile; 6) The use of new free-flowing cylinder heads; 7) The use of four-bolt main bearing caps on the three center bearings and 8) The use of new synthetic 5W-30 engine oil (also eliminating the need for a separate engine-oil cooler).

An LT-1-powered Corvette with automatic transmission was tested at 0-to-60 mph in 5.26 seconds. It did the quarter mile in 13.9 seconds at 102.2 mph. An LT-1-powered Corvette with the six-speed manual transmission was even faster. It did 0-to-60 mph in 4.92 seconds and the quarter mile in 13.7 seconds at 103.5 mph. For comparison, the '92 ZR-1 with standard manual transmission did 0-to-60 mph in 4.3 seconds and the quarter mile in 12.9 seconds. The closeness of the performances proved that the LT-1 had dramatically narrowed the

Supposedly, this ZR-1 is one of just seven painted Quasar Blue Metallic in 1992. *Tom Glatch*

1992 'VETTE FACTS

VEHICLE IDENTIFICATION NUMBER	Base Corvettes for 1992 were numbered 1G1YY|2/3|3P6N5100001 to 1G1YY|2/3|3P6N5119977. ZR1 Corvettes for 1992 were numbered 1G1YZ23|6N5800001 to 1G1YZ23|6N5800501. (On base coupes the sixth symbol was a 2 and on base convertibles the sixth symbol was a 3). The first symbol 1 indicated U.S. built. The second symbol G indicated a General Motors product. The third symbol 1 indicated a Chevrolet Motor Division vehicle. The fourth and fifth symbols were YY (Base Corvette) or YZ (Corvette ZR-1). The sixth symbol indicated the body style: 2 = Two-door hatchback or liftback, GM styles 07, 08, 77, 87 and 3 = Two-door convertible, GM style 67. The seventh symbol indicated the restraint code: 1 = Active manual belts, 2 = Active manual belts with driver and passenger inflatable restraint system, 3 = Active manual belts with driver-inflatable restraint system, 4 = Passive automatic belts and 5 = Passive automatic belts with driver inflatable restraint system. The eighth symbol indicated the engine: P = RPO LT1 5.7-liter Multi-Port-Fuel-Injection (MFII) Chevrolet/GM of Canada V-8 and J = RPO LT5 5.7-liter MFI V-8. The ninth symbol was a check digit that varied. The 10th symbol indicated the model year N = 1992. The 11th symbol indicated the assembly plant: 5 = Bowling Green, Kentucky. The last six symbols indicated the sequential production numbers starting with 100001 at each factory for base coupes and convertibles and 800001 for ZR-1s.
ENGINE	**Base MPFI V-8 (LT-1):** Type: V-8 Bore and stroke: 4.00 x 3.48 in. Displacement: 350 cid Brake hp: 300 at 5,000 rpm. Induction: MPFI **ZR-1 V-8 (LT-5):** Type: V-8 Bore and stroke: 3.90 x 3.66 in. Displacement: 350 cid Brake hp: 375 at 5,800 rpm. Induction: MPFI
VITAL STATS	**Hatchback Coupe:** Original Price: $33,635 Production: 14,604 Wheelbase: 96.2 in. Length: 178.6 in. Tires: P275/40-ZR17 Goodyear Eagle GT **Convertible:** Original Price: $40,145 Production: 5,875 Wheelbase: 96.2 in. Length: 178.6 in. Tires: P275/40-ZR17 Goodyear Eagle GT **ZR-1:*** Original Price: $65,318 Production: 502 Wheelbase: 96.2 in. Length: 178.5 in. Tires: (Front) P275/40-ZR17 Goodyear Eagle GT (Rear) P315/35-ZR17 Goodyear Eagle GT *ZR-1 option quantity included in hatchback coupe production of 14,604.
COOL STUFF	A sleek-looking Sting Ray III concept car was seen in 1992. It previewed many technical innovations that would arrive in the C5 and C6 Corvettes. The Acceleration Slip Regulation system introduced on the 1992 Corvette was designed by Bosch and was the next step after ABS. In 1992, Dave Hill took over the reins as Corvette chief engineer. Inspired by Corvette's reputation and heritage, Hill was determined to take the car to a new level.

performance gap between the base Corvette and the much-more-expensive ZR-1 Corvette.

The 1992 ZR-1 was basically a carry-over from the year previous with new model badges above the front fender vents. It was again powered by the 32-valve DOHC 5.7-liter V-8 matched with a six-speed 2F tranmission. Standard Corvette models received the bulk of attention, as described above. Both models had new rectangular exhausts. A new all-black dash treatment, relocated digital speedometer and improved instrument graphics were also adopted.

On August 28, 1992, Chevrolet Motor Division announced that David McLellan would be retiring as Corvette chief engineer.

McLellan had taken over the Corvette program after the retirement of Zora Arkus-Duntov in 1975. Chevy's assistant manager of public relations Tom Hoxie said in 1992, "During McLellan's 18-year tenure he transformed the Corvette from an American muscle car into an internationally-acclaimed, high-performance sports car that runs rings around a host of more expensive European and Japanese models." Said McLellan, "I can't think of a better time for me to be leaving. No manufacturer has ever built one million sports cars and at the age of 40 the Corvette is stronger than it's ever been. Our all-new car is a few years old and it's time to let someone else put their stamp on it."

1992 Corvette Status Guide	Basket Case		Average Driver		Rare, Unique or Completely Original	
Condition of CORVETTE:	Production Status					
Suggested Actions:	Average	Rare/ Unique	N-O-M	O-M	Needs Work	Unrestored Low Mileage
Collect It		▓				▓
Drive, Show and Enjoy			▓	▓		
Race, Autocross Competitively	▓		▓			
Store for a Future Project/Investment					▓	
Candidate for Resto Rod	▓		▓			
Restore to Curb Appeal Condition			▓	▓		

1993 Corvette

Chevrolet had not produced a 30th Anniversary Corvette for the "fiberglass flyer's" 30th birthday in 1983. A decade later, the company was careful not to miss the promotional opportunities of a car to commemorate the Corvette's fourth decade. The 40th anniversary of the hallowed nameplate was loudly recognized with a good-looking special appearance package that included an exclusive "Ruby Red" color used on the exterior and interior.

The 40th Anniversary package – RPO Z-25 – retailed for $1,455 and it also included color-keyed wheel centers, headrest embroidery and bright metal "40th Anniversary" emblems on the hood, deck and side-gills. This anniversary package was optional equipment on coupes, convertibles and ZR-1 coupes. The 40th Anniversary Convertibles were delivered with an exclusive Ruby Red cloth top.

The ZR-1's 5.7-liter LT-5 V-8 was upgraded

A pair of history making Corvettes—both 40th anniversary editions.   *Tom Glatch*

this year and featured significant power and torque increases. Improved air flow derived from cylinder head and valve train refinements boosted its output rating from 375 hp to 405 hp. Improvements in the LT-5 engine's cylinder head and valve train included "blending" the valve heads and creating three-angle valve inserts, plus the use of a sleeve spacer to help maintain port alignment of the fuel injector manifold. These refinements added the 30 extra "ponies" and also resulted in a higher torque rating. In addition, the LT-5 was now equipped with four-bolt main bearings, meaning that the crankcase, front cover, oil pan and oil pump had to be redesigned. The LT-5 also got platinum-tipped spark plugs and an electrical linear exhaust gas recirculating (EGR) system. The ZR-1 still used a six-speed transmission.

Standard Corvette models were again powered by the 5.7-liter LT-1 V-8 connected to a four-speed overdrive automatic or optional six-speed manual transmission. Both the coupe and convertible changed to narrower 255/45-ZR17 front tires to make handling more predictable and improve steering functions. The rear tire size was increased to 285/45 ZR17. Standard features included a removable body-color roof panel for hatchbacks or a convertible top. All Corvette convertibles except those with the Z-25 40th Anniversary Package could be ordered with the choice of a beige, black or

Engines came in the 300 hp LT-1 version (shown) and the 405-hp LT-5 edition in 1993. *Tom Glatch*

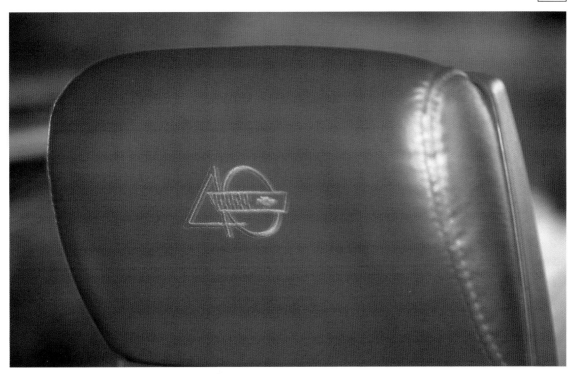

The head rest shows the 40th anniversary Corvette logo. *Tom Glatch*

Another sign this car was special was the 40th anniversary badge it wore. *Tom Glatch*

MIKE YAGER SAYS:	
CHEERS	It was the year of the 40th Anniversary Corvette with its special anniversary package and emblems. A total of 245 rare ZR-1 40th Anniversary edition Corvettes were built. The ZR-1 now had 405 horses in its stable. There were new interior enhancements in 1993, a passive key entry system and new machined look wheel finish. Parts that are easy to find include suspension items, the base engines, transmissions, interior and exterior trim plus lights and lenses.
JEERS	One problem with the 1993 Corvettes is their original window and door seals degrade quickly. Hard to find parts include sport seats, Delco-Bose stereo components, stock power antennas and original Goodyear tires.
GAME PLAN	Start with the most original and untouched example that you can find. If you're looking for a 1993 Corvette, find a rare 40th Anniversary ZR-1, an extremely attractive car.

The official Chevrolet portrait of its 40th anniversary Corvette. *KP Archives*

1993 'VETTE FACTS

VEHICLE IDENTIFICATION NUMBER	Base Corvettes for 1993 were numbered 1G1YY|2/3|3PXP5100001 to 1G1YY|2/3|3PXP5121142. ZR1 Corvettes for 1993 were numbered 1G1YZ23J3P5800001 to 1G1YZ23J3P5800448. (On base coupes the sixth symbol was a 2, on base convertibles the sixth symbol was a 3). The first symbol 1 indicates U.S. built. The second symbol G indicated a General Motors product. The third symbol 1 indicated a Chevrolet Motor Division vehicle. The fourth and fifth symbols were YY (Base Corvette) or YZ (Corvette ZR-1). The sixth symbol indicated the body style: 2 = Two-door hatchback or liftback, GM styles 07, 08, 77, 87 and 3 = Two-door convertible, GM style 67. The seventh symbol indicated the restraint code: 1 = Active manual belts, 2 = Active manual belts with driver and passenger inflatable restraint system, 3 = Active manual belts with driver-inflatable restraint system, 4 = Passive automatic belts and 5 = Passive automatic belts with driver inflatable restraint system. The eighth symbol indicates engine: P = RPO LT1 5.7-liter Multi-Port-Fuel-Injection (MFI) Chevrolet/GM of Canada V-8; J = RPO LT5 5.7-liter MFI V-8. The ninth symbol was a check digit that varied. The 10th symbol indicated the model year P = 1993. The 11th symbol indicated the assembly plant: 5 = Bowling Green, Kentucky. The last six symbols indicated the sequential production numbers starting with 100001 at each factory for base coupes and convertibles and 800001 for ZR-1s.
ENGINE	**Base MPFI V-8 (LT1):** Type: V-8 Bore and stroke: 4.00 x 3.48 in. Displacement: 350 cid Brake hp: 300 at 5,000 rpm. Induction: MPFI **ZR-1 V-8 (LT5):** Type: V-8 Bore and stroke: 3.90 x 3.66 in. Displacement: 350 cid Brake hp: 405 at 5,800 rpm. Induction: MPFI
VITAL STATS	**Hatchback Coupe:** Original Price: $34,595 Production: 15,898 Wheelbase: 96.2 in. Length: 178.5 in. (Front) P255/45-ZR17 Goodyear Eagle GT (Rear) P285/40-ZR17 Goodyear Eagle GT **Convertible:** Original Price: $41,195 Production: 5,712 Wheelbase: 96.2 in. Length: 178.5 in. (Front) P255/45-ZR17 Goodyear Eagle GT (Rear) P285/40-ZR17 Goodyear Eagle GT **ZR-1:*** Original Price: $66,278 Production: 448 Wheelbase: 96.2 in. Length: 178.5 in. Tires: (Front) P275/40-ZR17 Goodyear Eagle GT (Rear) P315/35-ZR17 Goodyear Eagle GT *ZR-1 option quantity included in hatchback coupe production of 15,898.
COOL STUFF	Even Corvettes without the optional RPO Z25 40th Anniversary package had the special anniversary-style embroidered headrests. The RPO Z25 40th Anniversary Package was added to 6,749 cars with no body style breakout available. Calendar-year sales totaled 20,487 Corvettes. Model-year production totaled 21,590. The regular Corvettes were getting so good that few buyers saw the need to spend $28,000 to move up to a ZR-1. The Mercury Marine ZR-1 engine assembly line in Stillwater, Oklahoma was shut down in 1993. The ZR-1 was offered through April 1995, but car production was programmed at 448 units per year from 1993-on, enough to use up engines that had already been produced.

white cloth top. Also standard was black cloth upholstery. If the coupe or convertible owner sprung for the leather seat option, the seats came with a "40th Anniversary" logo on them.

A first on all 1993 Corvettes was the original GM Passive Keyless Entry system whereby simply leaving or approaching the Corvette automatically unlocked or locked the appropriate doors. The 1993 Corvette was also the first North American automobile to use recycled sheet-molded-compound body panels.

1993 Corvette Status Guide	Basket Case		Average Driver		Rare, Unique or Completely Original	
Condition of CORVETTE:	Production Status					
	Average	Rare/ Unique	N-O-M	O-M	Needs Work	Unrestored Low Mileage
Suggested Actions: Collect It						
Drive, Show and Enjoy						
Race, Autocross Competitively						
Store for a Future Project/Investment						
Candidate for Resto Rod						
Restore to Curb Appeal Condition						

1994 Corvette

Several refinements that focused on safety and smoother operation were the order for 1994 Corvettes. A passenger-side airbag was added to help the Corvette conform with new Federal safety regulations. All Corvettes now offered dual airbags. In addition, other interior changes were required including richer new carpeting, new door-trim panels, new standard leather seats, a new steering wheel, a redesigned instrument panel and a restyled console. The interior changes greatly enhanced the fit and finish quality of the Corvette interior.

Other new equipment included an optional rear-axle ratio, revised spring rates, a convertible backlight with heated

This 1994 Corvette color was called Admiral Blue—shown here on a coupe. *KP Archives*

MIKE YAGER SAYS:	
CHEERS	Corvette was the featured parade car for the inaugural Indy Brickyard 400 race and 25 special commemorative cars were made. Choice 1994 parts include base LT-1 engines, transmissions, suspension systems, trim items and the lights and lenses.
JEERS	All C4 Corvettes suffered from large, high sills and 1994 was the same. Original hardtops, sport seat components, ZR-1 parts, Z07 suspension pieces and Delco-Bose components all are difficult parts to find.
GAME PLAN	This was the twilight year of the C4 Corvette. Not much was new or changed in 1994. It was still a great car and a great way to end an era of tremendous performance engineering. Look for one of the Brickyard 400 Corvettes!

glass and new exterior colors. The ZR-1 also received new non-directional five-spoke wheels for 1994. Extended Mobility Tires became a limited-availability option for '94 Corvettes combining the base suspension with the FX-3 Selective Ride Control option.

The 5.7-liter V-8 powering the standard Corvettes now used sequential fuel injection, which provided a smoother idle, better drivability and lower emissions. That engine was mated to a refined 4L60-E electronic four-speed automatic overdrive transmission that provided a more consistent shift feel. A brake-transmission shift interlock safety feature was also new for 1994.

The ZR-1 again used the LT-5 5.7-liter V-8. It was fitted with a six-speed manual

New carpeting, door trim and leather seats were standard features of the 1994 Corvettes. *KP Archives*

1994 'VETTE FACTS	
VEHICLE IDENTIFICATION NUMBER	Base Corvettes for 1994 were numbered 1G1YY|2/3|2P9R5100001 to 1G1YY|2/3|2P9R5122882. ZR1 Corvettes for 1994 were numbered 1G1YZ22|9R5800001 to 1G1YZ22|9R5800448. (On base coupes the sixth symbol was a 2 and on base convertibles the sixth symbol was a 3). The first symbol 1 indicated U.S. built. The second symbol G indicated a General Motors product. The third symbol 1 indicated a Chevrolet Motor Division vehicle. The fourth and fifth symbols were YY (Base Corvette) or YZ (Corvette ZR-1) The sixth symbol indicates the body style: 2 = Two-door hatchback or liftback, GM styles 07, 08, 77, 87 and 3 = Two-door convertible, GM style 67. The seventh symbol indicated the restraint code: 1 = Active manual belts, 2 = Active manual belts with driver and passenger inflatable restraint system, 3 = Active manual belts with driver-inflatable restraint system, 4 = Passive automatic belts, 5 = Passive automatic belts with driver inflatable restraint system and 6 = Passive automatic belts with driver and passenger inflatable restraint system. The eighth symbol indicated the engine: P = RPO LT1 5.7-liter Multi-Port-Fuel-Injection (MFI) Chevrolet/GM of Canada V-8 and J = RPO LT5 5.7-liter MFI V-8. The ninth symbol was a check digit that varied. The 10th symbol indicated the model year R = 1994. The 11th symbol indicated the assembly plant: 5 = Bowling Green, Kentucky. The last six symbols indicated the sequential production numbers starting with 100001 at each factory for base coupes and convertibles and 800001 for ZR-1s.
ENGINE	**Base MPFI V-8 (LT-1):** Type: V-8 Bore and stroke: 4.00 x 3.48 in. Displacement: 350 cid Brake hp: 300 at 5,000 rpm. Induction: MPFI **ZR-1 V-8 (LT-5):** Type: V-8 Bore and stroke: 3.90 x 3.66 in. Displacement: 350 cid Brake hp: 405 at 5,800 rpm. Induction: MPFI
VITAL STATS	**Hatchback Coupe:** Original Price: $36,185 Production: 17,984 Wheelbase: 96.2 in. Length: 178.5 in. (Front) P255/45-ZR17 Goodyear Eagle GT (Rear) P285/40-ZR17 Goodyear Eagle GT **Convertible:** Original Price: $42,960 Production: 5,320 Wheelbase: 96.2 in. Length: 178.5 in. (Front) P255/45-ZR17 Goodyear Eagle GT (Rear) P285/40-ZR17 Goodyear Eagle GT **ZR-1:*** Original Price: $67,443 Production: 448 Wheelbase: 96.2 in. Length: 178.5 in. Tires: (Front) P275/40-ZR17 Goodyear Eagle GT (Rear) P315/35-ZR17 Goodyear Eagle GT *ZR-1 option quantity included in hatchback coupe production of 17,984.
COOL STUFF	The five most expensive 1994 Corvette options were: RPO CC2 Auxiliary hardtop for convertible ($1,995). RPO C2L Dual removable roof panels for coupe. ($950). RPO FX3 Electronic Selective Ride & Handling system ($1,695). RPO Z07 Adjustable suspension package for hatchback coupe ($2,045). RPO ZR1 Special Performance package for hatchback coupe ($31,258). On the opening day of the National Corvette Museum over 15,000 supporters showed up to celebrate the grand opening. They brought more than 5,000 Corvettes along, which caused quite a traffic tie-up in both directions on Interstate-65 in Bowling Green, Kentucky. An enthusiastic crowd of 1,200 fans and 350 assorted Corvettes showed up for the first Corvette "Funfest" at Mid America Designs in Effingham, Illinois in September 1994. Today this event draws about 12,000 Corvettes and 50,000 Corvette fans each fall.

A 1994 Corvette convertible in one of two shades of red available that model year. *KP Archives*

1994 Corvette Status Guide	Basket Case		Average Driver		Rare, Unique or Completely Original	
Condition of CORVETTE:	Production Status					
	Average	Rare/ Unique	N-O-M	O-M	Needs Work	Unrestored Low Mileage
Suggested Actions: Collect It						▓
Drive, Show and Enjoy			▓	▓	▓	
Race, Autocross Competitively	▓	▓				
Store for a Future Project/Investment						
Candidate for Resto Rod	▓	▓	▓			
Restore to Curb Appeal Condition	▓	▓				

transmission, which was again a no-cost option for LT-1-powered Corvette models.

For 1994, Corvettes came in a choice of 10 exterior colors and interior hues. Standard features included a removable body-color roof panel for hatchbacks or a convertible top. All Corvette convertibles except those with Polo Green Metallic finish could be ordered with one of three top colors: Beige, Black or White cloth top. The White convertible top was not available for Polo Green Metallic cars. Leather seats became standard upholstery.

Reeves Callaway took his "tuner" versions of the Corvette one step further in 1994 by designing a competition-style body for the C4 that was tested at Le Mans in both 1994 and 1995. Crafted by Callaway stylist Paul Deutschmann, the car had a Ferrari-like nosepiece, added gill-style air slots behind the front and rear wheel openings and a tall racing type airfoil on its rear deck lid. This design became the Callaway SuperNatural Corvette LM that teamed Deutschmann's beauty of line with Callaway's race-proven SuperNatural-modified 6.3-liter 435-hp Corvette V-8.

On September 2, 1994, the National Corvette Museum opened in a specially-designed facility located near the Corvette factory in Bowling Green, Kentucky. It had been six years since the NCM board of directors sat down in 1988 to map out plans to raise funds to build the facility. The ribbon-cutting ceremony drew a huge crowd and caused a massive Corvette traffic jam in Bowling Green.

1994 was also the kick-off year for Mid America Motorwork's fall "Corvette Funfest."

We started the first Funfest event was started by Mike and Laurie Yager to celebrate the 20th anniversary of our Corvette parts and accessories company – which was then known as Mid America Designs. It was held at company headquarters in Effingham, Illinois, the couple's hometown, and was truly the beginning of something big!

Fittingly, the 1994 ZR-1 coupe was arrayed in Competition Yellow for this photo.   *KP Archives*

1995 Corvette

In the Corvette fraternity, the big news of 1995 was the final appearance of the ZR-1 performance coupe after a half dozen years of availability. The ZR-1 had first been announced in 1989, but was not actually offered until 1990. At first, there had been strong demand for the concept of a ultra-high-performance "King of the Hill" Corvette, largely because collectors bought the cars to hoard away. But as the Corvette C4 coupe and convertible were improved, the typical Corvette customer saw no need to pay tens of thousands of extra dollars for a ZR-1 that wasn't much faster than the LT-1 Corvette.

By 1993, Chevy saw the writing on the wall and stopped production of LT-5 engines for the ZR-1. After that, only 448 of the cars were built each year for three years. The final ZR-1 was a Torch Red version that left the assembly line in April of 1995.

A ceremony was held with both Chevrolet and Mercury Marine executives in attendance, along with some 800 ZR-1 owners and enthusiasts. The last car built was then sent to the National Corvette Museum in Bowling Green, Kentucky, where it can be seen on display today.

Changes on the Corvette included the addition of heavy-duty brakes with larger front rotors as standard equipment, along with new

The '95 Indy 500 Pace Car was painted in Deep Purple Metallic over Arctic White.   *Tom Glatch*

Just 527 drivers had a chance to step into their own 1995 Corvette Indy Pace Car. *Tom Glatch*

The LT-1 V-8 engine that produced 300 hp was the '95 Indy Pace Car's power plant. *Tom Glatch*

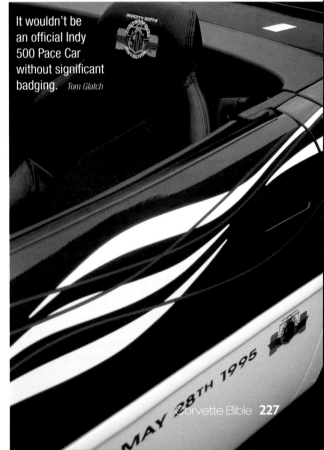

It wouldn't be an official Indy 500 Pace Car without significant badging. *Tom Glatch*

MIKE YAGER SAYS:	
CHEERS	In 1995, Corvette served as the Indianapolis 500 Pace Car once again. A large brake package was standard in 1995 and side grille styling had changed. Plentiful pickings from the parts bin included interior and exterior trim, base engines, wheels, transmissions and suspension componentry.
JEERS	It was the final year for the "King of the Hill" ZR-1. The era of the large, high sills continued and so did the "up and over" exit strategy. Those rarities in the 1995 parts bin include the GM hardtops, ZR-1 parts and trim, the Z07 suspension components, rear antennas, the Delco-Bose stereos and original Goodyear tires.
GAME PLAN	Choose carefully as always. In 1995, Corvette produced a very attractive Indy 500 Pace Car, a good choice for a collectible car. Also, think about a hardtop to put over a 1995 Corvette convertible or the clean lines of a luggage rack for that '95 Corvette roadster.

The official Chevrolet press photo of the 1995 Corvette Indy Pace Car.

low-rate springs (except ZR-1). De Carbon gas-charged shock absorbers were used for improved ride quality. In addition to exterior color changes, Corvettes featured a new "gill" panel behind the front wheel openings to help quickly distinguish the 1995 models from predecessors. Other improvements included reinforced interior stitching and a quieter-running cooling fan.

Engine and transmission offerings remained unchanged from the year previous. Base engine in the coupe and convertible was the aluminum-head LT-1 90-degree overhead valve 350-cid V-8 with the 4.00 x 3.48-inch bore and stroke measurements. Other specs included a 10.5:1 compression ratio, 300 hp at 5,000 rpm, 340 lbs.-ft. of torque at 3,600 rpm, hydraulic valve lifters and sequential multi-port-fuel injection. The ZR-1's LT-5 350-cid V-8 had the different 3.90 x 3.66-inch bore and stroke measurements, plus four valves per cylinder and four overhead cams. It ran an 11.0:1 compression ratio and produced 405 hp at 5,800 rpm and 385 lbs.-ft. of torque at 5,200 rpm. It also employed an aluminum cylinder head, hydraulic valve lifters and sequential multi-port fuel-injection.

For the third time in its existence (also 1978 and 1986), Corvette was selected as the official pace car for the Indianapolis 500. The 1995 Dark Purple Metallic over Arctic White Corvette was driven by 1960 Indy 500

1995 'VETTE FACTS

VEHICLE IDENTIFICATION NUMBER	Base Corvettes for 1995 were numbered 1G1YY|2/3|P7S5100001 to 1G1YY|2/3|P7S5120294. ZR1 Corvettes for 1995 were numbered 1G1YZ22|OS5800001 to 1G1YZ22|OS5800448. (On base coupes the sixth symbol was a 2 and on base convertibles the sixth symbol was a 3). The first symbol 1 indicated U.S. built. The second symbol G indicated a General Motors product. The third symbol 1 indicated a Chevrolet Motor Division vehicle. The fourth and fifth symbols were YY (Base Corvette) or YZ (Corvette ZR-1). The sixth symbol indicated the body style: 2 = Two-door hatchback or liftback, GM styles 07, 08, 77, 87 and 3 = Two-door convertible, GM style 67. The seventh symbol indicated the restraint code: 1 = Active manual belts, 2 = Active manual belts with driver and passenger inflatable restraint system, 3 = Active manual belts with driver-inflatable restraint system, 4 = Passive automatic belts, 5 = Passive automatic belts with driver inflatable restraint system and 6 = Passive automatic belts with driver and passenger inflatable restraint system. The eighth symbol indicated the engine: P = RPO LT1 5.7-liter Multi-Port-Fuel-Injection (MFI) Chevrolet/GM of Canada V-8 and J = RPO LT5 5.7-liter MFI V-8. The ninth symbol was a check digit that varied. The 10th symbol indicated the model year S = 1995. The 11th symbol indicated the assembly plant: 5 = Bowling Green, Kentucky. The last six symbols indicated the sequential production numbers starting with 100001 at each factory for base coupes and convertibles and 800001 for ZR-1s.
ENGINE	**Base MPFI V-8 (LT-1):** Type: V-8 Bore and stroke: 4.00 x 3.48 in. Displacement: 350 cid Brake hp: 300 at 5,000 rpm. Induction: SFI **ZR-1 V-8 (LT-5):** Type: V-8 Bore and stroke: 3.90 x 3.66 in. Displacement: 350 cid Brake hp: 405 at 5,800 rpm. Induction: SFI
VITAL STATS	**Hatchback Coupe:** Original Price: $36,785 Production: 15,771 Wheelbase: 96.2 in. Length: 178.5 in. (Front) P255/45-ZR17 Goodyear Eagle GT (Rear) P285/40-ZR17 Goodyear Eagle GT **Convertible:** Original Price: $43,665 Production: 4,971 Wheelbase: 96.2 in. Length: 178.5 in. (Front) P255/45-ZR17 Goodyear Eagle GT (Rear) P285/40-ZR17 Goodyear Eagle GT **ZR-1:*** Original Price: $6,8043 Production: 448 Wheelbase: 96.2 in. Length: 178.5 in. Tires: (Front) P275/40-ZR17 Goodyear Eagle GT (Rear) P315/35-ZR17 Goodyear Eagle GT *ZR-1 option quantity included in hatchback coupe production of 15,771.
COOL STUFF	The five most expensive 1995 Corvette options were: RPO CC2 Auxiliary hardtop for convertible ($1,995). RPO FX3 Electronic Selective Ride & Handling system ($1,695). RPO Z07 Adjustable suspension package for hatchback coupe ($2,045). RPO Z4Z Indy 500 Pace Car Replica for convertibles only ($2,816). RPO ZR1 Special Performance package for hatchback coupe ($31,258). It was the first time all of the five most expensive Corvette options all cost over $1,000. The last ZR-1 built, on exhibit at the National Corvette Museum, has a window banner that says, "The Legend Lives." In June of 1995, the J.D. Powers Survey found the Corvette to be one of the most improved cars in America. This was largely a result of a Quality Initiative program put into affect at the Bowling Green factory. The Callaway SuperNatural Corvette designed by Paul Deutschmann again appeared at the French Grand Prix at Le Mans in 1995.

The Barrymores had their profiles and the 1995 Corvettes also had a memorable one.   *KP Archives*

winner Jim Rathmann. Chevrolet General Manager Jim Perkins drove another Pace Car. Chevy built a total of 527 cars – all ragtops – equipped with the RPO Z4Z Indy 500 Pace Car Replica package that sold for $2,816 over the price of a standard LT-1-powered Corvette convertible.

A 1995 show car called the Stingray III was developed at GM's Advanced Concept Center in Thousand Oaks, California. This open car had a Porsche-style convertible top, a V-6, slit-style headlights, modern spoked wheels and a smoothly-rounded body.

1995 Corvette Status Guide	Basket Case		Average Driver		Rare, Unique or Completely Original	
Condition of CORVETTE:	Production Status					
	Average	Rare/ Unique	N–O–M	O–M	Needs Work	Unrestored Low Mileage
Suggested Actions: Collect It						▒
Drive, Show and Enjoy			▒	▒		
Race, Autocross Competitively	▒	▒				
Store for a Future Project/Investment	▒	▒	▒			
Candidate for Resto Rod	▒	▒	▒			
Restore to Curb Appeal Condition	▒	▒				

1996 Corvette

A sad, but historic milestone in the Corvette legend took place in April of 1996 when Zora Arkus-Duntov died of lung cancer in his home at Grosse Pointe Woods, Michigan. The man who had served as Corvette Chief Engineer during the car's early formative years was 86 years old at the time of his passing.

Though the "Father of the Corvette" was gone, his offspring was doing well. In fact, 1996 would be a landmark year for Corvette enthusiasts. With the demise of the ZR-1, Chevrolet tried to offset the void by introducing two new special edition Corvettes, the Grand Sport and Collector Edition models.

The RPO Z16 Grand Sport package retailed for $2,880 on the convertible or $3,250 on the coupe. It evoked memories of its 1962 and 1963 racing predecessors. The 1996 version

With the help of Jim Perkins, General Manager of Chevrolet in 1996, I was able to add the last C4 off the assembly line to my collection. *Tom Glatch*

Larry Shinoda signed his approval to a car that carries over 2000 great signatures. *Tom Glatch*

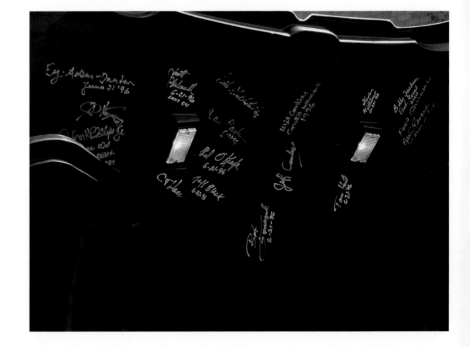

Elfy Arkus-Duntov (Zora's beautiful wife) and many other notables autographed the clam shell hood. *Tom Glatch*

Thanks to Jim Perkins and Team Chevrolet - and Team McClellan - for a fantastic car! *Tom Glatch*

The C4's interior would be memorialized with time as the new C5 interior had major changes. *Tom Glatch*

It was an absolute privilege to watch this car go from its "birdcage" to the end of the assembly line - and it's a thrill to own it. *Tom Glatch*

MIKE YAGER SAYS:	
CHEERS	It was the final Corvette of the C4 series. In 1996, there was a Grand Sport special option package as well as the Collector's Edition special trim package. There also was a performance package available. The LT-4 was an engine option and all of them were equipped with six-speed transmissions. Three aluminum wheel styles were offered in 1996 and a real-time suspension dampening was available. The easy parts to find from 1996 include the base LT-1 engines, transmissions, suspension parts, interior and exterior trim, plus lights and lenses.
JEERS	The C4 styling was getting old. People were wondering when the C5 would be available. Scarce in the 1996 parts bin are original Grand Sport edition wheels, Collector Edition wheels, the LT-4 engines, hardtops and the ECM computers.
GAME PLAN	It was the end of the C4 era. The C4 had been an engineering triumph for Dave McLellan and his team. We say "Thanks for a great Corvette!" It is one we have all owned and loved!

There are many Corvettes to keep—like this 1996 Collector's Edition convertible. *KP Archives*

sported Admiral Blue Metallic Paint, a white stripe, red "hash" marks on the left front fender and black five-spoke aluminum wheels. Powering the Grand Sport – and optional in all other Corvettes – was a 330-hp 5.7-liter LT-4 V-8 featuring a specially-prepared crankshaft, steel camshaft and water pump gears driven by a roller chain. The LT-4 was available only with the six-speed manual transmission.

The RPO Z15 Collector Edition Corvette package retailed for $1,250. It was produced as a tribute to the final year of production of the fourth-generation Corvette (the fifth-generation model was to debut the following year). The 1996 Collector Edition

Corvette featured exclusive Sebring Silver paint, Collector Edition emblems, silver five-spoke aluminum wheels and a 5.7-liter LT-1 V-8 fitted with a four-speed automatic transmission (The LT-4 V-8 and six-speed manual transmission were both optional).

On all Corvettes, 1996 marked the introduction of the optional Selective Real Time Damping system that employed sensors at each wheel to measure movement. Data retrieved from each wheel and the Powertrain Control Module was processed by an electronic controller that calculated the damping mode to provide optimum control. Also optional was a Z-51 Performance Handling Package available on

1996 'VETTE FACTS

VEHICLE IDENTIFICATION NUMBER	Base Corvettes for 1996 were numbered 1G1YY|2/3|257T5100001 to 1G1YY|2/3|257T5120536. Grand Sport-optioned Corvettes for 1996 were numbered 1G1YY2251T5600001 to 1G1YY2251T5601000. (On base coupes the sixth symbol was a 2 and on base convertibles the sixth symbol was a 3). The first symbol 1 indicated U.S. built. The second symbol G indicated a General Motors product. The third symbol 1 indicated a Chevrolet Motor Division vehicle. The fourth and fifth symbols were YY Corvette. The sixth symbol indicated the body style: 2 = Two-door hatchback or liftback, GM styles 07, 08, 77, 87 and 3 = Two-door convertible, GM style 67. The seventh symbol indicated the restraint code: 1 = Active manual belts, 2 = Active manual belts with driver and passenger inflatable restraint system, 3 = Active manual belts with driver-inflatable restraint system, 4 = Passive automatic belts, 5 = Passive automatic belts with driver inflatable restraint system, 6 = Passive automatic belts with driver and passenger inflatable restraint system and 7 = Active manual driver's belt and passive automatic passenger's belt with driver and passenger inflatable restraint system. The eighth symbol indicated the engine: P = RPO LT1 5.7-liter Sequential multiport-fuel-injection (MFI) Chevrolet/Pontiac/Buick/Cadillac V-8; 5 = RPO LT4 5.7-liter Sequential multiport-fuel-injection (MFI) Chevrolet only. The ninth symbol was a check digit that varied. The 10th symbol indicated the model year T = 1996. The 11th symbol indicated the assembly plant: 5 = Bowling Green, Kentucky. The last six symbols indicated the sequential production numbers starting with 100001.
ENGINE	**Base V-8 (LT-1):** Type: V-8 Bore and stroke: 4.00 x 3.48 in. Displacement: 350 cid Brake hp: 300 at 5,000 rpm. Induction: SFI **Optional V-8 (LT-4):** Type: V-8 Bore and stroke: 4.00 x 3.48 in. Displacement: 350 cid Brake hp: 330 at 5,800 rpm. Induction: SFI
VITAL STATS	**Hatchback Coupe:** Original Price: $37,225 Production: 17,167 Wheelbase: 96.2 in. Length: 178.5 in. (Front) P255/45-ZR17 (Rear) P285/40-ZR17 **Convertible:** Original Price: $45,060 Production: 4,369 Wheelbase: 96.2 in. Length: 178.5 in. (Front) P255/45-ZR17 (Rear) P285/40-ZR17 **Grand Sport Coupe:** Option Price: $3,250 Tires: (Front) P275/40-ZR17 (Rear) P315/35-ZR17 **Grand Sport Convertible** Option Price: $2,880 Tires: (Front) P255/45-ZR17 (Rear) P285/40-ZR17 Note: The Z-16 Grand Sport Package option was installed on 1,000 cars (coupes and convertibles combined). **Collector Edition:** Option Price: $1,250 Note: The Z-15 Collector's Edition option was installed on 5,412 cars (coupes and convertibles combined).
COOL STUFF	The stamping on the bottom of the Johnny Lightning "Last C4" model shows it was actually based on that company's replica of the 1995 ZR-1. If you find one without the packaging look for the red hash marks and the black "Last C4" decals on the hood. Nearly every Bowling Green Assembly Plant employee and assembly line worker present at the "Last of a Legend" ceremony personally signed Mike Yager's "Last C4," as did all of the GM dignitaries in attendance. The "Last C4" is currently a featured attraction of the "My Garage" Corvette Museum at Mid America Motorworks in Effingham, Illinois. All Corvette convertibles, except those with code 13, 28 or 45 paint colors, could be ordered with one of three cloth top colors: Beige, Black or White. Sebring Silver Metallic (code 13) cars came only with Black cloth tops. Admiral Blue (code 28) Grand Sports came only with White cloth tops. Polo Green Metallic (code 45) cars came with Beige or Black cloth tops, but not White.

the Corvette coupe, and tuned for autocross and gymkhana competition.

Regular Corvette models again used the 5.7-liter V-8 with sequential fuel injection and four-speed automatic transmission. Leather seats were standard equipment.

Though it was 13 years old and a bit long in the tooth by 1996, the C4 had turned the Corvette into a true "World Class" sports car. To commemorate the C4's contributions, my company – then known as Mid America Designs – worked closely with Chevrolet Motor Division to create a truly unique, one-of-a-kind Corvette to mark the end of C4 history.

In keeping with marque tradition, the last 1996 Corvette off the Bowling Green assembly line received special equipment including Grand Sport flares and hash marks. The car was a white coupe. It was also factory fitted with white ZR-1 wheels, specially embroidered seat emblems, windshield graphics and unique "Last C4" logos.

A special-edition Johnny Lightning replica of the "Last C4 Corvette" was produced in a limited run of 4,800 copies complete with authentic Corvette paint colors and the white-painted five-spoke ZR-1 wheels. The packaging included the Mid America logo and a copyright date of 1997.

1996 Corvette Status Guide	Basket Case		Average Driver		Rare, Unique or Completely Original	
Condition of CORVETTE:	Production Status					
Suggested Actions:	Average	Rare/ Unique	N–O–M	O–M	Needs Work	Unrestored Low Mileage
Collect It						●
Drive, Show and Enjoy			●			
Race, Autocross Competitively	●	●				
Store for a Future Project/Investment						
Candidate for Resto Rod	●	●	●			
Restore to Curb Appeal Condition	●	●				

1997 Corvette

Inspired by the Corvette's 44-year reputation and heritage, Dave Hill – who replaced Dave McClellan as Corvette chief engineer in 1992 – was determined to take his charge to a new level of perfection. With the introduction of the C5 in 1997, he and his team proved they were up to the goal he had set for himself. The C5 was another landmark design for "America's Sports Car." It was the first all-new Corvette in 13 years and only the fifth (or sixth depending upon your point of view) major change in the Corvette's 44-year-long history.

This all-new-from-the-ground-up Corvette was offered only as a coupe in its debut year. Among the equipment featured for the C5 was a new, more compact 5.7-liter engine. This LS-1 overhead valve V-8 had a cast-aluminum engine block and cylinder heads. With its new 3.90 x 3.62 bore and stroke it displaced 346 cubic inches. The LS-1 had a 10.1:1 compression ratio and generated 345

I asked that this First C5 be painted to match the Last C4 - and Chevrolet graciously obliged. *Tom Glatch*

A team led by John Cafaro designed the C5 Corvette. *KP Archives*

The 1997 Corvette instrument panel offered thorough readings for any driver. *KP Archives*

It could have been called a Corvette family reunion—with five generations present. *KP Archives*

The Corvette emblem has always signified something special in a sports car. *KP Archives*

MIKE YAGER SAYS:	
CHEERS	There was a complete redesign of the chassis and body. The Corvettes were all new cars with new engines including the all new LS-1 small block. The transmissions were in the rear. The most rigid Corvette platform ever constructed. The Hydro-Formed frame was an industry leading feature. There was easier entry and exiting this version. The C5 had the same entry level pricing as the C4.
JEERS	Corvette was once again threatened with discontinuance. The C5 introduced the most rigid Corvette platform ever constructed.
GAME PLAN	With a production of only 9,700 units, this is going to be a future collector's item!

Torch Red was one of the popular Corvette colors offered in the 1997 model year. *KP Archives*

The 1997 Corvette LS-1 V-8 produced 345 hp and was rated at 346 cid. *KP Archives*

1997 'VETTE FACTS

VEHICLE IDENTIFICATION NUMBER	Corvettes for 1997 were numbered 1G1YY22G1V5100001 to 1G1YY22G1V5109093. The first symbol 1 indicated U.S. built. The second symbol G indicated a General Motors product. The third symbol 1 indicated a Chevrolet Motor Division vehicle. The fourth and fifth symbols YY indicated a Corvette. The sixth symbol indicated the body style 2 = two-door coupe, GM styles 27, 37, 47 or 57. The seventh symbol indicated the restraint code: 2 = Active manual belts with driver and front passenger inflatable restraint system, 4 = Active manual belts with frontal and side-impact driver and front passenger inflatable restraint system. The eighth symbol indicated the engine: G = RPO LS1 5.7-liter Sequential multiport-fuel-injection (MFI) Chevrolet V-8. The ninth symbol was a check digit that varied. The 10th symbol indicated the model year V = 1997. The 11th symbol indicated the assembly plant: 5 = Bowling Green, Kentucky. The last six symbols indicated the sequential production numbers starting with 100001.
ENGINE	**Engine (LS-1):** Type: V-8 Bore and stroke: 3.90 x 3.62 in. Displacement: 346 cid Brake hp: 345 at 5,600 rpm. Induction: SFI
VITAL STATS	Hatchback Coupe: Original Price: $37,495 Production: 9,092 Wheelbase: 104.5 in. Length: 179.7 in. (Front) P255/45-ZR17 (Rear) P275/40-ZR18
COOL STUFF	The all-new C5 Corvette was designed under the direction of John Cafaro. *American Woman Motorscene* magazine named the 1997 Corvette its "Most likely to be immortalized" car. The C5 Corvette could do five second 0-to-60-mph runs and cover the quarter mile in 13.28 seconds at 107.6 mph according to *'Vette* magazine. In contrast to a few years earlier, only one Corvette option was now priced over $1,000. The top five in price order were: RPO U1S Remote CD changer ($600). RPO AQ9 Adjustable leather bucket seats ($625). RPO CC3 Roof panel with blue tint ($650). RPO C2L Dual body color-keyed roof panel and blue transparent roof panel ($950). RPO F45 Continuously Variable Real Time Damping ($1,695).

hp at 5,600 rpm and 350 lb.-ft. of torque at 4,400 rpm. Other features included hydraulic valve lifters and sequential fuel injection. An Electronic Throttle Control system allowed engineers to give the motor a limitless range of throttle progression.

The C5 Corvette was offered with a 4L60-E electronic four-speed overdrive automatic as the base transmission and a six-speed manual transmission was optional. A tubular, U-jointed, metal matrix, composite driveshaft was used. Power-assisted rack-and-pinion steering was also standard equipment. Four-wheel power disc ABS brakes were supplied for quick stops from high speed.

The short-and-long-arm front suspension setup featured forged-aluminum upper and lower control arms, a forged-aluminum steering knuckle, a transverse-mounted monoleaf spring, a steel stabilizer bar and an offset spindle. The rear suspension used a five-link design with tow and camber adjustment, cast-aluminum upper and lower control arms and knuckle, a transverse monoleaf spring, steel tie rods and a stabilizer bar.

The 1997 Corvette's underbody structure was the stiffest in the car's history. It featured two full-length, hydro-formed perimeter frame rails coupled to a backbone tunnel. The rails consisted of a single piece of tubular steel, replacing the 14 parts used previously.

The cockpit of the all-new Corvette featured a twin-pod design reminiscent of the original 1953 Corvette's dashboard. The instrument panel contained traditional backlit analog gauges and a digital Driver Information Center that comprised a display of 12 individual readouts in four languages. The new-design blunt tail section allowed for smoother airflow and resulting 0.29 coefficient of drag.

Under Hill, a big part of the Corvette mission continued to be expanding the performance envelope and making the car a sure-fire winner on the racetrack. Hill was also dedicated to the notion that the Corvette could be civilized and refined at the same time – a goal seemingly at odds with the slam-bang durability required on the track.

The C5 proved right out of the box that Hill's performance and refinement goals were not mutually exclusive. C5 Corvettes quickly dominated SCCA events, as well as other regional and local competitions, while the refined nature of the car attracted thousands of new Corvette buyers looking for luxurious touring and great highway performance.

1997 Corvette Status Guide	Basket Case		Average Driver		Rare, Unique or Completely Original	
Condition of CORVETTE:	Production Status					
	Average	Rare/ Unique	N-O-M	O-M	Needs Work	Unrestored Low Mileage
Suggested Actions: Collect It						
Drive, Show and Enjoy						
Race, Autocross Competitively						
Store for a Future Project/Investment						
Candidate for Resto Rod						
Restore to Curb Appeal Condition						

1998 Corvette

In its 45th year, the Corvette regained a convertible. The "topless" version of the C5 Corvette featured a heated glass rear window and the top had an "express-down" feature that released the tonneau cover and automatically lowered the windows part way at the touch of a button.

New-for-1998 was a $3,000 magnesium wheel option featuring lightweight wheels with a unique bronze tone. Standard features included a stainless steel exhaust system, Extended Mobility Tires capable of running for 200 miles with no air pressure, dual heated electric remote breakaway outside rearview mirrors, daytime running lamps and five-mph front and rear bumpers.

The LS-1 V-8 and four-speed automatic transmission were again the standard offering. The T-56 six-speed manual transmission was optional. The 1998 convertible went 0-to-60 in 5.1 seconds and did the quarter mile in 13.5 seconds.

A convertible was once again among the body choices for 1998 Corvette buyers. *KP Archives*

A new Active Handling system was offered as an option (JL4) on all 1998-1/2 Corvette models. This represented a logical step in the evolution of enhanced chassis control systems like ABS brakes and traction control. Working in close concert with those systems, Active Handling enhanced the accident-avoidance capabilities of the already nimble Corvette.

The Active Handling system activated when there is a significant difference between how the driver intends for the car to corner and how the car is actually cornering. It automatically applied any of the four brakes to help correct the situation.

During the 1998 model year, just prior to the release of the Active Handling option, the Corvette's ABS brake hydraulic control unit was relocated to the front of the engine compartment to facilitate quicker Active Handling system "warm-up" and shorten front brake response time when the brake fluid was cold. In temperatures below 14 degrees, the Driver Information Center (DIC) displayed an "Active Handling Warming Up" message as soon as the vehicle reached six-mph to caution the driver that Active Handling was not fully functional yet. When the system warmed up, another message "Active Handling Warmed Up" was sent.

The Corvette's Active Handling system was the first of its type to offer dual-mode operation. In addition to an "off" mode, in which Active Handling was disabled, the

The Corvette convertible made open top lovers happy with its presence in 1998. *KP Archives*

Once again, Corvette was chosen as the Indianapolis 500 Pace Car in 1998. *KP Archives*

MIKE YAGER SAYS:	
CHEERS	Both a coupe and convertible were offered. The convertible offered a trunk for the first time since 1962. There were new option packages, new color choices and noise reduction was improved. Another edition of a Corvette Indianapolis Pace Car was made.
JEERS	The wheel design was an odd choice, based on wagon wheels from 1997. There were no engine performance options. There was no hardtop for the convertible.
GAME PLAN	Look for an Indy Pace Car Corvette from 1998. They have a stunning graphic and paint scheme.

system allowed selection of a "competitive driving" mode for autocross or gymkhana competitions. In this mode, the Active Handling system remained fully-functional –measuring steering, yaw rate and lateral acceleration inputs as well as applying individual wheel brakes as required – but the traction-control system was disabled, allowing for some wheel spin and over steer that rally drivers often find beneficial.

For the fourth time (1978, 1986, 1995, 1998), a Corvette was selected to pace the Indianapolis 500 with Indy 500 veteran Parnelli Jones driving the purple and yellow pace car. RPO Z-4Z was an Indy Pace Car replica package that retailed for $5,039 on

In 1998, buyers could choose optional magnesium wheels from the options list. *KP Archives*

1998 'VETTE FACTS	
VEHICLE IDENTIFICATION NUMBER	Corvettes for 1998 were numbered 1G1YY[2/3]2G1W5100001 to 1G1YY[2/3]2G1W5131069. The first symbol 1 indicated U.S. built. The second symbol G indicated a General Motors product. The third symbol 1 indicated a Chevrolet Motor Division vehicle. The fourth and fifth symbols YY indicated a Corvette coupe or convertible. The sixth symbol indicated the body style 2 = two-door coupe, GM styles 27, 37, 47 or 57 or 3 = two-door convertible, GM body style 67. The seventh symbol indicated the restraint code: 2 = Active manual belts with driver and front passenger inflatable restraint system, 4 = Active manual belts with frontal and side-impact driver and front passenger inflatable restraint system. The eighth symbol indicated the engine: G = RPO LS1 5.7-liter Sequential multiport-fuel-injection (MFI) Chevrolet V-8. The ninth symbol was a check digit that varied. The 10th symbol indicated the model year W = 1998. The 11th symbol indicated the assembly plant: 5 = Bowling Green, Kentucky. The last six symbols indicated the sequential production numbers starting with 100001.
ENGINE	Engine (LS-1): Type: V-8 Bore and stroke: 3.90 x 3.62 in. Displacement: 346 cid Brake hp: 345 at 5,600 rpm. Induction: SFI
VITAL STATS	**Hatchback Coupe:** Original Price: $37,495 Production: 19,235 Wheelbase: 104.5 in. Length: 179.7 in. (Front) P245/45-ZR17 (Rear) P275/40-ZR18 **Convertible:** Original Price: $44,425 Production: 11,849 Wheelbase: 104.5 in. Length: 179.7 in. (Front) P245/45-ZR17 (Rear) P275/40-ZR18 Note. A total of 1,163 Corvettes had the Indy Pace Car package.
COOL STUFF	On November 24, 1997 *Motor Trend* magazine picked the 1998 Corvette convertible to be its "Car Of The Year." November 6, 1997 was the date that Chevrolet Motor Division and Indianapolis Motor Speedway announced that a 1998 Corvette Convertible would pace the Indy 500 Race in May 1998. It required a total of 55 hours to manufacture the C5 Corvette, which represented a cut of 70 hours from the time needed to build the C4 model. On November 4, 1997 the 9,752nd 1998 Corvette built rolled down the assembly line. This meant that the total 1997 C5 model production total had been surpassed before the start of the calendar year. The last Fairway Green C5 built was a 1998 model assembled on November 10, 1997. The color was then discontinued.

cars with automatic transmission or $5,804 on cars with manual transmission. The new Active Handling System was required on all Indy Pace Car replicas.

Corvette made its long-awaited return to Trans-Am racing successful by placing first in the 1998 season-opening event on the street circuit at Long Beach, California in the No. 8 AutoLink Corvette driven by veteran road racer Paul Gentilozzi.

Once again in 1998, the LS-1 engine produced 345 hp from 346 cubic inches. *KP Archives*

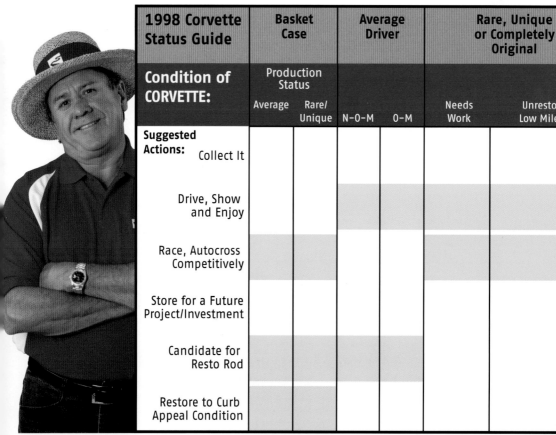

1998 Corvette Status Guide	Basket Case		Average Driver		Rare, Unique or Completely Original	
Condition of CORVETTE: Suggested Actions:	Production Status Average	Rare/ Unique	N-O-M	O-M	Needs Work	Unrestored Low Mileage
Collect It						
Drive, Show and Enjoy						
Race, Autocross Competitively						
Store for a Future Project/Investment						
Candidate for Resto Rod						
Restore to Curb Appeal Condition						

1999 Corvette

The fifth-generation Corvette, in its third model year, added a fixed-roof hardtop to the lineup that already consisted of coupe and convertible body styles.

The fixed-roof coupe model was the first true hardtop Corvette offered since the Stingray convertible/hardtop cars built through 1975. Its styling and rooflines created a third unique profile alongside the removable-roof coupe and the convertible models. Its standard equipment included the six-speed manual transmission, a limited-slip rear axle with 3.42 ratio gearing, the Z-51 suspension with stiff springs, large stabilizer bars and large mono-tube shock absorbers. An automatic transmission was not available in the fixed-roof Corvette.

All 1999 Corvettes were powered by a 5.7-liter LS-1 V-8 with 345 hp. The coupe and convertible used the 4L60-E electronically-controlled four-speed automatic overdrive transmission, with the six-speed manual unit

New in 1999 was a fixed-roof coupe version of the Corvette. *KP Archives*

MIKE YAGER SAYS:	
CHEERS	There were three Corvette models offered in 1999—the coupe, convertible and hardtop. New option packages and offerings included the power telescopic steering wheel, the new power steering system and the "head up" display. The hardtop had a lower base price in 1999. Another edition of the Indianapolis 500 Pace Car was produced in 1999.
JEERS	Once again in 1999, there were no engine performance options and there was no hardtop for the convertible. Wheels look like they came off a wagon.
GAME PLAN	The 1999 Corvette hardtop is highly sought after due to its low production numbers and its unique design.

A family portrait—the 1999 Corvette models included coupe, convertible and hardtop. *KP Archives*

There was always something interesting about Corvettes, even technical drawings! *KP Archives*

1999 'VETTE FACTS	
VEHICLE IDENTIFICATION NUMBER	Corvettes for 1999 were numbered 1G1YY|1/2/3|2G5X5100000 to 1G1YY|1/2/3|2G5X5133283. The first symbol 1 indicated U.S. built. The second symbol G indicated a General Motors product. The third symbol 1 indicated a Chevrolet Motor Division vehicle. The fourth and fifth symbols YY indicated a Corvette. The sixth symbol indicated the body style: 1 = fixed-roof hardtop, GM Style 07, 2 = two-door coupe, GM styles 27, 37, 47 or 57 and 3 = two-door convertible, GM body style 67. The seventh symbol indicated the restraint code: 2 = Active manual belts with driver and front passenger inflatable restraint system, 4 = Active manual belts with frontal and side-impact driver and front passenger inflatable restraint system. The eighth symbol indicated the engine: G = RPO LS-1 5.7-liter sequential multiport-fuel-injection (MFI) Chevrolet V-8. The ninth symbol was a check digit that varied. The 10th symbol indicated the model year X = 1999. The 11th symbol indicated the assembly plant: 5 = Bowling Green, Kentucky. The last six symbols indicated the sequential production numbers starting with 100001.
ENGINE	Engine (LS-1): Type: V-8 Bore and stroke: 3.90 x 3.62 in. Displacement: 346 cid Brake hp: 345 at 5,600 rpm. Induction: SFI
VITAL STATS	**Fixed Roof Coupe:** Original Price: $39,171 Production: 18,078 Wheelbase: 104.5 in. Length: 179.7 in. (Front) P245/45-ZR17 (Rear) P275/40-ZR18 **Hatchback Coupe:** Original Price: $38,777 Production: 4,031 Wheelbase: 104.5 in. Length: 179.7 in. (Front) P245/45-ZR17 (Rear) P275/40-ZR18 **Convertible:** Original Price: $45,579 Production: 11,161 Wheelbase: 104.5 in. Length: 179.7 in. (Front) P245/45-ZR17 (Rear) P275/40-ZR18
COOL STUFF	The new fixed-roof hardtop came only in five of the available 1999 Corvette colors: Arctic White, Light Pewter Metallic, Nassau Blue, Black and Torch Red. The C5-R was the first official factory Corvette race car in history. From the time the car was first tested at Grattan Raceway, in 1997, it was clear that the C5-R was destined to be a champion. The second annual Corvette Hall of Fame event was staged at the National Corvette Museum in Bowling Green, Kentucky on September 3, 1999. NCM Executive Director Wendell Strode introduced Chevrolet's General Marketing Manager Kurt Ritter and John Middlebrook, Vice President and General Manager of Vehicle Brand Marketing for General Motors as the year's speakers. For 1999, NCM Chairman of the Board Jim Minneker inducted race driver Dick Guldstrand, Corvette Chief Engineer Dave McLellan and Chevrolet General Manager Jim Perkins into the Corvette Hall of Fame.

optional. The Z-51 suspension was also on the options list for coupes and convertibles.

Other new options for the "regular" Corvette models included a Head-Up Display (HUD) system which projected key instrumentation readouts onto the windshield to allow drivers to view vehicle vitals without taking their eyes off the road and a "Twilight Sentinel" system with delayed headlight shut off. That system allowed exterior illumination after the ignition was turned off. Corvettes also featured a power telescoping steering column that allowed drivers to more accurately tailor the position of the steering wheel to their specific needs.

All 1999 Corvettes could also be had with an optional Active Handling System (AHS). AHS operated in harmony with the anti-lock braking and traction-control systems to selectively apply any of the four brakes in an effort to help the driver counteract and diffuse dangerous handling characteristics such as over steer and under steer.

Standard Corvette equipment included next-generation dual airbags, air conditioning, leather seating, power door locks and windows, a PassKey II theft-deterrent system, electronic speed control, an electronic Driver Information Center and Remote Function Actuation with Remote Keyless entry system. Leather interiors were standard and came in black, Light Oak, Light Gray and red. Convertible tops were available in white, black and Light Oak.

A fifth-generation Corvette C5 was the official pace car of the 67th running of the 24 Hours of Le Mans in France. Additionally, Chevrolet introduced the Corvette C5-R, a General Motors-engineered and factory-backed GT-2-classed sports car that raced in select U.S. and international events.

This new addition – officially called the

1999 Corvette Status Guide	Basket Case		Average Driver		Rare, Unique or Completely Original	
Condition of CORVETTE:	Production Status					
	Average	Rare/ Unique	N-O-M	O-M	Needs Work	Unrestored Low Mileage
Suggested Actions: Collect It						
Drive, Show and Enjoy						
Race, Autocross Competitively						
Store for a Future Project/Investment						
Candidate for Resto Rod						
Restore to Curb Appeal Condition						

C5-R Corvette GTS racer – was the updated expression of a dream that Zora Arkus-Duntov worked hard to realize throughout his career with GM and honored the Corvette's long and distinguished competition record with a return to road racing.

Starting with the new C5 Corvette, GM created the C5-R, which went on to become the greatest Corvette racing car ever made. The C5-R made its debut with a two-car effort at the Rolex 24 at Daytona in January 1999.

"We hope to use the Corvette race program to illustrate the great characteristics of the Corvette as both a sports car and a race car," said Dave Hill at the time. "This should cause new people to take a look at the Corvette as an alternative to other sports cars. And we've found that once we get people to take a look at the new Corvette, the car sells itself."

All Corvettes came with the 5.7-liter 345-hp LS-1 V-8 engine in 1999. *KP Archives*

There were many options and amenities offered to keep Corvette drivers happy in 1999. *KP Archives*

2000 Corvette

"Still eliciting the passion of bargain-minded speed fiends, the Chevrolet Corvette delivers power, handling and style at a relatively reasonable price," said *Motor Trend* magazine in its October 1999 "Complete Buyer's Guide 2000 & 2001 New Cars" issue. Offered again for the New Millennium were three models powered by the marvelous LS-1 V-8 and suited to a wide range of buyer needs from a luxury touring machine to a street-performance car.

As in 1999, the fixed-roof hardtop was the "loss leader" model from a pricing and marketing standpoint, although it represented a stripped-for-high-performance model from the view of the enthusiast. The Goodyear Eagle F1 tires and an upgraded version of the Z-51 Performance Handling

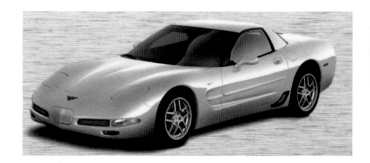

New colors joined older versions in the Corvette lineup. The Z06 would soon follow. *KP Archives*

Corvette designers attempted to please as many tastes as possible with interior choices. *KP Archives*

Another year and more stares, the 2000 Corvette joined a long line of head turners. *KP Archives*

suspension package were offered with this unique-looking body style, which had quickly become the most popular offering in the Corvette model line up.

A coupe and a convertible remained available as well. New exterior and interior color options were the main changes in these models for 2000. A new five-spoke aluminum wheel design with an optional high-polish version was also made available.

The Corvette's standard equipment list again included next-generation dual airbags, air conditioning, leather seating, power door locks and windows, a PassKey II theft-deterrent system, electronic speed control, an electronic Driver Information Center and a Remote Function Actuation system with Remote Keyless Entry.

In sports car racing, the CR-5 Corvette proved itself to be a winner. Early in the

MIKE YAGER SAYS:	
CHEERS	Once again, the 2000 Corvette was offered in three models: the coupe, convertible and hardtop. An improved performance suspension was offered. There was a new wheel design and more interior colors were offered.
JEERS	As in 1999, there was no hardtop offered for the convertible and there were no engine performance options. Single engine choice. No hardtop for convertible. Tires are noisy and wear more easily.
GAME PLAN	The 2000 hardtop is more sought after than the 1999 edition because of its low production numbers and unique design.

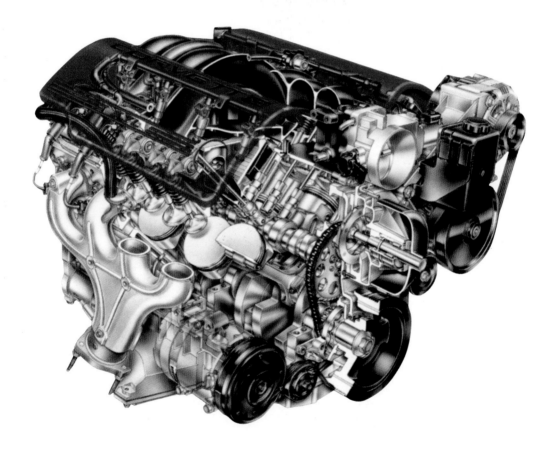

The LS-1 continued to offer 345 horsepower under the hoods of 2000 Corvettes. *KP Archives*

2000 'VETTE FACTS	
VEHICLE IDENTIFICATION NUMBER	Corvettes for 2000 were numbered 1G1YY|1/2/3|2G5Y5100000 to 1G1YY|1/2/3|2G5Y5133682. The first symbol 1 indicated U.S. built. The second symbol G indicated a General Motors product. The third symbol 1 indicated a Chevrolet Motor Division vehicle. The fourth and fifth symbols YY indicated a Corvette. The sixth symbol indicated the body style: 1 = fixed-roof hardtop, 2 = two-door coupe, GM styles 27, 37, 47 or 57 and 3 = two-door convertible GM body style 67. The seventh symbol indicated the restraint code: 2 = Active manual belts with driver and front passenger inflatable restraint system. The eighth symbol indicated the engine: G = RPO LS-1 5.7-liter sequential multiport-fuel-injection (MFI) Chevrolet V-8. The ninth symbol was a check digit that varied. The 10th symbol indicated the model year Y = 2000. The 11th symbol indicated the assembly plant: 5 = Bowling Green, Kentucky. The last six symbols indicated the sequential production numbers.
ENGINE	Engine (LS-1): Type: V-8 Bore and stroke: 3.90 x 3.62 in. Displacement: 346 cid Brake hp: 345 at 5,600 rpm. Induction: SFI
VITAL STATS	**Fixed Roof Coupe:** Original Price: $39,475 Production: 2,090 Wheelbase: 104.5 in. Length: 179.7 in. (Front) P245/45-ZR17 (Rear) P275/40-ZR18 **Hatchback Coupe:** Original Price: $38,900 Production: 18,113 254Wheelbase: 104.5 in. Length: 179.7 in. (Front) P245/45-ZR17 (Rear) P275/40-ZR18 **Convertible:** Original Price: $45,900 Production: 13,479 Wheelbase: 104.5 in. Length: 179.7 in. (Front) P245/45-ZR17 (Rear) P275/40-ZR18
COOL STUFF	Model-year production was 33,682 Corvettes. A total of 3,578 of the cars left the Bowling Green factory with optional Millennium Yellow paint in honor of the Y2K year. This was available on the coupe and convertible only for $500 extra. The National Corvette Museum hosted the 10th anniversary celebration of the World Record Run that was made by a Corvette in 1990. A classic 1969 Corvette coupe with the rare L-88 engine option was sold for $107,000 at a government auction setting a record high price for such a model.

year, in Florida, the 48th Annual Superflo 12 Hours at Sebring race was held and CR-5 Corvette No. 4, driven by Ron Fellows, Chris Kneifel and Justin Bell, placed 16th overall. CR-5 Corvette No. 3, driven by Andy Pilgrim, Kelly Collins and Frank Freon followed up with a 24th overall finish. In March, General Motors took the wraps off a Corvette Pace Car for the 24 Hours of Le Mans and displayed this car at the Chevy/Vette Fest in Chicago.

By that time, it had become clear that it was only a matter of time before the Corvette would be making national and international racing headlines. The big day came on June 17, 2000 when "America's Sports Car" took on the best competitors in the world at Le Mans. By the time France's famous 24-hour endurance race was over, the CR-5 had surprised more than a few skeptics with an impressive finish. The Corvettes came in third and fourth in their class.

The CR-5 racing cars that attacked the Le Mans Mulsanne Corner did so with many of the same parts found in the production car, including its aerodynamic styling, rigid body structure and tremendous suspension geometry. Even the racing engine was derived from the production car's LS-1 power plant. Modifications upped the engine's output to an amazing 620 hp.

On May 4, 2000, the Speedvision automotive cable television network introduced its "Corvette — The American Dream" series. Later, at Lowe's Motor Speedway in Charlotte, Round One of the Speedvision GT Championship was held. Bill Cooper, driving the Les Stanford/Pirate Racing Corvette C5, won the race. MTI Racing's Corvette C5, driven by Reese Cox, took second place.

2000 Corvette Status Guide	Basket Case		Average Driver		Rare, Unique or Completely Original	
Condition of CORVETTE:	Production Status					
	Average	Rare/ Unique	N–O–M	O–M	Needs Work	Unrestored Low Mileage
Suggested Actions: Collect It						
Drive, Show and Enjoy						
Race, Autocross Competitively						
Store for a Future Project/Investment						
Candidate for Resto Rod						
Restore to Curb Appeal Condition						

2001 Corvette

The 2001 Chevrolet Corvette continued as a two-door, two-passenger performance sports car available in three trims. It came as a base coupe and a convertible as well as a new high-performance coupe called the Z06. The coupe and convertible came equipped with a standard 346-cid LS-1 V-8, which had an output increase to 350 hp.

The LS-1 featured an aluminum cylinder block and heads, a 10.1:1 compression ratio, hydraulic valve lifters and sequential multiport fuel injection. It generated 360 lbs.-ft. of torque at 4,800 rpm. The engine was attached to a four-speed automatic transmission. A six-speed manual transmission was optional. A built-in temperature-sensing unit was designed to alert the driver when the transmission oil temperature got too high.

Standard on the C5 coupe were air conditioning, a driver's side airbag, a passenger airbag, alloy wheels, anti-lock brakes, an anti-theft system, cruise control, a rear window defogger, a remote keyless entry system, power locks, power mirrors, heated side mirrors, power steering, power windows, an AM/FM anti-theft radio with cassette, a leather-trimmed power driver's

The first-year Z06 featured special wheels, titanium exhaust and functional brake air vents. *KP Archives*

MIKE YAGER SAYS:	
CHEERS	The new Z06 performance model was an exciting addition in 2001. The LS-6 engine also was new. Titanium exhausts were used for the first time on a production car. The wheel design was improved and the polished wheels were striking. The 2001 Corvettes offered improved performance suspensions and more interior colors.
JEERS	Once again, there was no hardtop offered for the convertible. Corvettes had no provision for a spare tire. The LS6 engine not available in open car configuration.
GAME PLAN	Find a 2001 Corvette convertible made in Dark Bowling Green for your collection!

seat, a tilt steering column, automatic transmission and a Traction Control system. The C5 convertible came with all of the same standard equipment, plus a power antenna.

The newly-introduced Z06 immediately claimed distinction as the quickest, best handling Corvette ever. Its 385-hp LS-6 V-8 and unique six-speed manual transmission with overdrive were combined with a specially engineered lightweight hardtop body to provide a Corvette for the extreme performance enthusiast. The Z06 transmission featured more aggressive gearing for quicker acceleration and more usable torque at various speeds.

The Goodyear tires on the Z06 were made especially for it and were an inch wider than standard tires front and rear, but 23 pounds

The coupe, Z06 and convertible posed for the 2001 Corvette family photo. *KP Archives*

2001 'VETTE FACTS

VEHICLE IDENTIFICATION NUMBER	Corvettes for 2001 were numbered 1G1YY[1/2/3]2[G/S]515100000 and up. The first symbol 1 indicated U.S. built. The second symbol G indicated a General Motors product. The third symbol 1 indicated a Chevrolet Motor Division vehicle. The fourth and fifth symbols YY = Corvette coupe and convertible or YZ = Z06 Hardtop. The sixth symbol indicated the body style: 1 = Z06 hardtop, 2 = two-door coupe, GM styles 27, 37, 47 or 57 and 3 = two-door convertible, GM body style 67. The seventh symbol indicated the restraint code: 2 = Active manual belts with driver and front passenger inflatable restraint system. The eighth symbol indicated the engine: G = RPO LS-1 5.7-liter sequential multiport-fuel-injection (MFI) Chevrolet V-8. S = RPO LS-6 5.7-liter sequential multiport-fuel-injection (MFI) Chevrolet V-8. The ninth symbol was a check digit that varied. The 10th symbol indicated the model year 1 = 2001. The 11th symbol indicated the assembly plant: 5 = Bowling Green, Kentucky. The last six symbols indicated the sequential production numbers.
ENGINE	**Base Engine (LS-1):** Type: V-8 Bore and stroke: 3.90 x 3.62 in. Displacement: 346 cid Brake hp: 350 at 5,600 rpm. Induction: SFI **Optional Engine (LS-6):** Type: V-8 Bore and stroke: 3.90 x 3.62 in. Displacement: 346 cid Brake hp: 385 at 6,000 rpm. Induction: SFI
VITAL STATS	**Coupe:** Original Price: $40,475 Production: 15,681 Wheelbase: 104.5 in. Length: 179.7 in. (Front) P245/45-ZR17 (Rear) P275/40-ZR18 **Convertible:** Original Price: $47,000 Production: 14,173 Wheelbase: 104.5 in. Length: 179.7 in. (Front) P245/45-ZR17 (Rear) P275/40-ZR18 **Z06 Coupe:** Original Price: $47,500 Production: 5,773 Wheelbase: 104.5 in. Length: 179.7 in. (Front) P265/40-ZR17 (Rear) P295/35-ZR18
COOL STUFF	Corvette claimed an important quality control achievement in 2001, winning first place in the respected Initial Quality Study (IQS) by J.D. Power & Associates. The Corvette topped the Premium Sports Car category, populated by makes such as Porsche, Honda and BMW. Bill DeLong – a mechanic on the Corvette ALMS Racing team – won "Mechanic of the Year Award" honors for the Corvette in 2001. On August 16, 2001 General Motors Racing announced it would implement a customer care program to deliver a race-ready version of its successful Chevrolet Corvette C5-R to buyers with what it described as "a passion for performance."

lighter. The Z06 also featured a windshield and backlight made of thinner glass and a titanium exhaust system to reduce its weight by nearly 40 pounds. The Z06 was basically equipped like the coupe, but with AM/FM cassette and radio optional and no automatic transmission availability.

Automobile Magazine awarded the 2001 Corvette Z06 "Automobile of the Year" honors. In its August 2000 issue, Road & Track said of the Z06 "The Empire has struck back in big numbers." That same month, a Motor Trend test driver tested a Z06 and reported, "I did things in the Corvette I wouldn't consider in the Cobra R, things that would result in an off-track excursion and maybe a big crash in the Dodge RT/10." The Automobile Journalists Association of Canada gave the Corvette Z06 its 2001 "Car of the Year Award" for best new sports and performance car.

The competition-proven C5-R began the 2001 racing season with an historic overall win at the Rolex 24 at Daytona. A car with Dale Earnhardt, Dale Earnhardt Jr., Andy Pilgrim and Johnny O'Connell driving finished second in the GTS class and fourth overall. Later that year, the Corvette won at Le Mans when a C5-R took the top two spots in the GTS class. It was only the car's second appearance at Le Mans.

2001 Corvette Status Guide	Basket Case		Average Driver		Rare, Unique or Completely Original	
Condition of CORVETTE:	Production Status					
	Average	Rare/Unique	N-O-M	O-M	Needs Work	Unrestored Low Mileage
Suggested Actions: Collect It						
Drive, Show and Enjoy						
Race, Autocross Competitively						
Store for a Future Project/Investment						
Candidate for Resto Rod						
Restore to Curb Appeal Condition						

The 2001 engines came in 350-hp LS-1 form and 385-hp LS-6 version in 2001. *KP Archives*

The 2001 Z06 Corvettes came with this side fender badge to explain their identities. *KP Archives*

Many power and convenience niceties were standard on the 2001 Corvettes. *KP Archives*

2002 Corvette

All 2002 Corvettes had a second-generation Active Handling system. It featured dynamic rear brake proportioning to prevent rear wheel lockup, plus rear brake stability control to assist drivers in maintaining control under light braking and high-acceleration conditions. It also had integral traction control calibrated to allow better power and handling, while controlling excessive wheel spin. The system's on/off switch and "Competitive Mode" enabled drivers to disengage traction control without giving up Active Handling's other benefits.

The 2002 automatic transmission cooler case was constructed of lightweight cast aluminum, replacing stainless steel. Coupes and convertibles received an AM/FM/In-dash CD system as the new standard entertainment system. An AM/FM/cassette system was available when buyers ordered the remote 12-disc CD changer, which was also available with a CD radio.

The open top advocates enjoyed absorbing sun and sky in their 2002 Corvettes. *KP Archives*

There was no shortage of amenities inside the 2002 Corvettes. *KP Archives*

Corvette models were the convertible, coupe and Z06 for the 2002 model year. *KP Archives*

MIKE YAGER SAYS:	
CHEERS	The new Z06 performance V-8 produced 405 hp! Active handling in the 2002 Corvette was improved. The 2002 Corvette offered new engineering enhancements.
JEERS	No engine choices for targa top or convertibles. No provision for a spare tire on all 2002 Corvettes and there was no hardtop offered for the convertible.
GAME PLAN	This is a fantastic series of cars—a great value, especially the 2002 convertible and the Z06.

A 2002 Corvette coupe was posed for this official company image. *KP Archives*

Standard on the C5 coupe was air conditioning, a driver airbag, a passenger airbag, alloy wheels, anti-lock brakes, an anti-theft system, cruise control, a rear defogger, remote keyless entry, power locks, power mirrors, heated side mirrors, power steering, power windows, an AM/FM anti-theft radio with cassette, a leather-trimmed power driver's seat, tilt steering, an automatic transmission and the Traction Control system. The C5 convertible came with all of the same standard equipment, plus a power antenna.

The Z06 Corvette was aimed at the upper end of the high-performance market. For 2002, a 20-hp boost made the Z06 the quickest production Corvette ever. This improvement was the result of new hollow-stem valves, a higher-lift camshaft, a low-restriction mass air flow (MAF) sensor and a new low-restriction air cleaner. Eliminating the PUP converter from the exhaust system enabled better flow of spent gasses and reduced vehicle weight without compromising the car's National Low Emission Vehicle (NLEV) status.

A Z06-specific FE-4 high-performance

2002 'VETTE FACTS	
VEHICLE IDENTIFICATION NUMBER	Corvettes for 2001 were numbered 1G1YY|1/2/3|2|G/S|515100000 and up. The first symbol 1 indicated U.S. built. The second symbol G indicated a General Motors product. The third symbol 1 indicated a Chevrolet Motor Division vehicle. The fourth and fifth symbols YY = Corvette coupe or convertible and YZ = Corvette Z06 Hardtop. The sixth symbol indicated the body style: 1 = Z06 hardtop, 2 = two-door coupe, GM styles 27, 37, 47 or 57 and 3 = two-door convertible, GM body style 67. The seventh symbol indicated the restraint code: 2 = Active manual belts with driver and front passenger inflatable restraint system. The eighth symbol indicated the engine: G = RPO LS1 5.7-liter sequential multiport-fuel-injection (MFI) Chevrolet V-8. S = RPO LS6 5.7-liter sequential multiport-fuel-injection (MFI) Chevrolet V-8. The ninth symbol was a check digit that varied. The 10th symbol indicated the model year 2 = 2002. The 11th symbol indicated the assembly plant: 5 = Bowling Green, Kentucky. The last six symbols indicated the sequential production numbers.
ENGINE	**Base Engine (LS-1):** Type: V-8 Bore and stroke: 3.90 x 3.62 in. Displacement: 346 cid Brake hp: 350 at 5,600 rpm. Induction: SFI **Optional Engine (LS-6):** Type: V-8 Bore and stroke: 3.90 x 3.62 in. Displacement: 346 cid Brake hp: 405 at 6,000 rpm. Induction: SFI
VITAL STATS	**Hatchback Coupe:** Original Price: $41,855 Production: 14,760 Wheelbase: 104.5 in. Length: 179.7 in. (Front) P245/45-ZR17 (Rear) P275/40-ZR18 **Convertible:** Original Price: $48,380 Production: 12,710 Wheelbase: 104.5 in. Length: 179.7 in. (Front) P245/45-ZR17 (Rear) P275/40-ZR18 **Z06 Coupe:** Original Price: $50,555 Production: 8,297 Wheelbase: 104.5 in. Length: 179.7 in. (Front) P265/40-ZR17 (Rear) P295/35-ZR18
COOL STUFF	Corvette Racing won its first American Le Mans Series driving championship in 2002. The ALMS Driver's Championship that went to Corvette pilot Ron Fellows was also the first of four in a row that Corvette Racing would capture. *Automobile Magazine* named the Corvette the "Racing Car of the Year" and noted its incredible track success, as well as the CR-5's strong connection to the C5 production car The Corvette won its second consecutive J. D. Power IQS award. J. D. Power gave the Bowling Green Assembly Plant its Silver Award for being the industry's 2nd-highest quality plant in North America.

suspension featured a larger front stabilizer bar, revised shock valving, a stiffer rear leaf spring and specific camber settings – all calibrated for maximum control during high-speed operation. The Z06 also had new rear shock valving for a more controlled ride.

Although retaining the 2001 design and color, the unique aluminum Z06 wheels were cast, rather than forged. Hydroformed frame rails and a four-wheel independent suspension with cast-aluminum upper and lower front A-arms were other Z06 features.

The Z06 (and C-5 Corvettes equipped with the Z-51 package) now had aluminum front stabilizer bar links and reduced weight. The rear suspension had a transverse leaf spring system. Now standard on Z06s, the Head-Up Display (HUD) system projected gauges digitally on the windshield, ahead of the steering wheel, enabling the driver to keep his or her eyes on the road.

New high-performance front brake pads on the Z06 provided improved lining durability and fade resistance in high-performance situations. Electron Blue took the place of Speedway White as one of five Z06 colors. An AM/FM cassette/radio was optional and no automatic transmission was offered.

Corvette Racing ran 11 races in 2002 and won 10 of them. Ron Fellows took the ALMS Driver Championship and Chevrolet was the winning manufacturer. CR-5s took first and second places in GTS class at the 24 Hours of Le Mans.

2002 Corvette Status Guide	Basket Case		Average Driver		Rare, Unique or Completely Original	
Condition of CORVETTE:	Production Status					
	Average	Rare/ Unique	N-O-M	O-M	Needs Work	Unrestored Low Mileage
Suggested Actions: Collect It						
Drive, Show and Enjoy						
Race, Autocross Competitively						
Store for a Future Project/Investment						
Candidate for Resto Rod						
Restore to Curb Appeal Condition						

The new LS-6 V-8 offered the return of muscle, in this case, 405 horsepower. *GM*

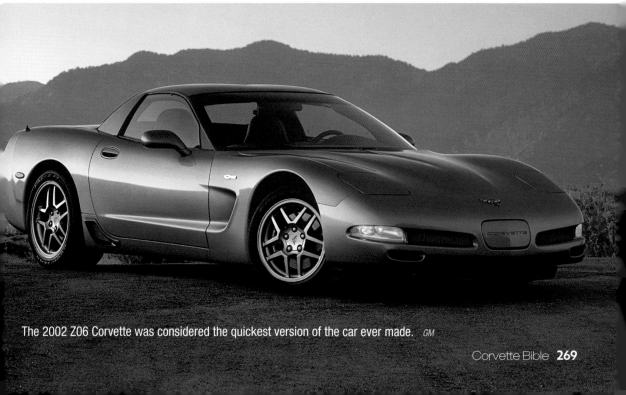

The 2002 Z06 Corvette was considered the quickest version of the car ever made. *GM*

2003 Corvette

For 2003, Chevrolet's image machine continued to reign as one of GM's technology and style bellwethers. Highlights included a 50th Anniversary Edition package, more standard equipment on the coupe and convertible models and the availability of Magnetic Selective Ride Control. This used a revolutionary damper design that controlled wheel and body motion with Magnetic-Rheological fluid in the shock absorbers.

CORVETTE

The 2003 50th anniversary Corvette coupe and convertible make a beautiful pair. *Phil Hall Collection*

The Corvette sporting heritage was combined with the 50th anniversary logo. *Phil Hall Collection*

This was the interior of the 50th anniversary Corvette depicted in its 2003 brochure. *Phil Hall Collection*

MIKE YAGER SAYS:	
CHEERS	The special 50th Anniversary model was a highlight of 2003 Corvettes.
JEERS	There was a new Indy Pace Car but no replicas were offered. No provision for spare tire. No hardtop offered for the convertible. Lack of engine choices. Tire noise.
GAME PLAN	One collector car I passed up was the 50th Anniversary Edition convertible!

New standard equipment for coupe and convertible models included fog lamps, sport seats, a power passenger seat, dual-zone auto HVAC and a parcel net. The coupe had a luggage shade. Also standard on the C5 coupe was air conditioning, a driver's side airbag, alloy wheels, anti-lock brakes, an anti-theft system, cruise control, a rear window defogger, remote keyless entry system, power locks, power mirrors, heated side mirrors, power steering, power windows, an AM/FM anti-theft radio with cassette, a leather-trimmed power driver's seat, a tachometer, tilt steering wheel, an automatic transmission and the Traction Control system. Child Restraint Attachment System (CRAS) child seat hooks on the passenger seat allowed easier connection of child safety seats. The air bag "off" switch was used to disable the passenger side air bag when a child seat was installed. All 2003 Corvettes featured a special 50th anniversary emblem on the front and rear. The emblem was Silver and featured the number "50" with the signature cross-flag design. In addition, Medium Spiral Gray Metallic exterior paint replaced Pewter in 2003.

The 50th Anniversary Edition package was available only during the 2003 model year on coupes and convertibles. It included special 50th Anniversary Red exterior paint, specific badges, a unique Shale interior and champagne-painted anniversary wheels with special emblems. It also featured embroidered badges on the seats and floor mats, padded door armrests and grips and a Shale convertible top. The Anniversary Edition had the standard Corvette LS-1 engine as well as Magnetic Selective Ride Control. A special 50th Anniversary Edition of the 2003 Corvette was the Official Pace Car of the Indianapolis 500 in May.

At the time of the Indianapolis 500, the three 2003 Corvettes provided to the Speedway for pace car duties were the only 2003 models in existence. Actor Jim Caviezel led the field to the green flag on May 26. The Corvette Pace Car was virtually identical to the 50th Anniversary Edition Coupe. It was equipped with the LS-1 V-8. A few modifications included special exterior graphics wrapped over the "Anniversary Red" exterior and a lower-restriction muffler system. A four-point racing-type safety belt

2003 'VETTE FACTS	
VEHICLE IDENTIFICATION NUMBER	Corvettes for 2003 were numbered 1G1YY|1/2/3|2|G/S|535100001 to 1G1YY|1/2/3|2|G/S|835135468. The first symbol 1 indicated U.S. built. The second symbol G indicated a General Motors product. The third symbol 1 indicated a Chevrolet Motor Division vehicle. The fourth and fifth symbols YY = Corvette coupe or convertible and YZ = Corvette Z06 Hardtop. The sixth symbol indicated the body style: 1 = Z06 hardtop, 2 = two-door coupe, GM styles 27, 37, 47 or 57 and 3 = two-door convertible, GM body style 67. The seventh symbol indicated the restraint code: 2 = Active manual belts with driver and front passenger inflatable restraint system. The eighth symbol indicated the engine: G = RPO LS1 5.7-liter sequential multiport-fuel-injection (MFI) Chevrolet V-8. S = RPO LS6 5.7-liter sequential multiport-fuel-injection (MFI) Chevrolet V-8. The ninth symbol was a check digit that varied. The 10th symbol indicated the model year 3 = 2003. The 11th symbol indicated the assembly plant: 5 = Bowling Green, Kentucky. The last six symbols indicated the sequential production numbers.
ENGINE	**Base Engine (LS-1):** Type: V-8 Bore and stroke: 3.90 x 3.62 in. Displacement: 346 cid Brake hp: 350 at 5,600 rpm. Induction: SFI **Optional Engine (LS-6):** Type: V-8 Bore and stroke: 3.90 x 3.62 in. Displacement: 346 cid Brake hp: 405 at 6,000 rpm. Induction: SFI
VITAL STATS	**Coupe:** Original Price: $43,475 Production: 12,812 Wheelbase: 104.5 in. Length: 179.7 in. (Front) P245/45-ZR17 (Rear) P275/40-ZR18 **Convertible:** Original Price: $50,375 Production: 14,022 Wheelbase: 104.5 in. Length: 179.7 in. (Front) P245/45-ZR17 (Rear) P275/40-ZR18 **Z06 Coupe:** Original Price: $51,275 Production: 8,635 Wheelbase: 104.5 in. Length: 179.7 in. (Front) P265/40-ZR17 (Rear) P295/35-ZR18
COOL STUFF	"Few vehicles have had the staying power of Corvette," said Rick Baldick, Corvette brand manager, when the 2003 models arrived. "We believe much of that success comes from a willingness to embrace advancing technology while remaining true to Corvette's glorious history. As we celebrate our golden anniversary in 2003, we honor our past and cast a bright eye toward the future." Early in May 2003, GM Racing and the U. S. Armed Forces teamed up for a good will tour following the Corvette Racing team's practice session at Le Mans. The Corvette C5-R team also played host to dozens of U. S. Naval officers throughout the racing season, as part of the Navy Pit Crew. It was a program that selected 10 sailors from across America to join the Corvette Racing team as special guests at three American Le Mans Series races. The sailors selected got involved in pit activities and spent time with the Corvette racing drivers. After a dominating victory at the 12 Hours of Sebring in March (where Johnny O'Connell, driver of the #53 Corvette, took the checkered flag) the Corvette Racing team returned to the 24 Hours of Le Mans in June with two all-new race cars to defend their GTS title. Already the most successful Corvette in racing history, the Corvette C5-R competition coupe was the two-time defending GTS class champion at the legendary Le Sarthe circuit and in the American Le Mans Series. During 2003, the Morgan Mint honored the Corvette on genuine legal tender U. S. coins. One coin featured the original 1953 Corvette and the other featured the exclusive 50th Anniversary Edition. Both coins were colorized by the Morgan Mint. A limited number of 2003 Silver Eagles was set aside for this Corvette collector's edition. The National Corvette Museum served as the overall host of the third National Corvette Caravan in June 2003. Starting from the borders of the continental United States and joined by participants from all over the world, caravans swept across the country, converging on Bowling Green, Kentucky, from June 25 to 27 for special anniversary events. There were numerous activities along the route traveled by the merging caravans that made their way to Nashville, Tennessee, on June 27 and 28 to take part in the Chevrolet-sponsored Corvette 50th Anniversary Celebration.

setup and a safety strobe light system were also required by the Indy Racing League. A heavy-duty transmission and power steering cooler were added to the three Corvette Pace Cars.

The Z06 Corvette included a special engine, a unique six-speed manual gearbox, hollow-stem valves, a high-life camshaft, a low-restriction mass air flow (MAF) sensor, a low-restriction air cleaner, a high-performance exhaust system, a Z06-specific FE4 high-performance suspension system, a fat front stabilizer, revised shock absorber valving, a stiffer rear spring, specific camber settings, hydroformed frame rails, a four-wheel independent suspension with cast aluminum upper and lower A arms, aluminum front stabilizer links, a transverse spring system, the Head-Up Display (HUD) system and high-performance front brake pads. An AM/FM cassette/ radio was optional in the Z06 and no automatic transmission was offered.

2003 Corvette Status Guide	Basket Case		Average Driver		Rare, Unique or Completely Original	
Condition of CORVETTE:	Production Status					
	Average	Rare/ Unique	N–O–M	O–M	Needs Work	Unrestored Low Mileage
Suggested Actions: Collect It						
Drive, Show and Enjoy						
Race, Autocross Competitively						
Store for a Future Project/Investment						
Candidate for Resto Rod						
Restore to Curb Appeal Condition						

2004 Corvette

Chevrolet continued to celebrate the Corvette's golden anniversary in 2004 with efforts to keep the car fresh and "cutting edge." Standard equipment included a 5.7-liter V-8, a four-speed automatic transmission, rear-wheel drive with a limited-slip rear axle, 17 x 8.5 front and 18 x 9.5-in. rear alloy wheel rims, Goodyear Eagle F1 GS Extended Mobility run-flat tires, four-wheel independent suspension, front and rear stabilizer bars, front and rear ventilated disc ABS brakes, a passenger airbag deactivation switch, daytime running lights, dusk-sensing headlights, automatic delay on/off headlights, front fog lights, variable intermittent windshield wipers, a rear window defogger, two-passenger seating with leather bucket seats, a six-way power height adjustable driver's seat with adjustable lumbar support, remote power door locks, one-touch power windows, heated power mirrors, an AM/FM stereo cassette, four Bose premium-brand radio speakers, an element antenna, speed-proportional power steering, air conditioning, front reading lights, dual illuminating visor vanity mirrors, a leather-wrapped steering wheel, front floor mats, a cargo area light, a trip computer, a clock and low-fuel indicator. In addition to or in place

The 2004 Corvette Z06 Commemorative Edition coupe featured some obvious hints of a racing heritage. *Tom Glatch*

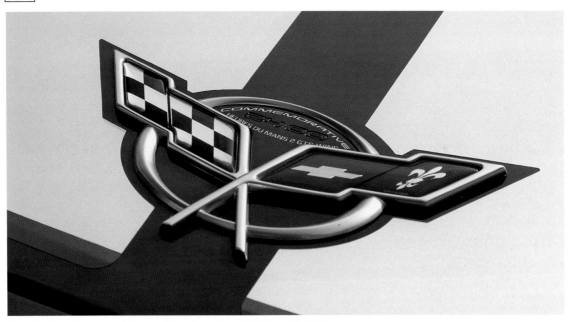

A shot of the Commemorative emblem from the 2004 Corvette Z06. *Tom Glatch*

The interior of the 2004 Z06 was all Corvette—plush, sporty and functional. *Tom Glatch*

The 2004 Commemorative Edition was available in coupe, convertible and Z06 forms. *KP Archives*

The 2004 Z06 Commemorative Edition was a tribute to the Le Mans wins. *Tom Glatch*

MIKE YAGER SAYS:	
CHEERS	The Commemorative Edition was something special—and it was available on the Z06, too! There was yet another Indy Pace Car and, once again, no replicas were offered. This was the last year for the C5 Corvette.
JEERS	Nothing new. No provision for a spare tire. No hardtop offered for convertibles. No performance engines for targa tops or convertibles.
GAME PLAN	Choose any of the Commemorative Editions—the convertible or the Z06!

The 2004 Commemorative Edition sported this stylistic Z06 logo. *Tom Glatch*

Inside the engine bay was the Z06 LS-6 350-cid V-8 that produced 405 hp. *Tom Glatch*

2004 'VETTE FACTS	
VEHICLE IDENTIFICATION NUMBER	Corvettes for 2004 were numbered 1G1YY|1/2/3|2|G/S|345100001 to 1G1YY|1/2/3|2|G/S|X45134064. The first symbol 1 indicated U.S. built. The second symbol G indicated a General Motors product. The third symbol 1 indicated a Chevrolet Motor Division vehicle. The fourth and fifth symbols YY = Corvette coupe or convertible and YZ = Corvette Z06 Hardtop. The sixth symbol indicated the body style: 1 = Z06 hardtop, 2 = two-door coupe, GM styles 27, 37, 47 or 57 and 3 = two-door convertible, GM body style 67. The seventh symbol indicated the restraint code: 2 = Active manual belts with driver and front passenger inflatable restraint system. The eighth symbol indicated the engine: G = RPO LS1 5.7-liter sequential multiport-fuel-injection (MFI) Chevrolet V-8. S = RPO LS6 5.7-liter sequential multiport-fuel-injection (MFI) Chevrolet V-8. The ninth symbol was a check digit that varied. The 10th symbol indicated the model year 4 = 2004. The 11th symbol indicated the assembly plant: 5 = Bowling Green, Kentucky. The last six symbols indicated the sequential production numbers.
ENGINE	**Base Engine (LS-1):** Type: V-8 Bore and stroke: 3.90 x 3.62 in. Displacement: 346 cid Brake hp: 350 at 5,600 rpm. Induction: SFI **Optional Engine (LS-6):** Type: V-8 Bore and stroke: 3.90 x 3.62 in. Displacement: 346 cid Brake hp: 405 at 6,000 rpm. Induction: SFI
VITAL STATS	**Coupe:** Original Price: $44,535 Production: 16,165 Wheelbase: 104.5 in. Length: 179.7 in. (Front) P245/45-ZR17 (Rear) P275/40-ZR18 **Convertible:** Original Price: $51,535 Production: 12,216 Wheelbase: 104.5 in. Length: 179.7 in. (Front) P245/45-ZR17 (Rear) P275/40-ZR18 **Z06 Coupe:** Original Price: $52,385 Production: 5,683 Wheelbase: 104.5 in. Length: 179.7 in. (Front) P265/40-ZR17 (Rear) P295/35-ZR18
COOL STUFF	On April 24, 2003, Chevrolet announced a special Commemorative Edition 2004 Corvette to celebrate Corvette Racing's historic Le Mans victories and the 2001 and 2002 GTS class championships at the famed 24 Hours of Le Mans. The 2004 Commemorative Edition Z06 featured a new hood using carbon fiber material, new exterior graphics and unique Le Mans Blue paint. A Silver and Red center graphic designed for the 2003 Le Mans racing car was also used on a limited number of 2004 Commemorative Edition Z06 Corvettes. Commemorative Edition coupes and convertibles also were built in 2004. The 2004 Commemorative Edition coupes and convertibles shared an exclusive package of styling amenities with the Z06 version. They included Le Mans Blue paint, a Shale-colored interior, a Commemorative Edition exterior badge noting Corvette's Le Mans titles and special embroidery on the headrests of each seat. Led by the new, sixth-generation Corvette, General Motors reinforced its commitment to producing compelling vehicles with the introduction of several new concept and production models at the 2004 North American International Auto Show in Detroit. Marking the sixth generation of its legacy, the 2005 Corvette C6 was designed to deliver more power, passion and precision to reach a new standard of performance car excellence. The Corvette performed the Indianapolis 500 pace car duties for a record sixth time. This also marked the third consecutive year and the 15th time overall that a Chevrolet product had served as the official pace vehicle—the most appearances by any brand.

of those features, the convertible featured a folding manual roof, a glass convertible rear window, a remote trunk release and a trunk light.

A 2004 Corvette convertible was selected to serve as the Official Pace Car at that year's Indianapolis 500. Very few modifications were made. They included a heavy-duty transmission, power steering coolers, a lower restriction muffler system, four-point racing-type safety belts and a safety strobe light system. A two-tone white and blue Indy Pace Car paint treatment incorporated Americana-themed graphics to tie into Chevrolet's new "An American Revolution" marketing theme. The theme highlighted innovation and success in motorsports.

All 2004 model Z06 Corvettes featured revised chassis tuning for quicker, smoother response in challenging environments. GM engineers refined the Z06's shock damping characteristics to provide improved handling. Refinement of the shock valves, in particular, resulted in more damping control and force delivered more smoothly. The new tuning was aimed at diminishing the impact of yaw and roll on the car. It was the result of testing at Germany's Nurburgring circuit. The Z06 Corvette also included a unique six-speed manual gearbox, a Z06-specific FE-4 high-performance suspension system, hydroformed frame rails, the Head-Up Display (HUD) system and high-performance front brake pads.

2004 Corvette Status Guide	Basket Case		Average Driver		Rare, Unique or Completely Original	
Condition of CORVETTE:	Production Status					
	Average	Rare/ Unique	N–O–M	O–M	Needs Work	Unrestored Low Mileage
Suggested Actions: Collect It						
Drive, Show and Enjoy						
Race, Autocross Competitively						
Store for a Future Project/Investment						
Candidate for Resto Rod						
Restore to Curb Appeal Condition						

The 2004 Commemorative Edition package recognized the success of the C5-R competition coupes. It featured new Le Mans Blue paint with a Shale interior, special badges and polished wheels. The convertible's top also was Shale to match the interior. The Commemorative Edition package included special badges, special seat embroidery and RPO QF5 high-polished, five-spoke aluminum wheels with specific center caps. For coupes and convertibles, the Commemorative Edition package was only available with the 1SC package, a $3,700 option. A lightweight, race-inspired carbon fiber hood was used on Z06s with the Commemorative Edition option. It weighed 10.6 pounds less than the standard hood. The only visual clue that the hood is made from carbon fiber was a red border surrounding the silver graphic on the car. It was arranged in a woven pattern signifying the material underneath.

A Corvette often is unmistakable from any angle, like this 2004 coupe. *Tom Glatch*

2005 Corvette

The C6 Coupe bowed at the North American International Auto Show in Detroit in January 2004. Production started later and a C6 convertible followed. The C6 blended technical sophistication and expressive style. It was shorter than the C5 and had a tighter profile with virtually no loss of space. It had handling, acceleration and braking upgrades. With a 0.28 drag coefficient it was the most aerodynamic Corvette ever. Anti-lift characteristics were improved.

Power came from a new LS-2 6.0-liter V-8 based on GM's new Gen IV small-block family of engines. It generated 400 hp and 400 lb.-ft. of torque and was the largest, most powerful standard small-block used in a Corvette.

The 2005 Corvette coupe was captured in its sleek splendor on a sunny day. *Mike Mueller*

Millennium Yellow is a great color option for this All-American beauty. *Mike Mueller*

It also boasted the best horsepower to fuel economy ratio of all performance cars.

Major transmission revisions aided performance driving. The Tremec six-speed manual was available with two sets of ratios – the quicker one part of a Z-51 Performance Package. New synchronizers reduced travel by 10 percent and improved shifting characteristics. An inch shorter shifter knob improved driver operation. The Hydra-Matic 4L65-E was an upgraded version of the 4L60-E strengthened for the LS-2. It included advanced Performance Algorithm Shifting and shifted at higher revs to match engine output.

The signature of the C6 was an expressive new design combining classic Corvette cues in a completely fresh and contemporary fashion. It was five inches shorter and roughly one inch narrower than the C5 for greater agility and performance, plus a lean, muscular form. The C6 included larger 18-inch front/19-inch rear wheels topped by dramatic fender forms, plus a crisply tapered rear deck and fascia that supported improved high-speed performance. The C6 had more character in its front and rear fascias, exposed headlights (the first since 1962), round taillights and integrated exhaust tips.

MIKE YAGER SAYS:	
CHEERS	The all new Corvette C6 debuted in 2005 with a coupe and a convertible model. The C6 included fixed headlights—the hidden headlamps were gone. The cars had a push button start. The base engine was the LS-2 6.0 liter V-8 with more than 400 hp. The C6 also had a stronger 4L65 automatic transmission. The C6 had a touch-activated entry system. The power convertible top was back for the first time since 1962! The C6 featured enlarged wheels with cross-drilled rotors and EMT tires.
JEERS	Unfortunately, there was no Z06 offered. The 2005 Corvette tires were a weak point. Transparent top = very warm interior.
GAME PLAN	Look for a rare Monterey-colored coupe. I have one. There were only 700 Corvettes made in this rare early color.

186mph

A subtle hint that the 2005 Corvette could easily exceed the speed limit. *KP Archives*

2005 'VETTE FACTS	
VEHICLE IDENTIFICATION NUMBER	Corvettes for 2005 were numbered 1G1YY[2/3](2/4)U855100001 and up. The first symbol 1 indicated U.S. built. The second symbol G indicated a General Motors product. The third symbol 1 indicated a Chevrolet Motor Division vehicle. The fourth and fifth symbols YY = Corvette coupe or convertible. The sixth symbol indicated the body style: 2 = two-door coupe, GM styles 27, 37, 47 or 57 and 3 = two-door convertible, GM body style 67. The seventh symbol indicated the restraint code: 2 = Active manual belts with driver and front passenger inflatable restraint system; 4 = Active manual belts with front and side inflatable restraint system. The eighth symbol indicated the engine: U = RPO LS2 364-cid sequential multiport-fuel-injection (MFI) Chevrolet V-8. The ninth symbol was a check digit that varied. The 10th symbol indicated the model year 5 = 2005. The 11th symbol indicated the assembly plant: 5 = Bowling Green, Kentucky. The last six symbols indicated the sequential production numbers.
ENGINE	Base Engine (LS-2): Type: V-8 Bore and stroke: 4.00 x 3.62 in. Displacement: 364 cid Brake hp: 400 at 6,000 rpm. Induction: SFI
VITAL STATS	**Coupe:** Original Price: $44,245 Production: 26,728 Wheelbase: 105.7 in. Length: 174.6 in. (Front) P245/40-ZR18 (Rear) P285/35-ZR19 **Convertible:** Original Price: $52,245 Production: 12,710 Wheelbase: 105.7 in. Length: 174.6 in. (Front) P245/40-ZR18 (Rear) P285/35-ZR19
COOL STUFF	As soon as the 2004 Los Angeles Automobile Show opened on Monday, January 5th, hundreds of Corvette owners and enthusiasts clustered around the first C6 to go on public view. "The C6 is more competition-influenced – given our championship experience with Corvette Racing – than any previous Corvette," Dave Hill said. "Our goal was a performance car at home in virtually any environment. The C6 manual transmission had a lock-out forcing a driver to shift from 1st directly to 4th when operating at lower RPMs to boost fuel economy and allow the C6 to avoid the "gas guzzler tax." An aftermarket CAGS eliminator that costs about $20 can be installed to allow a normal 1-2-3-4-5-6 pattern at any speed range. The same six racing drivers that piloted the C5-Rs to an historical undefeated season in 2004 returned to the track in 2005: Ron Fellows, Johnny O'Connell and Max Papis drove the No. 3 Corvette C6-R and Oliver Gavin, Olivier Beretta and Jan Magnussen drove the No. 4 car.

A twin-cockpit interior incorporated sophisticated contours, leather-like surfaces and details like metallic accents and expressive use of color. The instrument panel and door trim areas had a cast skin that retained the feel of genuine leather with excellent softness and a low gloss, low glare premium-quality appearance. Anodized aluminum accented the interior in functional areas, such as the manual shift knob and door release buttons and included a screen-printed appliqué that minimized sun glare, heat and fingerprints.

The C6 had many new electronic

technologies including Keyless Access with push-button start. Options included a reconfigurable head-up display, a DVD-navigation system with voice activation, XM Satellite Radio and OnStar.

The body combined low weight, high strength, cored composite floors, an enclosed center tunnel, a rear axle-mounted transmission and an aluminum cockpit structure with enhanced structural integrity, feel, refinement and quietness. A short-long arm and transverse leaf spring independent suspension remained, but the cradles, control arms, knuckles, springs, dampers, bushings, stabilizer bars and steering gear were redesigned. Extended Mobility Tires were new. Standard,

Magnetic Selective Ride Control and Z-51 suspensions could be selected. An improved MSRC setup allowed more differentiation between "Tour" and "Sport" settings. The Z-51 Performance Package brought the Corvette Coupe performance very close that of the Z06.

A new C6-R race car debuted at the 12 Hours of Sebring in March 2005 after a year of rigorous testing and development. A two-car, factory-backed team competed in the production-based GT-1 class (formerly GTS) of the American Le Mans Series as well as the legendary 24 Hours of Le Mans in France. The new C6-R was the most technically advanced sports car ever developed by GM.

2005 Corvette Status Guide	Basket Case		Average Driver		Rare, Unique or Completely Original	
Condition of CORVETTE:	Production Status					
	Average	Rare/ Unique	N-O-M	O-M	Needs Work	Unrestored Low Mileage
Suggested Actions: Collect It						
Drive, Show and Enjoy						
Race, Autocross Competitively						
Store for a Future Project/Investment						
Candidate for Resto Rod						
Restore to Curb Appeal Condition						

2006 Corvette

The 2006 C6's features and refinements enhanced a car that was new-for-2005. The 2006 coupe and convertible continued to use the 6.0-liter LS-2 V-8 matched to a rear transaxle that helped improve vehicle weight balance. The six-speed manual was standard. A new six-speed paddle shift transmission with automatic modes was available. The front and rear short/long arm suspensions were the most competition-oriented in Corvette history.

Dramatic fender forms and exposed headlamps combined with the grille to create a strong visual identity for the Corvette, while the tapered rear deck and fascia aided high-speed performance. Fixed Xenon high-intensity discharge headlights provided superior lighting.

The 2006 convertible featured an optional power-operated soft top. An easy-to-operate manual top was standard. Both used a five-layer fabric that concealed the underlying structure for a good top-up appearance, while preserving the car's excellent aerodynamics and reducing road noise.

The interior had a blend of high-quality materials, craftsmanship and functionality provided premium quality and enhanced

The engineers at Chevrolet tell me this car is "95% perfect".　*Mike Mueller*

MIKE YAGER SAYS:	
CHEERS	There was another all-new Corvette, the late arriving Z06! Some positives of the Z06 were its aluminum and carbon fiber construction and its 7.0-liter, 505-hp V-8. The six-speed, paddle shifting automatic transmission was exciting in 2006. Red, white and blue Indy Pace Cars were made but were not offered for sale.
JEERS	The Corvette's tires continued to be a weak point. Transparent top = very warm interior.
GAME PLAN	Drive it and love it!

The dramatic red valve covers show off the 2006 Corvette Z06 V-8 engine. *Mike Mueller*

One futuristic look on the 2006 Corvette Z06 back end were twin dual exhausts. *Mike Mueller*

2006 'VETTE FACTS	
VEHICLE IDENTIFICATION NUMBER	Corvette coupes and convertibles for 2006 were numbered 1G1YY|2/3|(2/4)U855100001 and up. The first symbol 1 indicated U.S. built. The second symbol G indicated a General Motors product. The third symbol 1 indicated a Chevrolet Motor Division vehicle. The fourth and fifth symbols YY = Corvette coupe or convertible. The sixth symbol indicated the body style: 2 = two-door coupe, GM styles 27, 37, 47 or 57 and 3 = two-door convertible, GM body style 67. The seventh symbol indicated the restraint code: 2 = Active manual belts with driver and front passenger inflatable restraint system; 4 = Active manual belts with front and side inflatable restraint system. The eighth symbol indicated the engine: U = RPO LS2 364-cid sequential multiport-fuel-injection (MFI) Chevrolet V-8. The ninth symbol was a check digit that varied. The 10th symbol indicated the model year 6 = 2006. The 11th symbol indicated the assembly plant: 5 = Bowling Green, Kentucky. The last six symbols indicated the sequential production numbers.
ENGINE	**Base Engine (LS-2):** Type: V-8 Bore and stroke: 4.00 x 3.62 in. Displacement: 364 cid Brake hp: 400 at 6,000 rpm. Induction: SFI **Z06 Engine (LS-7):** Type: V-8 Bore and stroke: 4.125 x 4.00 in. Displacement: 427 cid Brake hp: 505 at 6,300 rpm. Induction: SFI
VITAL STATS	**Coupe:** Original Price: $44,490 Production: 34,021 Wheelbase: 105.7 in. Length: 174.6 in. (Front) P245/40-ZR18 (Rear) P285/35-ZR19 **Convertible:** Original Price: $52,190 Production: 11,151 Wheelbase: 105.7 in. Length: 174.6 in. (Front) P245/40-ZR18 (Rear) P285/35-ZR19 **Z06 Fixed Roof Coupe** Original Price: $65,690 Production: 6,272 Wheelbase: 105.7 in. Length: 175.6 in. (Front) P275/35-ZR18 (Rear) P325/30-ZR19
COOL STUFF	Previous Z06 models, from the original 1963 model to the 2001 through 2004 editions, incorporated upgrades to existing Corvettes. None was as heavily revised as the 2006 Z06. Two racing icons united when Lance Armstrong, seven-time Tour de France winner, drove the 2006 Corvette Z06 pace car to lead the field to the start of the 90th running of the Indy 500 on May 28, 2006. For a record 17th time, a Chevy paced the race and a Corvette led the pack for the eighth time. Corvette racing achieved its goal for 2006. In a battle for the championship in a year the marked the Corvette's 50th year of racing the bow-tie brand captured ALMS manufacturers, drivers and team championships. Corvette pilots Oliver Beretta and Oliver Gavin took top spot in the driver's championship with 176 points. Ron Fellows and Johnny O'Connell placed fourth with 152 points. Rival Aston Martin took second and third.

performance driving. An MP3-capable AM/FM radio with CD player was standard. New technology enhanced conventional radio reception. An improved optional Bose audio system with an in-dash six-disc changer and XM Satellite Radio were options. The OnStar system was also available.

Strong, lightweight body construction, New Goodyear Extended Mobility Tires (EMT) and a choice of three suspensions – the same as in 2005 – made the Corvette an easy-to-drive machine with superior handling.

A new high-performance Z06 model for 2006 delivered a superb combination of capability and technology and one of the best performance values on the market.

With its muscular appearance, the new Z06 had "attitude." "It combines the strong attributes of the new, sixth-generation Corvette with the spirit, technology and know-how from the race program to form an American supercar with outstanding credentials," said Dave Hill.

A new 7.0-liter LS-7 V-8 promised 0-to-60 mph performance of less than 4 seconds, a quarter-mile elapsed time of less than 12 seconds and a top speed of more than 190 mph on a racetrack.

The production Z06 had direct and indirect links to Corvette Racing, since it was developed in conjunction with a new C6-R competition coupe. Engineers developed it as a unique vehicle with power train, body

2006 Corvette Status Guide	Basket Case		Average Driver		Rare, Unique or Completely Original	
Condition of CORVETTE:	Production Status					
	Average	Rare/Unique	N–O–M	O–M	Needs Work	Unrestored Low Mileage
Suggested Actions: Collect It						
Drive, Show and Enjoy						
Race, Autocross Competitively						
Store for a Future Project/Investment						
Candidate for Resto Rod						
Restore to Curb Appeal Condition						

structure and chassis features distinct from those of other Corvettes.

The Z06 engine was a GM Gen IV 427-cid V-8 fitted with lightweight reciprocating components that redlined at 7,000 rpm. It featured such things as a dry-sump lubrication system and titanium rods and valves.

The aluminum "fixed-roof" body used one-piece hydroformed perimeter frame rails, a magnesium front cradle and a magnesium roof panel. The Z06 front fascia incorporated a larger grille, a cold-air scoop and a lower air splitter. It had a "wide-body" rear fender treatment and unique rear spoiler. It was three inches wider than other Corvette

models and weighed 3,130 pounds.

A three-inch-diameter exhaust system with bi-mode mufflers and larger polished stainless steel tips added horsepower. Engine, transmission and differential oil coolers – plus a steering cooler – were included.

Huge 14-inch cross-drilled front disc brakes with six-piston calipers and 13.4-inch cross-drilled rear rotors with four-piston calipers stopped the car handily. It rode on special wheels and tires. A rear-mounted battery improved the car's weight distribution. Its unique interior features included a revised gauge cluster and lightweight two-tone seats with more supportive bolsters.

The 2006 Corvette Z06 has strong development ties to racing. *Mike Mueller*

2007 Corvette

The 2007 Corvette featured a number of equipment enhancements and refinements. The features improved a groundbreaking sports car design that was all-new in 2005 and substantially upgraded for 2006. Coupe and convertible models came with the LS-2 6.0L V-8 engine that produced 400 hp matched to a rear transaxle. The front and rear short/long arm suspensions had the most racing-influenced suspension tuning in the Corvette's history. New Atomic Orange Tintcoat Metallic color replaced Daytona Sunset Orange Metallic. The specific tintcoat added depth to an exciting new color.

Interior enhancements were available on the coupe and convertible. They included two-tone perforated leather seating surfaces with crossed flag embroidery and contrasting stitching, in Red, Cashmere or Titanium. Steering wheel-mounted audio controls are included with premium Bose systems. The safety and security of OnStar was made available on the Z06 as part of the 2-LZ option package. Higher tech air

The "Corvette family" in 2007 with the coupe, convertible and Z06 edition. *Phil Hall Collection*

Here's the 2007 Indy 500 Pace Car Corvette on track at the "Brickyard." *Chevrolet*

The 2007 Ron Fellows ALMS GT1 Special Edition Corvette. *Chevrolet*

MIKE YAGER SAYS:	
CHEERS	The base car had a 400-hp V-8 and suspension modifications as standard equipment. Color choices on the 2007 Corvettes were optional at extra cost. There steering-mounted controls and Selective Ride were positive points.
JEERS	The tires were a weak point. They had a short life span and were expensive to replace. Transparent top = very warm interior.
GAME PLAN	There were only 700 made in this rare early color. Again, at this stage just enjoy driving a car that is "95% perfect".

Drivers were always welcome in the 2007 Corvette, with the right key, of course. *Phil Hall Collection*

An inside look at the LS-2 V-8 showed the valves for the 400 hp engine. *Phil Hall Collection*

2007 'VETTE FACTS	
VEHICLE IDENTIFICATION NUMBER	Corvette coupes and convertibles for 2007 were numbered 1G1YY|2/3|(2/4)U855100001 and up. The first symbol 1 indicated U.S. built. The second symbol G indicated a General Motors product. The third symbol 1 indicated a Chevrolet Motor Division vehicle. The fourth and fifth symbols YY = Corvette coupe or convertible. The sixth symbol indicated the body style: 2 = two-door coupe, GM styles 27, 37, 47 or 57 and 3 = two-door convertible, GM body style 67. The seventh symbol indicated the restraint code: 2 = Active manual belts with driver and front passenger inflatable restraint system; 4 = Active manual belts with front and side inflatable restraint system. The eighth symbol indicated the engine: U = RPO LS2 364-cid sequential multiport-fuel-injection (MFI) Chevrolet V-8. The ninth symbol was a check digit that varied. The 10th symbol indicated the model year 7 = 2007. The 11th symbol indicated the assembly plant: 5 = Bowling Green, Kentucky. The last six symbols indicated the sequential production numbers. Note: No data on Z06 VINs.
ENGINE	**Base Engine (LS-2):** Type: V-8 Bore and stroke: 4.00 x 3.62 in. Displacement: 364 cid Brake hp: 400 at 6,000 rpm. Induction: SFI **Z06 Engine (LS-7):** Type: V-8 Bore and stroke: 4.125 x 4.00 in. Displacement: 427 cid Brake hp: 505 at 6,300 rpm. Induction: SFI
VITAL STATS	**Coupe:** Original Price: $44,995 Production: TBA Wheelbase: 105.7 in. Length: 174.6 in. (Front) P245/40-ZR18 (Rear) P285/35-ZR19 **Convertible:** Original Price: $53,335 Production: TBA Wheelbase: 105.7 in. Length: 174.6 in. (Front) P245/40-ZR18 (Rear) P285/35-ZR19 **Z06 Fixed Roof Coupe** Original Price: $70,000 Production: TBA Wheelbase: 105.7 in. Length: 175.6 in. (Front) P275/35-ZR18 (Rear) P325/30-ZR19
COOL STUFF	At the Detroit Auto Show in early 2007, Bob Lutz acknowledged that the new 600-hp 2008 Dodge Viper SRT10 had surpassed the Corvette Z06 in horsepower. "But the Corvette vehicle line executive will not take that lying down," Lutz continued. It was an open secret that a Corvette known as the Blue Devil, Devil Ray, Stingray or SS (depending on whom you talked to) was in development as 2007 started. "We all know the new Corvette is out there," said Bob Gritzinger, senior editor for news at *AutoWeek* magazine. "The car is in development and it's been speculated that it will have about 650 horsepower. It's supposed to be here in 2009." In early January 2007, Corvette driver Oliver Gavin told the press that Corvette Racing had not decided to enter the Europe-based Le Mans Series or the American Le Mans Series. Due to budget cuts, Aston Martin appeared to be leaving the series, which would leave the Corvette without serious competition. Following some successful late-2006 fund-raising efforts, the National Corvette Museum announced it was planning a 40,000-sq.-ft. addition to include a 400-seat conference center, a 75-seat cafe, an enlarged gift shop and archives. The addition is scheduled to be completed in the summer of 2009, in time for the museum's 15th anniversary.

bags allowed designers to remove the old passenger-side air bag on/off switch box and use a bigger glove compartment. A power top was now included with the 3-LT option package for convertibles.

For 2007, cross-dilled brake rotors were now included when the optional Magnetic Selective Ride Control suspension was ordered. This allowed customers to combine the larger brakes from the Z-51 performance package with the comfort of Magnetic Selective Ride Control. Magnetic Selective Ride Control featured magneto-rheological dampers that detected road surfaces and adjusted damping rates almost instantly for optimal ride control.

The Z-51 Performance Package brought Corvette performance very close to the widely admired previous generation Z06. It included more aggressive dampers and springs, larger stabilizer bars, Goodyear Eagle F1 Supercar EMT tires, enhanced cooling and larger cross-drilled brake rotors.

As the fastest, most technologically advanced production model in Corvette's 54-year history, the 2007 Z06 offered an unprecedented level of capability and technology and an exterior design incorporating aerodynamic features that were co-developed with the Le Mans winning C6.R race car.

The Z06's LS-7 7.0L engine delivers 505

2007 Corvette Status Guide	Basket Case		Average Driver		Rare, Unique or Completely Original	
Condition of CORVETTE:	Production Status					
	Average	Rare/ Unique	N–O–M	O–M	Needs Work	Unrestored Low Mileage
Suggested Actions: Collect It						
Drive, Show and Enjoy						
Race, Autocross Competitively						
Store for a Future Project/Investment						
Candidate for Resto Rod						
Restore to Curb Appeal Condition						

horsepower in a 3,132-pound package – a combination that gave 0-60 performance of 3.7 seconds in first gear, quarter-mile times of 11.7 seconds at 125 mph and a top speed of 198 mph on Germany's Autobahn. It also provides maximum lateral acceleration of 1.04 g and 60-0 braking in 111.3 feet. Along with its astounding performance, the Corvette Z06 delivered 26 mpg on the highway.

The LS-7 reintroduced a 427-cid Corvette V-8. Unlike older "big-block" 427s, the 7.0-liter LS-7 is the largest-displacement *small-block* V-8 ever produced by Chevrolet. It can be identified by red engine covers with black lettering. The LS-7 shared Gen IV architecture with the LS2, but used a different cylinder block casting with pressed-in steel cylinder liners to accommodate the engine's larger cylinder bores. It also had a different front cover, oil pan, exhaust manifolds and cylinder heads among other parts.

Z06 power train and drive train systems were matched to the LS-7's performance capability. The light, four-into-one headers discharged in to new, close-coupled catalytic converters and through to new "bi-modal" mufflers featuring vacuum-actuated outlet valves that controlled exhaust noise during low-load operation. The valve opened for maximum power.

The Z06 retains the 105.7-inch wheelbase of other Corvettes, as well as the short-long arm suspension and transverse leaf spring design, but it rides on all-new wheels, tires, brakes, as well as its own rear spring and roll stabilizer. For 2007, an available enhanced acoustic package reduced road noise inside.

The interior of the 2007 Ron Fellows GT1 Corvette, a very special car. *Chevrolet*

A Visit to the MY Garage Museum

The MY Garage Museum is located on the Mid America Motorworks campus in Effingham, Illinois. The museum exhibits range from low-mileage, original Corvettes to racing Corvettes to styling Corvettes that appeared at the famed 1964-1965 New York World's Fair.

"The scope of the museum is not only the cars, but also the automotive memorabilia I've collected after more than 35 years as a Corvette enthusiast," says Mike Yager. "It's a super way to share my car collection with enthusiasts."

Over 75,000 people per year visit the free MY Garage Museum. It is open Monday-Saturday from 8:00 a.m. - 5:00 p.m. and closed on Sundays. For information write Mid America Motorworks, P.O. Box 1368, Effingham, IL 62401 or call (217) 540-4200 or email: mail@mamotorworks.com

Here are some of the MY Garage Museum attractions:

The 1964 World's Fair Car was a complete exercise in styling at a time when the U.S. was intent on showcasing its industrial muscle. It blows me away. *Mid America Motorworks*

The 1964 Bill Mitchell Styling Car was specially built for Chevrolet General Manager, Bunkie Knudson, as his personal car in September 1963.

Mid America Motorworks

1964 NEW YORK WORLD'S FAIR MITCHELL STYLING CORVETTE

Chevrolet had become famous for creating radical dream cars like the exotic Stingray designed under the supervision of Bill Mitchell and the mid-engined XP-819. In 1964, Chevrolet decided to build a less radical creation for the World's Fair of New York and subsequent auto shows. This fuel-injected 327-cid coupe was designed with a multitude of special features by Mitchell's Styling Department in Detroit.

The car is totally unrestored today, but it is beautifully preserved. Its most unique special features include special show-car side mirrors, a functional side exhaust and a hood cut-out for the completely chromed engine.

The exterior of the 1964 World's Fair Corvette retains its original finish and body modifications. It sports six Corvette taillights that are stock units with the lenses reversed to make them appear larger. The car also has unique brake-venting insets in the top of its rear body. These look similar to those used on early Sting Ray race cars, although they are simulated versions on the show car. The unique original paint color consists of a base coat of Gold Metallic under 15 coats of Candy Apple Red. This is all complimented by a large one-piece cast-nose grille.

The interior styling of the World's Fair Corvette is also special and includes leather seat covers dyed an iridescent red to match the brilliant exterior paint job and interior door panels with sequential flashing reflectors.

1964 NEW YORK WORLD'S FAIR CUTAWAY DISPLAY 427 V-8/TURBO HYDRA-MATIC

Can you say futuristic? This very unique engine was certainly ahead of its time, as first production-type 427-cid V-8 didn't appear in a Corvette until the 1966 model year. The same can be said for the General Motors Turbo Hydra-Matic three-speed transmission, which didn't appear on the scene until 1968.

This amazingly-detailed cutaway exhibition power train allows MY Garage Museum visitors to see every aspect of the engine and transmission's operation. Viewers can watch as the engine splits in half and rotates. This display gives visitors a close-up look at the operation of each internal system.

1960 CERV 1

Dubbed CERV I — for Chevrolet Engineering Research Vehicle — this car was the first of four such vehicles produced by Chevrolet over a 35-year period. Corvette chief engineer Zora Arkus-Duntov was responsible for the mechanical engineering of this "state-of-the-art" late-'50s racer, while famed car designer Larry Shinoda created the stunning body contours.

The CERV I originally sported a 283-cid V-8, an exotic version of Rochester fuel-injection and narrow tires. To gain more speed, before the car was retired, Duntov added a 377-cid aluminum small-block V-8, a low-profile Hilborne fuel-njection system and updated lower and wider wheels and tires.

1964 XP-819

The experimental Corvette known as XP-819 was unique for a number of reasons. Most importantly, it almost became a rear-engined production Corvette. This car was created under the auspices of a "Safety Proposal" program headed by Frank Winchell. Zora Arkus-Duntov, the patriarch of the Corvette, was unimpressed with the XP-819's handling and stability. The innovative exterior was the handiwork of legendary designers Larry Shinoda and John Schinella. It incorporates many futuristic modifications. This design was a key ingredient in the creation of the C3 Corvette, which made its debut in 1968.

1968 CORVETTE LE MANS RACE CAR

Dave Heinz and Bob Johnson drove this car in the French Grand prix at Le Mans in 1972. It was a true American grassroots racing effort, since this Corvette had once been a discarded and wrecked 1968 roadster. The car's original L-88 big-block V-8 and M-22 Rock Crusher four-speed manual gearbox were secretly supplied by Chevrolet as part of their back-door "no race involvement" program.

When driven by Heinz & Johnson, the Corvette took 15th overall in the 1972 Lemans 24-hour race and first place at the 1973 Sebring 12-hour competition. It was also first in class and second overall at the 1973 Daytona GTO-2. This Corvette features the Chevrolet "Distance Kit," which includes fixed headlight buckets, clear headlight lens covers, large ZL-1 type fender flares and wheel spacers.

The 1968 LeMans Race Car was a wrecked street car that was built into a serious competitor in eight weeks. Nickname: Ole Scrappy. *Mid America Motorworks*

1990 CORVETTE R9G COUPE

In 1990, Chevrolet dealers could order Corvette coupes destined for the new World Challenge race series. This is one of just 23 such coupes ever made.

By checking off merchandising option code R9G, these cars would be equipped, right from the factory, with such items as heavy-duty springs and the FX3 adjustable suspension. The cars featured 5.7-liter V-8s, although not the special-order race-bred engines as offered in 1988-1989. The owners of these cars were responsible for additional modifications and no racing-oriented changes could be ordered through Chevrolet.

This car did not undergo a race conversion. To date, it has gone only 77 original miles.

1954 CORVETTE

With a mere 3,010 original miles, this 1954 Corvette is one of 3,640 built that year and one of some 300 cars originally done in Pennant Blue. Like all 1954 Corvettes, this car is equipped with a "Blue-Flame" six-cylinder engine and a two-speed Powerglide transmission.

Corvette judges recently deemed that this is the most nearly-perfect example of an unrestored 1954 Corvette in existence. It won the highly-coveted National Corvette Restorers Society Three-Star Bowtie award. This impressive Corvette also appeared in the 1996 "Special Collection" at the well-known Bloomington Gold Corvette show.

1988 CORVETTE THIRTY-FIFTH ANNIVERSARY TWIN TURBO CALLAWAY

The year 1988 marked the 35th anniversary of the Corvette. This milestone was celebrated by the release of a $4,795 Special Edition package for coupes only. This option featured a two-tone white exterior with black roof, white leather seats, a white steering wheel, special exterior and interior accents, a console-mounted anniversary plaque, special emblems and white wheels.

The MY Garage Museum car is a truly stunning example of this package because it is also equipped with the super-rare Callaway Twin-Turbo conversion and a four-speed manual transmission. It is one of only 125 Callaway Twin Turbos made that year and is even rarer because it has the 35th Anniversary Package. In 1988 you could get all this for a sticker price of $61,495!

Only two such cars were built, as far as anyone knows. This one has gone a total of just 346 original miles since it was new.

"CORVETTE SUMMER" MOVIE CAR

Imagine it's 1978 and you're off to the movies. What's playing? A film called "Corvette Summer!" Who's starring in it? Two young actors at the beginning of their careers: Mark Hamill (of later "Star Wars" fame) and Annie Potts (who later became a major TV star). Oh... and one very unusual Corvette.

Shown exactly as it appeared in the movie, this 1973 Corvette underwent some major "cosmetic surgery" before it made its original screen debut. In addition to the custom body panels, wild paint, tilting front-end, mag wheels and more, it also features right-hand steering to keep the driver close to the curb (and girls) when cruising the boulevard.

1996 CORVETTE ("LAST C4" COUPE)

The year 1996 was a milestone year in Corvette history because it marked the final year of the fourth-generation Corvette. Mid America Designs (the name of Mike Yager's company at that time) worked

1996 Corvette ("Last C4" Coupe) side view. *Mid America Motorworks*

closely with Chevrolet to produce a truly unique, one-of-a-kind Corvette to commemorate the event.

In keeping with tradition, the last car to leave the assembly line at the Corvette factory in Bowling Green, Kentucky, received special equipment.

The unique features of this car include flares and hash marks like those that came on cars with a Grand Sport package, ZR-1 wheels, specially-embroidered seat emblems, special windshield graphics and unique "Last C4" logos. GM dignitaries and nearly every plant employee and assembly line worker present when the car came down the assembly line personally autographed the "Last C4" Corvette. In addition, a model of the car was also created.

1964 CHEVROLET CORVETTE STYLING CAR

The newest addition to the MY Garage collection is this 1964 Corvette "styling" car. In September, 1963, this unique coupe was specially built for Chevrolet general manager Semon E. "Bunkie" Knudson.

The car's second owner was a Mr. Gailey who worked at the Chevrolet Engineering Center. Gailey purchased the car in the summer of 1964 after it was offered at a special GM party where names were drawn from a hat for the right to purchase surplus engineering and styling cars.

The car still retains its original drive train, which featured a 327-cid 365-hp V-8. It has

many custom parts that were added in the Styling and Engineering departments.

Firefrost Blue custom Cadillac paint was sprayed over the car's specially-prepared body. The hood features a special design with large, custom-cast grilles. This Corvette also has a unique front bumper treatment, custom high-back bucket seats, all-white leather trim, custom Cadillac carpeting, special polished stainless steel toe board grates, one-off door panels, power-operated windows and power vent wings.

Bill Mitchell's styling genius is reflected in the use of custom side pipes that share the design characteristics of both 1965 and 1969 production Corvettes. The 1964 Chevrolet Corvette Styling Car retains its original Engineering Department tag. It is located next to the vehicle identification number tag just under the glove box.

Today, this one-of-a-kind styling car has been restored to the same condition it was in when it left the GM Engineering Center. It certainly offers an insightful glimpse into Corvette history and GM's future vision in the mid 1960s.

1996 Corvette ("Last C4" Coupe) rear. *Mid America Motorworks*

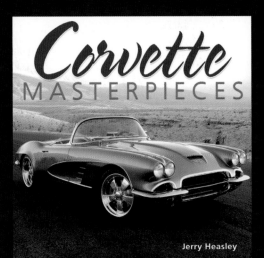
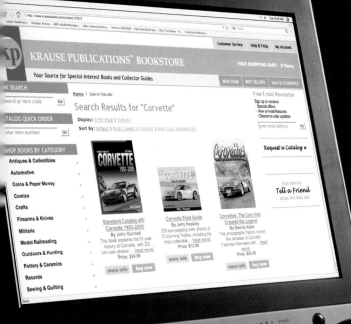